FROM THE LIBRARY OF

Colleen M. Hall

WE WERE INTERRUPTED

BOOKS BY BURTON RASCOE

THEODORE DREISER. 1925.
A BOOKMAN'S DAYBOOK. Edited with an Introduction by
C. Hartley Grattan, 1929.
TITANS OF LITERATURE. 1932.
PROMETHEANS. 1933.
BEFORE I FORGET. 1937.
THE JOYS OF READING. 1937.
BELLE STARR: "The Bandit Queen." 1941.
WE WERE INTERRUPTED. 1947.

Collaborator:

FANFARE. Pamphlet on H. L. Mencken. 1920. Contributor of title
essay.

THE LITERARY SPOTLIGHT. 1924. Contributor of the anonymous
personal sketches of H. L. Mencken, Joseph Hergesheimer,
Sherwood Anderson, John Farrar and Henry Blake Fuller.

THE BOOKMAN ANTHOLOGY OF ESSAYS. 1924. Contributor of an
essay on George Santayana.

THESE UNITED STATES. 1924. Contributor of *Oklahoma: Low Jacks
in a Crooked Game.*

THE AMERICAN CARAVAN. 1928. Contributor of an interior monologue, *What Is Love?* from a novel in progress.

MORROW'S ALMANACK. 1928. Editor. Wrote horoscopes and compiled calendar.

MORROW'S ALMANACK. 1929. Editor. Wrote horoscopes and compiled calendar.

MORROW'S ALMANACK. 1930. Wrote short essay for each month of
the year.

THE CRITIQUE OF HUMANISM. 1930. Contributor of satire on Humanist movement.

THE SMART SET ANTHOLOGY. Edited by Burton Rascoe and Groff
Conklin. 1934. Wrote introductory history of the magazine
and contributed short story "Caste."

AMERICAN LITERATURE. Edited by Henry Garland Bennett. 1935.
Contributed essay "What Are Intellectuals?"

AN AMERICAN READER. 1938. Editor. Wrote introductory history of
publishing in America and introductory essay to each division of the text.

THE PATRIOTIC ANTHOLOGY. Edited by Barbara Moses Olds. Introduction by Carl Van Doren. 1941. Contributed essay "Self-Evident Truths."

THE AMERICANA ANNUAL. 1947. Contributed articles on American literature and on book publishing for 1946.

TEN EVENTFUL YEARS. Encyclopaedia Britannica. 1947. Contributed article "Tendencies in the Drama."

ESSAY ANNUAL. 1933. Contributor of an essay on Montaigne, from *Titans of Literature.*

SPOOFS. 1933. Contributor of a burlesque of Bankers, brokers and financiers.

MODERN AMERICAN PROSE. Edited by Carl Van Doren. 1934. Contributor of essay on Lucian.

THE NEW REPUBLIC ANTHOLOGY. 1936. Contributor of *The Grim Anniversary,* an account of the panic of October 1929.

Introductions for:

MADAME BOVARY. By Gustave Flaubert. 1919. Borzoi Edition.

MANON LESCAUT. By the Abbe Prevost. 1919. Borzoi Edition.

MADEMOISELLE DE MAUPIN. By Theophile Gautier. 1920. Borzoi Edition.

ERIK DORN. By Ben Hecht. 1921. Modern Library Edition.

NANA. By Emile Zola. 1922. Borzoi Edition.

CHIVALRY. By James Branch Cabell. 1922. Modern Library Edition.

THE TRIUMPH OF DEATH. By Gabrielle D'Annunzio. 1923. Modern Library Edition.

TRICKS OF WOMEN AND OTHER ARMENIAN TALES. Translated by P. F. Cooper. 1928.

A HIGH WIND IN JAMAICA. By Richard Hughes. 1930.

FLOYD GIBBONS. By Douglas Gilbert. 1930.

BOOM IN PARADISE. By T. H. Weigall. 1932.

THE DECAMERON. By Boccaccio. 1930. Limited Editions Club Edition.

THE NATURAL PHILOSOPHY OF LOVE. By Remy de Gourmont. 1932. Black and Gold Library Edition.

EXTRA! EXTRA! DEADLINES AND JOSSLYN. By Henry Justin Smith. 1933.

THE MEMOIRS OF VINCENT NOLTE. 1934.

THE GREAT TREK. By Max Miller. 1936.

THE BALLAD OF READING GAOL. By Oscar Wilde. 1937. Limited Editions Club Edition.

SISTER CARRIE. By Theodore Dreiser. 1939. Limited Editions Club Edition.

FOR HAZEL

BURTON RASCOE

We Were Interrupted

DOUBLEDAY & COMPANY, INC.

Garden City, N. Y.

CONTENTS

Contents

WE WERE INTERRUPTED

CHAPTER 1

The Roaring Twenties—A Panorama

SUMMARY OF A DECADE. LOOKING BACKWARD TO
THE TWENTIES. THE END OF AN EPOCH. THE
BEGINNING OF A NEW LIFE FOR ME.

This book treats of one life, my own, during a decade—that of 1920 to 1930—as I lived it, felt it, observed it, thought upon it, and drew conclusions and opinions about it while the events I relate were occurring. Such a book will be of no interest to any reader unless I can either make him share vicariously in the life I have known or awake in him remembrances of his own experiences of the kind common to men.

Although this book is complete in itself, it is a continuation of an autobiographical work entitled *Before I Forget,* published in 1937, in which I told of my people, childhood, youth, and young manhood in Kentucky, Oklahoma, and Chicago. At least I told of such periods in my life as had left definite impressions upon my memory.

I had found those years pleasant to recall, even in their disappointments, fears, and unhappy moments; for life is an unpredictable adventure, which a boy enters upon eagerly and hopefully, being naïvely sure at nearly all times that everything is going to turn out quite wonderful for him. And, if he has high faith in the promise of life and is almost continually charmed and excited by the spectacle of life, he is never deeply disappointed in his expectations, even when things do not turn out altogether as he hoped they would.

I found those twenty-eight years of my existence, which I

wrote about in *Before I Forget,* enormously exhilarating, on the whole, as well as a continual process of self-education. That book should not concern you now and I mention it only to explain why this book begins in 1920.

As in *Before I Forget,* I have tried to deal with each phase of my past as the contemporary experience seemed to me then, and not as I think of it now. I am not the same person I was twenty-seven years ago or the same person I was seventeen years ago. Fundamentally, no doubt I am the same, for I matured early, through the circumstance of beginning to earn my living as a newspaper reporter, editorial writer, and signed columnist when I was fourteen years old and just entering high school. Also a voracious appetite for living, coupled with a voracious appetite for reading, enabled me very early to arrive at certain concepts of life and to adopt a certain set of principles of conduct, as well as to achieve a point of view from which I have seen no cause to deviate since I came of age.

But as one grows older one finds one's views modified, one's tastes developed, one's complacencies shaken up, one's old enthusiasms replaced by newer ones, one's attitudes altered by circumstances and environment, one's temporary illusions displaced by an entirely new set of them, and one's satisfactions in life differing in kind, as well as in measure, from the satisfactions of youth. At fifty-five I do not wish to betray the person I was between twenty-eight and thirty-eight by giving him a character which I may think, now, that he should have had, or attribute to him a knowledge which he could have gained only through experience he had not yet enjoyed. I have tried not to judge that person, who was myself, during the decade of 1920–30 in the light of my present wisdom or, with the facile criteria of hindsight, to judge of the events of the years he lived through.

The decade 1920–30 was an interesting one, I think, to anyone with an awareness of life. It was a revolutionary and explosive era which began with a spiritual malaise that seemed to have

2

settled all over the world. This was a letdown and a reaction after the orgy of bloodletting on European battlefields in World War I, during which emotions had been whipped to a high pitch and hysteria had prevailed while a savage madness swept the earth.

The realities that people faced in the spring of 1920 were: that a great war which had been fought in the name of freedom and democracy had apparently been fought in vain; that there was no real democracy or brotherhood discernible anywhere but only strife and hatred, greed and cruelty, internecine wars in Europe and clamorings of nations for territorial expansion and aggrandizement; that some few had grown rich out of the war while millions had experienced only tragedy and impoverishment, and some few had become powerfully entrenched in ruthless domination of others through the mandate a despairing people had given them, or through power they had seized without the people's mandate; and that frustration and disappointment were driving the exploited and dispossessed to blind, malignant fury against whatever human symbols they held to be responsible for their condition, even when those symbols were exploited and dispossessed persons like themselves.

The decade, therefore, began in a general atmosphere of cynicism, disillusion, and bitterness which was reflected not only in the fiction, essays, and poetry of the period but in the behavior of people in all classes of society. There were, of course, those who were serene and unperturbed either because of a tolerant faith in the brotherhood of men and in the ultimate triumph of good over evil or because of an abiding skepticism of mankind's ability to live up to its professed ideals or even of its ability to function without basely self-interested motives disingenuously disguised as efforts in behalf of the commonweal. And there were those (among whom I may include myself) who were too young and too full of great expectations to be indoctrinated with more than the temporary romantic despair of the hurt idealists

3

or with the disgust of the tired liberals, or to be misled by the rabble-rousing of demagogues and professional agitators who satisfy their egos by pitting human beings against other human beings in all sorts of expressions of discontent, from sabotage of industry to race riots and outrages of savage intolerance.

But things righted themselves after a fashion—at least in this country—under the competitive system of individual initiative, corporate enterprise, and a republican form of government, whereas the totalitarian theory of government was being tested with lamentable results in various parts of Europe. And our country went from a war hangover into a spurt of productive activity which led to a spree of overconfidence that ended in a debacle.

If the present period makes some who are of my age or older feel like saying, "Here's where I came in," let them remember that history never exactly repeats itself and the 1920s were wonderfully exciting for those of us who lived through them—even those of us who never shared the limelight with Aimee Semple McPherson or "Red" Grange, nor had as much money as had Charles Ponzi or Samuel Insull.

Some of my coevals have looked back upon the 1920s in books they have written about the period with something between a grin and a shudder, as a weird phantasmagoria in which they incredibly participated. Some of these popular historians—I except Mark Sullivan and Frederick Lewis Allen—have written of the period with passionate disapproval. They have been loftily sarcastic about the decade, as if they had lived during it but had taken no willing part in it. In effect, they now stand *above* ten years of their lives in a spirit of critical detachment and disapproval. Seizing only the cruder, surface manifestations of life of the period, they can find nothing to praise in the whole decade.

For myself, I don't know how to live in a state of suspended animation, a Jeremiah to a period that has already vanished. Jeremiah, at least, talked of a period in which he was living as he wrote. He called upon the men around him in Judea to reform their ways. He did not ask people not to commit mistakes they had already been guilty of and could do nothing about except repent and atone. He called upon people to desist from the sins they were *then* committing.

But if those historians of the 1920s examined their hearts in honest memory they would find, I think, that they had many moments of pleasure during the 1920s, even if they only listened to "Amos 'n' Andy" over the radio, heard Gershwin's "Rhapsody in Blue" on a phonograph record, read Anita Loos's "Gentlemen Prefer Blondes," went once to a speakeasy, saw and heard just one good talking picture, learned the words of "Yes, We Have No Bananas," "Tea for Two," "I'll See You in My Dreams," and "Lover, Come Back to Me," saw Charlie Chaplin in "The Gold Rush," and followed Herriman's "Krazy Kat" comic strip.

No, our past is always with us. It is a part of us. We cannot repudiate it. We are the products of our errors as well as of our triumphant virtues. This is true of nations as well as of individuals. So, although I am only a mite in a nation of 140,000,000 souls I do not hesitate to say that my own life is linked up with the destiny of our nation, nor do I apologize for the presumption of observing that whereas the spring of 1920 was the ending of a period in my life and the beginning of a new one, it was also the petering out of a period in the political, economic, social, and cultural development of America and the gestation of a new one.

Economically, that period in America's history lasted three weeks short of ten years before another period began, so accurately can it be charted. It quasi-officially began on November 12, 1919, when the price of securities on the New York Stock Exchange dropped precipitously in a 2,700,000-share turnover of ownership in a panic which ended the war boom that had flourished under the Democratic administration of Woodrow Wilson. It quasi-officially ended on October 23, 1929, when, in

5

one day, 16,410,000 shares were dumped on the market of the New York Stock Exchange in a panic which ended the most frenzied speculative boom in history and, at the same time, ended the Republican regime of Harding, Coolidge, and Hoover, and ushered in a depression that was to last another ten years.

That depression quasi-officially ended on September 3, 1939, when Prime Minister Neville Chamberlain of Great Britain announced that a state of war existed between Great Britain and Germany. Then, among the nations that were to become involved in a second world war, productive energies were galvanized into a furious activity for destruction. In a machine age, quick obsolescence of manufactured goods is the surest means toward quick profit and full employment, and war is the surest route toward that end, for not only are the materials of war rapidly consumed and expended but millions of able-bodied men are killed or maimed in the process, thereby solving the problem of unemployment for at least that many.

So from 1939 through 1945 we had a war boom and, at least, a paper prosperity,* which increased the public debt from about forty billion dollars to nearly three hundred billion dollars. Every child born into this nation in 1947 owes nearly $2,915 at the moment of his birth as against the $11 owed by a child born in 1915. Wars are the reason for his present liability; and wars are also the reason for the greater concentrations of wealth and power, accumulated under the banner of the Four Freedoms, whereunder all freedoms have perished in such a power state as Russia and have even been severely curtailed in such a representative government as our own.

Like an overwritten Eugene O'Neill play, the drama of our 1920s began to be played long before November 1919 and lasted long after October 1929, but its essence, in so far as this country

* Later reflection by the author: I have used an expression here which I thought had a specific connotation when I wrote it. But I wonder if there is any other kind of prosperity except a "paper prosperity." A dollar, a check, a letter of credit, a bond, a contract, an insurance certificate are all paper, backed by faith.

was concerned, was within the "playing time" between March 1920 and March 1930. For in March 1920 Harry M. Daugherty began laying plans to elect Warren G. Harding as President of the United States; and ten years later James A. Farley began laying his plans to put Franklin D. Roosevelt into the White House.

Politically for Europe and tangentially for the rest of the world, a new and dramatic phase of history began in November 1917 when several hundred workmen, meaning only to demonstrate peacefully against famine and unemployment in St. Petersburg, achieved a revolution without intending to do so and then found themselves without a leader or a plan of government. This turn of affairs resulted in a provisional government after the Czar's abdication and a civil war in which the Bolsheviks were triumphant over the Mensheviks and White Russians. Vladimir Ulianov (Lenin) and Leiba D. Bronstein (Trotsky) came to power as heads of the Council of Peoples' Commissars of the Russian Republic . . . The postlude came when, after the death of Lenin, Trotsky and eighty-six other original members of the successful Bolshevist faction were expelled from the Communist Party and banished from Russia and J. V. Dzugashvili (Stalin) became dictator of the Union of Soviet Socialist Republics.

The drama, then, like the Richard and Henry plays of Shakespeare, engendered sequels in which Benito Mussolini in Italy and Adolf Hitler in Germany rose to power as self-proclaimed champions of the downtrodden masses and as resuscitators of their nations and played their ignoble and destructive roles, aided and abetted (up to a certain dangerous point) by loans and credits granted by the ruling and monied powers of Great Britain and the United States as insurance against "the menace of Bolshevism." The war, which this game of power politics brought about, in which, for a time, the Nazis were not a "bulwark" against the Bolshevists but allied with them for the extermination of Great Britain and France, was given a road-company tryout

7

in a civil war in Spain, which the British and American governments watched with allegedly neutral complacency and negative aid and comfort while Franco overthrew a people's republic and established a dictatorship.

Socially, the decade 1920–30 was a revolutionary and experimental one, showing progress through temporary retrogressions and excesses. The Prohibition Amendment to the Federal Constitution took effect at midnight on January 16, 1920, as a "noble experiment," and, instead, inaugurated a thirteen-year reign of unprecedented lawlessness consequent upon the efforts to enforce an unpopular restraint upon personal freedom. This experiment not only deprived the government of more than two billion dollars annually in internal revenue but also cost the taxpayers many millions in vain efforts to make it effective. But on the side of social gains the Nineteenth Amendment went into effect on August 26, 1920, thus not only enfranchising some 27,000,000 citizens who had hitherto been officially voiceless in the political affairs of the nation, but further emancipating women from their ancient degradation as chattels in a male-dominated world.

The period of 1920–30 has been designated the "Jazz Age," "The Fantastic Interim," the "Speakeasy Era," the "Age of Wild and Flaming Youth," and the "Era of Wonderful Nonsense." But these are superficial designations. It was an age of America's coming of age in literature and the other arts; an age in which our national provincialism gave way to the infiltration of a degree of international culture and foreign ideas; an age which not only saw the development of the automobile, the radio, the talking pictures, and the airplane, but, contemporaneously with the advancement of the physical and chemical sciences, the dawn of an era that seems destined to be as remote from the nineteenth-century mechanistic theory of the universe as exemplified in the works of Thomas Henry Huxley as the theory of evolution was from the concepts of the Middle Ages. After an orgy of uncritical

8

acceptance of Freud's theory of the erotic basis of personality and character, Freud's explorations of the subconscious have proved to be a great boon to mankind, and psychotherapy (long stubbornly fought by the orthodox medicos) is a generally accepted adjunct to physiotherapy. And Einstein's theory of relativity (first called to the general public's attention in the early 1920s) has as many implications concerning a future theory of the cosmos as has the atomic bomb (derived from Einstein's equations) concerning the future of civilization.

Under the Harding-Coolidge-Hoover administrations now so roundly denounced by youngsters who have known no other Presidents except Franklin D. Roosevelt and Harry S. Truman and who therefore attribute all our social gains to the New Deal, child-labor laws eliminated 2,000,000 children from exploitation by industry, the first old-age pension law was passed in seventeen states, real wages went up thirty-six points from a norm of 100 in 1914, whereas they declined under the New Deal, and labor made tremendous gains, after terrific setbacks under Wilson when managements used the power of the national guard and appeals to popular concepts of "patriotism" to smash unions during the war and nearly broke the backbone of labor during the postwar depression.

My chief concerns during the 1920s were in the realm of ideas, aesthetic and social, as reflected in literature, drama, and the allied arts of the period. As a literary critic, as a drama critic, as an editor, and as an author my profession mainly has been journalistic and literary. But it was one of my earliest adult convictions that good literature is concerned with life, reflects life, and springs out of the life of the author's own time, voicing the needs and aspirations of a people and recording their behavior with honesty and insight.

Therefore I have never dwelt in an ivory tower; my forum has been the market place. I would enjoy Homer, Sophocles, Aristophanes, and Lucian less, I think, if I had not given myself

9

very much to life, nearly all aspects of it that I could seek out or that came within my ken. Shakespeare and the economic theories of Solly and Keynes would not have meant so much to me, I think, if I had not gambled intensely and successfully in the stock market for a brief while. I would appreciate Bach, Debussy, Kern, and Gershwin the less, I think, if I had not played the drums and traps for years to the music of my wife's piano playing. I would see less than I do, I think, in the work of Michelangelo and Rodin if I had not long sought diversion by modeling in clay, and I would know little about the problems and effects of Vermeer and Van Gogh if I did not paint. The rodeo would be as incomprehensible to me as are the fine points of bullfighting if I had not spent much of my life in the saddle. I would appreciate the literature of my native land the less if I had not roamed the country by train and automobile, getting acquainted with the natives of nearly every state and with their language and their customs. The dancing of Fred Astaire and of Ray Bolger would not thrill me quite so much, I think, if I had never practiced tap and soft-shoe dancing. Much of Rabelais and Petronius would be hidden from me if I had not studied Greek and Latin and acquired a vast knowledge of the meaning and nuances of words, but much of their work would also be hidden from me if I had never spent time in the company of lusty topers, had never seen the inside of a bordello, and had not written a daily syndicated column for four years about New York in the heyday of "Texas" Guinan and Gilda Gray.

Many aspects of the business of living have been hidden from me, except through reading and the exercise of my imagination, from building a bridge, running a corporation, or producing a play to facing the enemy on the field of battle—and there are thousands of other adventures, trivial and sublime, which it has not been my lot to experience; but I have done what I could with my equipment, my tastes, my curiosity, and my opportunities to enjoy life, taking the bitter with the sweet, and I have found my experience nourishing to the spirit and stimulating even when it has been as unpalatable as gall and wormwood.

In other words, during the 1920s I had fun. All life is irksome and unsatisfactory at times; tragedies hit and wound us, one creates enemies as well as friends; sometimes our moods are exalted and sometimes we are inexpressibly depressed; we are frustrated in our desires as often as we fulfill them; we are frequently resentful toward the prison of our being; we are ill sometimes when we need most to be well; finances worry us now and then, and the future of the race at times seems dark and forbidding; gremlins and poltergeists seem to delight in playing tricks on us at the most inappropriate times, and when a collar button hides under a caster or a desk drawer sticks when we are in a hurry, we are likely to damn the inherent cussedness of inanimate objects. We all pride ourselves on our sense of humor and too often for pride and comfort do we fail to display it. We wound others without intending to do so and we sometimes fear we have wounded someone unintentionally when the chances are that he, or she, is hardly aware of our existence. We are estranged from friends through differences of opinion or because we are no longer mutually dependent upon each other; long friendships are sometimes abruptly broken off over some trifle and those we once loved become our enemies. Love sometimes turns into hate and recrimination. And, as Anatole France says, we are born, we suffer, we die, and, he added, "and that is all we know." He omitted to say that we live, we enjoy, we work, we create, we laugh more often than we weep, and the most of us look forward, except on our blue days, with hope and expectancy; and, if not, if we are honest with ourselves, we look back on our lives with some degree of satisfaction and thankfulness to our Creator.

CHAPTER 2

Chicago—News Days and Night Life

THE CHICAGO "TRIBUNE" AND CAPTAIN PATTER-
SON. THE WILD CREW. RING LARDNER AND
OTHERS. BACK TO THE FARM IN OKLAHOMA.
MEMORIES OF THOSE CHICAGO DAYS LIVE ON.

On the morning of May 3, 1920, while I was cleaning out
my desk at the Chicago *Tribune* for the last time, after eight
exciting and fruitful years on that newspaper, I felt a strange and
gratifying elation.

I felt as if I had been released from a kind of bondage into a
new life of hope and promise, of unpredictable but fascinating
adventure. I felt that the books on a period in my life were
closed and in order and that I was about to open up a new
account book, all clean and fresh for the entries. Come sorrow,
come pain, come happiness, come disappointments, come failure,
and come successes, a new era lay before me of surprise, struggle,
change, growth, and development in new, untried fields.

It would not be a continuance in an old routine that had
become mechanical and therefore boring. I had been saved from
that secure but dreaded fate, the secret fear of all active and
ambitious young newspapermen—of either winding up on the
rim of the copy desk, or, what is worse, becoming a high-salaried
executive, with all the headaches of the post, opulent, secure,
kowtowed to, and a slave, married to a virago of an important
job, hag-ridden by its excessive demands, and afraid of the whims
of the higher-ups.

That morning I gave thanks to Captain Patterson from the

depths of my heart for firing me. I had profoundly admired certain aspects of his mind and character. I had admired his forthrightness, his intellectual honesty which admitted no compromise, his realistic sense of life, and his courage in his writings as on the field of battle in a war in which he did not believe. He had no sense of humor at all, no subtlety, only a crude and juvenile sense of the comic. But he was without hypocrisy, entirely lacking in that devious disingenuousness which passes for tact and diplomacy; he was genuinely interested in the welfare and interests of the common man, in the common man's emotions, conditioned reflexes, aspirations and anxieties, predilections and ways of amusing himself, because he shared all these factors in the common man's make-up, although he had inherited riches and power. And that was what made him one of the greatest, if not the greatest, journalistic geniuses of his time.

He was not intuitive as a woman is supposed to be intuitive, but farseeing, seeing so far, indeed, that he was generally ten years ahead of his time, and therefore antagonistic toward the prevailing opportunistic go-getterism of the profiteers and bandwagon jumpers, political or commercial, at any given moment of crisis in our own or world economy.

This was later to make him unpopular with many people, even feared and hated by them, because many people do not like to have their complacencies disturbed, particularly when they find it profitable to wrap themselves in the American flag and spout about freedom, justice, and democracy—without risking their hides as a combatant in war. Captain Patterson, though he did not believe in our interference with European squabbles, always assumed the responsibility of his convictions, and one of his convictions was that Stephen Decatur was right when he proposed a toast, "Our country! . . . May she always be in the right, but our country, right or wrong." Thus he enlisted in the Rainbow Division, though considerably past draft age, after resigning his commission as captain in the Illinois State Militia, and served

13

overseas in World War I, reaching his captaincy again through sheer merit on the field of battle. He got a very thorough baptism of fire in Lorraine, the defense of Champagne, the Second Battle of the Marne, at St. Mihiel, and in the Argonne.

He did this while many able-bodied, stay-at-home, self-advertised "patriots" were making fortunes gambling in "war babies," rooking the taxpayers on government war contracts, and encouraging their children to throw rocks at the great-grandchildren of 1840 immigrants who bore German names (few of whom knew a word of German), and led boycotts against second-generation German-American small merchantmen, so they could buy their property up at a cheap price.

Patterson, though in his sixties, volunteered for service in World War II as soon as war was declared by Congress, although he was opposed to our entering the conflict, and was rejected because of his age. He then appealed to President Roosevelt, in person, for a commission and was given a rude brush off: he had ardently supported Roosevelt's candidacy for two terms, but had balked at a third term, on principle. Franklin D. Roosevelt did not forgive those, even among his closest advisers and vote-getters, who opposed any idea, however absurd, dangerous, or whimsical, that popped into his head.

Patterson was pretty much like Franklin D. Roosevelt in that respect also. He was frank in saying he wanted "yes-men" about him, for "no-men" only delayed and complicated his carrying out what he had determined to do in the first place, and that he had been fortunate in choosing a father and a grandfather who had passed on to him the money and the power that enabled him to get his way. To many that seemed a callous and arrogant thing to say; but it was the simple truth, and Patterson was not one to dress up a truth with pretty words and hypocritical phrases in such a way that it became a lie, acceptable but deceitful.

Patterson had fired me on impulse in a moment of irritation because he had discovered I was not a "yes-man," just as he

14

fired Walter Howey, probably the best city editor newspapers in this country have ever known, and many others, for the same reason.

In the first shock of being fired, I had been very bitter toward Patterson, and I had been sunk for hours. My pride had been hurt. Moreover, I indulged myself in cynical reflections over the reward I had received for eight years of prideful and devoted loyalty to the paper, during which, for nearly two years, I had held down seven jobs at once, at a time of trained-help shortage —assistant Sunday editor, rotogravure editor, editor of the Sunday opposite-editorial page, literary editor and literary critic, drama editor and drama critic—and, happy sucker that I was, nearly killing myself for a salary that I never thought enough about to see that it was woefully inadequate.

There was no newspaper writers' union in those days and it would not have occurred to any newsman to ask for a raise, lest he get fired for his presumption, even if I had been of the temperament to ask for a raise, which I was not: my raises were voluntarily given by the management, and of course there were Christmas bonuses, based, pro rata, on one's salary and the profits of the company for the year. And you could borrow money from the company at a low rate of interest, instead of going to a loan shark. Later this paternalism was extended to loans to employees for the purchase of homes; and Patterson's annual bonuses to employees of the New York *News,* when the paper became successful, made the tabloid's employees the highest-salaried newspaper workers in the city, their annual pay being considerably higher than the Newspaper Guild's prevailing demands, and put executives into very high brackets of income. When the *News* signed a Guild contract, the bonuses, of course, ceased for non-executive employees and the annual wage of the non-executive employees thereby dropped down to the prevailing union level.

But that May morning in 1920, while I was cleaning out my desk, all my bitterness had vanished and I was feeling grateful to

Patterson for saving me from a life I had begun to consider stagnating and for booting me on toward what I considered to be inevitable. What I mean by that will become apparent later on.

I had no concrete reason for my elation that morning. I was out of a job with no immediate prospects of getting another one; signs of a severe economic depression were already beginning to appear; I had enough money to feed, clothe, and house my little family for a year or more, with strict economies, but no definite prospects beyond that and no desire whatever to do anything but physical labor for a long while and lie fallow, mentally, for several months.

But just as I had *known for a certainty* three years before I was out of Shawnee (Oklahoma) High School that I would go to the University of Chicago, live in Chicago after my schooling at that university, and work on the Chicago *Tribune*, without anything whatever to support my knowledge (my parents could not afford to send me to the University of Chicago, or, indeed, pay my fare up there), so also I *knew for a certainty* three years before I was fired from the Chicago *Tribune* that within five years I would be living in New York and working on the New York *Tribune* as literary critic.

I did not know by what a circuitous route I would arrive at that destination—it turned out to be not so circuitous but strange and unforeseen—because I have always had an excessive shyness about asking for a job. It is a shyness that has always defeated me on the very few occasions when I have voluntarily sought work. Thus I have always had to create jobs for myself or jobs have been offered to me. Every job I ever asked for I didn't get—except one—and I soon quit that. I have always been afraid when ushered into the presence of a boss from whom I have sought work; I have no ability whatever to sell myself; I have always stammered during such an interview, fidgeted, and given a very bad account of my abilities—even a deprecating account.

Once a job has been offered to me and I have accepted it, I have always been very good at it.

So I was elated that May morning as I cleaned out my desk and shook hands good-by with Bert Leston Taylor, the columnist, who shared a suite of offices with me. I was then twenty-seven years old and in six months would be twenty-eight. I had worked and played very hard ever since I was fourteen. For eighteen years I had been going at high tension. There had always seemed so much to do, so many pretty girls to adore, so much to read, so much to see, so much to learn, so much that was pleasurable, profitable, and instructive to engage in that I resented Nature's requirement of sleep as a day's exorbitant taxes on the energy she furnished me, and I paid it grudgingly with only four or five hours' sleep a night, compensated somewhat with catnaps, which I could take almost any time, anywhere—dozing a minute or two at my desk, in a streetcar or an elevated train, or sitting in my reading chair and waking up refreshed.

But the demands I had put on my constitution by overwork and strenuous pleasure had overstimulated me and as a result I was underweight and in need of a more balanced life. I seemed to have been afraid to miss anything—the newest acquisition at the Art Institute; the newest book of importance in French, German, or English; the first performances in Chicago of Pavlowa and of Nijinski; a concert by Casals, Kreisler, Grainger, or Paderewski; a play starring Doris Keane, John Barrymore, or Ethel Barrymore; W. C. Fields in his pool-playing and juggling act; the floor show at the Bismarck Gardens; the première of *The Birth of a Nation;* the opening of Jack Johnson's fabulous saloon, Hinky Dink's, "longest bar in the world and the biggest glass of beer for a nickel"; dancing at the Blue Fountain Room of the La Salle; attending nut sessions at the Dill Pickle; and golf at six o'clock in the morning in Jackson Park.

I wanted at least six months, or maybe a year, of the life of a farmhand—physical work in the open air from early breakfast to suppertime, to bed by nine or ten from sheer physical exhaustion, solid hours of sound sleep, and a good appetite—to put me in shape for the next decade's strenuously exciting life for me in new surroundings and among the heavy competition of New York.

For I knew I was going to New York and that presently I would be working on the New York *Tribune,* for it was the only paper I wanted to work for. It had at the time Franklin P. Adams, Heywood Broun, Robert Benchley, Frazier ("Spike") Hunt, W. O. (Bill) McGeehan, Clare Briggs, H. E. Krehbiel, Royal Cortissoz, James J. Montague, and other stimulating personalities on its staff (many of whom had gone to the *World* or elsewhere when I got there) ; it was founded by Horace Greeley, who had employed Margaret Fuller as his literary critic when she was an object of conservative abhorrence because of views on sex equality and had given Karl Marx one of his few sources of income as a special writer; and, besides, the *Tribune* had the best appearance, typographically, of any paper in the country.

So I felt fresh, clean, and free as I walked out of the old *Tribune* building at Madison and Randolph streets and down Madison to Wabash Avenue where I was to catch the Evanston Express elevated train to my home in Rogers Park. Soon I would be riding lickety-split, in a Texas saddle, across the open prairie and the grazing land of my father's acres; rounding up and cutting out horses or riding just for the fun of it; plowing (one of the noblest and most restful of occupations, conducive as it is to contemplation and revery) ; fishing and swimming in my father's artificial lake; cutting sugar cane for sorghum molasses (the most hellish job I know of on a farm, for the sap and pollen of the tall cane stalks mingle with your sweat in the hot sun, producing an almost intolerable itch and burn) ; hunting possum at night; picking cotton; going to candy-pulls and country dances; playing penny-ante poker with my dad and his cronies on blissful, quiet evenings; listening to coyotes bay in the moonlight; sleeping be-

18

neath the stars in a tree house on warm nights; eating enormous breakfasts of smoke-cured ham and sausages, eggs, home-grown fruit, sorghum molasses, toast, and coffee; cutting out deadwood timber and sawing it up for fuel against the winter's cold; listening to the old nestors swapping yarns on the shady side of the First National Bank in Seminole on Saturdays; attending town meetings and going to the nickelodeons to see Keystone comedies and Bill Hart in "Westerns"; and helping the neighbors with their hog-killings and harvestings (who would, in turn, help you).

Through some coincidence I was always running into John V. A. Weaver at State and Madison streets, and as I reached the corner of Mandel's Department Store there he was. Weaver was working as an advertising solicitor for the *Daily News* and acting as Henry Blackman Sell's and, following Sell, Harry Hansen's, unpaid assistant on the book pages of that evening newspaper. Johnny had had some of his *In American* verses accepted and published by Mencken and Nathan of the *Smart Set* (and they were very good too) and he was elated. But he was even more elated over the fact that, because my book pages on the *Tribune* came out on Saturdays whereas Sell's pages came out on Wednesdays, he had "scooped" me on the review of F. Scott Fitzgerald's *This Side of Paradise,* about which we had been very laudatory. Neither of us knew at the time that this book was to be a sort of symbol of at least one aspect of an era that was just beginning.

At the time I was chiefly impressed by the vibrant freshness of Fitzgerald's prose and the lyrical Celtic wildness and strangeness of his imagination, which I had already noted in some stories he had published in the *Smart Set*. It did not occur to me that there was anything new or revolutionary about the text; what Fitzgerald called "necking," which seemed to shock or titillate so many people, I had done from the time I was six years old when I had played pillow and post office and so had our fathers and mothers and grandfathers and grandmothers and great-grandfathers and great-grandmothers back to Adam, in one form or another. As a collegian, I hadn't drunk gin out of a pocket flask, nor heard of girls checking their girdles with their wraps at a dance—the girls I had known at college didn't wear girdles or corsets; gin was a liquid I thought was an ingredient only for cocktails or served raw only to Negroes in barrel houses; but on occasions of celebration I had drunk plenty of champagne, light and heavy wines, bonded bourbon, and beer without ever getting —except once—more than joyous and lighthearted.

I was interested in Fitzgerald as a gifted and promising new writer, not as the herald of the "Jazz Age" or as the novelist of a generation "seeking new freedoms" and "revolting against restraint." I didn't see any essential difference between the characters of *This Side of Paradise* and the characters of Joseph Medill Patterson's *A Little Brother to the Rich,* which had been published twelve years before, or the characters of some Rupert Hughes novels, except that Fitzgerald's young people drank gin, whereas Patterson's young wasters drank whisky, champagne, and old port, and spoke the slang of the time instead of the slang of Fitzgerald's time.

Nor, as I learned from Fitzgerald when I met him in New York later, was he aware that he had written a "bible of flaming youth." It was not his intention. He said he was desperately anxious to make some money to marry Zelda Sayre, whom he otherwise had been in danger of losing to a young man of considerable inherited wealth. He had tried advertising but wasn't a success at it, and had tried some short stories and sold them to Mencken and Nathan of the *Smart Set* at fifty dollars apiece. He thought he might try his hand at writing a novel, because he might make more money that way. But he didn't know how a novel was constructed.

"So," said Fitzgerald to me across a lunch table at Delmonico's, then at Fifth Avenue and Forty-fourth Street, "I propped up a copy of Booth Tarkington's *The Magnificent Ambersons* and a copy of James Branch Cabell's *Jurgen* before me and followed their leads and chapter divisions with a story about me and Zelda and persons I knew or could imagine. The book didn't make me as rich as I thought it would nor as you would suspect from its vogue and the way it was talked about. Most of those who read it seem to have read borrowed copies or got it from the public or rental libraries, for its actual sale wasn't more than 30,000 copies the first year. But it did make my stuff in demand by the *Saturday Evening Post* and other well-paying magazines, and Paul Reynolds, my agent, has been able to gouge good prices out of the editors. Zelda married me on the day of publication of *This Side of Paradise*, so everything turned out as I wished."

I was not, that May day in 1920, as I encountered Johnny Weaver at State and Madison, familiar with the milieu Fitzgerald described or referred to—Princeton, Bar Harbor, Lake Geneva, Pasadena, and other haunts of the sons and daughters of wealthy men. All I knew was that he had given his characters a special kind of romantic reality, with a brooding undercurrent of Celtic mysticism to the desperately gay excesses of his frantic young people, a tenderness of the author underlying the brittle sophomoric cynicism of the "line" or collegiate chatter.

I realized that Fitzgerald was a snob, who professed to be a socialist and who was infinitely concerned with the ways and clothes, amusements, food, drink, and habits of mind of the wealthy and the socially secure; and that he had endowed them with an aura of romantic glamour and spectacular adventure which he wished to achieve himself. For instance, in some of his stories Fitzgerald had laid so much emphasis upon the necessity of wearing Brooks Brothers clothes (as John Myers O'Hara was to do later), if one was not to be considered a social inferior, that I asked Johnny what a Brooks Brothers suit looked like.

"This is a Brooks Brothers suit I got on," grinned Johnny. "Ain't it a lulu?" It looked like something that had been cut by looking at a daguerreotype of the 1880s: buttons almost to the neck, a narrow lapel, and draped like a gunny sack (the sort of costume later worn by the Day youngsters in *Life with Father.* I decided then and there that I would never be acceptable in Fitzgerald's set, because nothing could persuade me to don such a museum piece of a suit.

On the strength of my review of *This Side of Paradise* and at a suggestion of mine, Mary King (later Mrs. J. M. Patterson), Sunday editor of the *Tribune,* had ordered a story from Fitzgerald just after I left the paper. He sent Miss King a story and wrote me a letter which was forwarded to me:

"DEAR MR. RASCOE: Just a line to ask you if you liked the story *The Lees of Happiness* which I wrote on order from your Sunday magazine. Its perhaps a little gloomy. You were kind enough to praise my first novel—I am now in the midst of a second—and its very much harder sledding. Hope it won't dissopoint you and the other critics were desposed to like *This Side of Paradise.*"

At first glance I was puzzled over those "its" without the apostrophe, the "dissopoint" and "desposed," thinking it was a special kind of Princetonian humor; but I decided that Fitzgerald shared the inability of Dr. Samuel Johnson and many other eminent writers to spell words correctly; and later I was to learn from Edmund Wilson, a classmate and friend of Fitzgerald's at Princeton, that Fitzgerald spelled "by ear," causing the editors at *Scribner's* a great deal of trouble in correcting his misspellings.

I could see from the difference between our reviews that *This Side of Paradise* meant one thing to Johnny and an entirely different thing to me. To me it was a disordered yet curiously coherent lyrical narrative of adolescent growing pains, voicing the enthusiasms and despairs, the search for certainty of belief and for an integrated character on the part of a gifted, romantic, sensitive, and chaste youngster whose values in life had received a severe shaking up as the result of the war and the diminishing of the family fortunes that had forced him to make his own way in the world after a spendthrift life of a pampered son of a fairly wealthy family. To Johnny, it was a challenge of the new youth to its elders, a realistic exposition of the freedom from restraint that young men and women were demanding for themselves.

Fitzgerald was only four years younger than I, yet he seemed to me then infinitely less mature than I. He was twenty-one when he left Princeton to join the Army and twenty-four when he wrote *This Side of Paradise,* yet he was still responding to life and literature like a bright and inquisitive high-school sophomore.

In fact he never did seem to me to reach emotional maturity, although he achieved artistic maturity in some of the short stories he published prior to *This Side of Paradise,* and, by curbing the extravagance of his fancy, achieved technical perfection in *The Great Gatsby,* and his greatest depth in *Tender Is the Night.* I was not surprised, then, when he wrote me on August 20, 1920, after I had got down to Oklahoma:

"Thank you very much for your most encouraging letter of August 14. [He had written me in a despondent mood and I had assured him that he faced a brilliant and prosperous future because he possessed unusual gifts of imagination and style and was touching the stars with his uplifted head.] I had an idea you were a much older man. I have read a good deal of your criticisms in newspapers but like Francis Hackett I seem to be able to find nothing you've written in book form."

What he meant to say was not that neither he nor Francis Hackett had been able to find anything I had written in book form but that he had sought books written by both Hackett and me and had not been able to find any. From that letter I observed that Fitzgerald not only could not spell well but that his Princeton education hadn't given him a mastery of elementary syntax. But he succeeded in writing beautifully and movingly at times in spite of these handicaps. Hackett had, by the way, published *Horizons,*

23

a collection of his *New Republic* essays; I had to my credit two paper-covered booklets, one of them on H. L. Mencken, and had written introductions for three French classics.

I often wondered if Fitzgerald wouldn't have been a much better writer if he had never gone to college and had had to shift for himself soon after leaving high school or earlier; for he had an exuberant poetic imagination, tinged with Celtic melancholy, and, in trying to be a Princetonian among the sons of wealthy men, a curious dichotomy developed in his mind, which made him a snob and caused him to make his hero in *This Side of Paradise* say that he despised the poor and yet kept him preoccupied with the delusion that he was a socialist. Thus he was to write me, characteristically misspelling Nietzsche:

"Mencken's 'code of honor' springs from Nietche, doesn't it?—the agreement among the powerful to exploit the less powerful and respect each other," and "why hasn't someone mentioned to him [Mencken] that he is in an intolerably muddled syllogism with several excluded middles on the question of aristocracy. What on earth does he mean by it? Every aristocrat of every race has come in for scathing comment yet he holds out the word as a universal panacea for art."

Mencken's code of honor did not spring from Nietzsche: it has long been a universal principle among great numbers of men, particularly among Americans from Washington, Jefferson, Franklin, Adams, Paine, Randolph, and Hamilton, down through the Concord group in New England and on through the whole fabric of American thinking; Mark Twain had it; Ring Lardner had it; the village grocer has it, bartenders have it, educators, men of God, doctors, and millions of others exist by it and have existed by it. Fitzgerald confused the Platonic and Aristotelian "aristocracy" (i.e., rule by the best minds which was Mencken's definition) with the inheritors of great wealth whom he knew at Princeton, Bar Harbor, Asheville, and Newport—descendants of acquisitive and energetic men who never thought of themselves as

24

aristocrats and who certainly did not agree among themselves to exploit the less powerful and respect each other; their throat-cutting was mainly done among themselves.

But this only shows that Fitzgerald at twenty-four had an eager and inquisitive, if immature and superficial, mind, and when he was to tell me about how he wrote *This Side of Paradise* with *Jurgen* and *The Magnificent Ambersons* propped up before him, I recalled how he had obviously been deeply impressed by the chapter entitled, "The Brown Man with Queer Feet" in *Jurgen* and had used the description in several of his stories and in *This Side of Paradise,* without understanding Cabell's use of the symbol. In *Jurgen,* the brown man with queer feet is Pan, which Fitzgerald would have known if he had not been ignorant of mythology. In *This Side of Paradise,* Amory Blaine, the hero, had the hallucination of twice seeing the brown man with queer feet on a drunken and sordid party: "A middle-aged man in a brown sack suit . . . And, suddenly, Amory perceived the feet and with a sudden rush of blood to the head he realized he was afraid. The feet were all wrong with a wrongness he felt rather than knew . . . He wore no shoes, but, instead, a sort of half moccasin, pointed, though, like the shoes they wore in the fourteenth century, and with the little ends curling up. They were darkish brown and his toes seemed to fill them to the end."

Thus Cabell's amoral Pan, an elementary force of Nature, passes through the alembic of Fitzgerald's imagination and emerges as an apparition of Evil, which stirs Amory's Puritan conscience and prevents him from spending the night with a little trollop of a chorus girl he had picked up at Bistolary's (Bustanoby's?) and who had taken him, Fred Sloane (a Princeton classmate, with him on a binge in New York) and another chorus girl to her flat. . . . And this was the book that within the year was to shock the prurient and to be identified as the promulgator of the "Jazz Age," to produce a host of imitations and vulgarizations, such as *Dancers in the Dark, Flaming Youth, The Wife of the Centaur,* and *Replenishing Jessica,* and—because life imitates art and most people, young and old, follow fashions—to set a standard of conduct for a decade, a standard no more generally loose, promiscuous, or immoral than standards of conduct in any other decade but more exhibitionistic and more articulate than usual in defiance of the conventions.

It was a decade during which many hypocritical taboos were broken down, American literature was liberated from its subservience to the smug moralities of British literature as represented by the work of Mrs. Humphry Ward, Marie Corelli, and Hall Caine, and even from subservience to the literature represented by the work of Sir Edmund Gosse and Sir Arthur Quiller-Couch. It was a decade during which the more constraining Victorian middle-class ideas of respectability (often a false front hiding the slums of the heart and mind) were pretty thoroughly routed in a dancing carnival of uninhibited youth. It was the culmination of a revolt against standards of domestic and social behavior, which had been voiced by Ibsen, Brandes, and others on the European continent, taken up independently by Samuel Butler in England, and echoed by G. Bernard Shaw, H. G. Wells, George Moore, James Joyce, Arnold Bennett, Lytton Strachey, and lesser lights in the British Isles and was having its effect upon Theodore Dreiser, James Branch Cabell, Sherwood Anderson, Sinclair Lewis, Ellen Glasgow, Willa Cather, Edna St. Vincent Millay and practically a whole generation of younger writers in America— the generation that preceded the generation of Hemingway, Dos Passos, E. E. Cummings, John Steinbeck, and William Saroyan. It was the troglodytic Dreiser, heedless of abuse, calumny, boycott, and ostracism, who had, in his clumsy but determined way, cleared a path through the swamps and jungles of sentimentality, prejudice, and hypocrisy over which younger American writers could tread, giving American literature a new vitality, a new honesty, a new freedom of expression.

There were, of course, the inevitable vulgarizations and excesses, like those of the Restoration days after the release of the Puritan restrictions that had prevailed under Cromwell, and there were many meretricious by-products of an era of heady freedom. Indeed it was a wine too strong for many of the celebrants, causing them to live too frantically and burning themselves out early in life; for the 1920s began with war dislocations, disillusions, and dissatisfactions which produced a restless and reckless era among a very considerable portion of the younger generation.

But that May morning in 1920 life seemed glorious in anticipation to me. I was presently to store the bulk of my large library in a friend's house, taking with me to Oklahoma only my Greek and Latin classics, twenty volumes of Anatole France, and twenty volumes of Remy de Gourmont and a miscellaneous collection of other books in French; and I was to rent my apartment furnished and attend two going-away parties given in my honor.

One of them was at the home of Jerome and Florence Frank in Hubbard Woods, at which, I recall, were Ruth and Harry Hansen, Etta and Keith Preston, Tennessee and Sherwood Anderson, Gene Markey, and many friends of the Franks whom I had not met before. Jerome was then a successful young corporation lawyer and was later to become one of Franklin D. Roosevelt's closest advisers, head of the Securities Exchange Commission, and finally a judge of the Circuit Court of Appeals, author of two books on the interpretation and philosophy of law and many magazine articles. Florence was a poet and playwright, connected with the Little Theater in Chicago, which had been founded by Maurice Browne and Ellen Von Falkenberg. Harry Hansen six years later was to be called to New York as literary critic for the *World,* later the *World-Telegram,* and was to write *Midwest Portraits* of the chief literary figures of our day in Chicago, a novel nostalgic of his boyhood in Davenport, Iowa, and a history of the Chicago River. Keith Preston, the brilliant wit, versifier, and Greek and Latin scholar, was to die untimely eight years later as the result of an infected tooth, after a happy career as a professor of Latin and Greek and as a columnist on the *News*. Sherwood Anderson was to move around to New York, Birmingham, Alabama, New Orleans, Paris, and Marion, Virginia, widening his fame through his novels and short stories, and to die on a trip to Chile as the result of swallowing a portion of a toothpick which punctured his intestines. Gene Markey was to draw caricatures for me to illustrate my pages on the New York *Tribune,* for Harry Hansen on the Chicago *Daily News* and for Ashton Stevens on the Chicago *Examiner,* branch out as a short-story writer, marry three of the most beautiful women in Hollywood, seriatim (Joan Bennett, Hedy Lamarr, and Myrna Loy), become a naval commander during the war, and a writer-producer in Hollywood; he was then a dilettante art student and a well-groomed, amiable, young man about town, the only man in Chicago I knew whose wardrobe was tailored in London.

The other party was given by Betty and Anthony M. Rud at their large house in Oak Park and it lasted all night, all the next day, and half the next night, with some dropping out and others dropping in, with Betty making pots of excellent coffee and helping the maid to keep piles of sandwiches available. Many of the Chicago *Tribune* crowd were there, including Margaret and Martin Stevers, Maude Martin Evers, and Charley MacArthur. Tony was later to write an excellent but neglected novel, *The Second Generation,* and hundreds of short stories and serve for a time as editor of *Adventure* magazine before dying in his early forties, just as he was getting back into his stride and writing his best stuff after a nervous breakdown. Charley was to go on to New York as a writer for the Hearst Sunday supplement, *The American Weekly,* become the elfin playboy of the Algonquin group, and celebrated as such by Alexander Woollcott, collaborate with Edward Sheldon on *Lulu Belle,* starring Lenore Ulric, and produced by Belasco, and collaborating with Ben Hecht on *The Front Page* and many subsequent motion-picture productions. Martin Stevers was to write *Steel Trails, Sea Lanes,* and

Mind Through the Ages and become editor in chief of Compton's Encyclopedia.

These were gay and happy parties, at which we all drank, but lightly, and nobody got intoxicated; we danced to phonograph music, told stories, and played games; there were many beautiful girls and young matrons at both parties and I think I was a little in love with nearly every one of them and I had a feeling of warm friendship for all the males present too; for Chicago is a homey town, at least among the people I knew, and the atmosphere at all parties was cordial, unaffected, and unstrained. And these were farewell parties flatteringly (if unconsciously) designed to make me loath to leave.

I was to recall these parties as I sat in the club car of the Rock Island train as it pulled out of the La Salle Street Station on the way to Kansas City and thence to Seminole, Oklahoma. And I was to recall also how nine years before I had come to Chicago in a black leather-upholstered coach car, sitting up all night with my imagination wildly playing over the wondrous adventures I would have in the huge, dynamic city which I had visited during a summer between my junior and senior years in high school. And I recalled too, in the manner of free association of images and ideas, isolated incidents such as:

Ring Lardner and his pint-sized companion, Ben Kendall, at Stillson's bar across the street from the *Tribune* and of Ring's need for Ben to bolster his wavering ego, asking Ben if he, Lardner, was as good a writer as F. P. Dunne, and Ben would say much better; then if he was as good as George Ade, Harry Leon Wilson, and dozens of others on to Mark Twain, and Ben would allow that Ring was the best humorist and the greatest writer in the world; and of the time when, after Ring had got into the money with a contract with the *Saturday Evening Post,* following the great success of his Busher stories, the Lardners had bought a house in Riverside and Mrs. Lardner would permit Ring to come into town on Friday night for session with his "boom companions," provided he got back Saturday night or Sunday morning and rested to be fresh for work from Monday through Friday; and how he contrived to break this routine by having Ben send him telegrams signed George Horace Lorimer and saying he was at the Congress Hotel for a day and wanted Ring to come in immediately to discuss his latest story; and how on one of these occasions Ring joined Ben and the next day they awoke to find themselves guests at the House of David, a religious community across the lake at St. Joseph, Michigan, and how from this episode resulted one of Ring's most hilarious stories; and how I wrote an article about Ring and sent it in turn to John Phillips of the *American* magazine and Henry Seidel Canby of the *Literary Review* of the New York *Post* and both of them had returned the article, saying that Lardner was not sufficiently well known to warrant an article about him (only about 20,000,000 males were using Ring's gag line from the Busher stories, "You know me, Al," at the time), and five years later sold the article just as I had originally written it. Hearing Mary Garden in *The Juggler of Notre Dame* from the top balcony and dashing around to the stage door of the auditorium in a blinding snowstorm to take "Primy" (we called her that because she expected to become a prima donna), a member of the chorus, to our hotel on the South Side, where other students would be waiting up for us with coffee, sandwiches, and brandy in Primy's room; watching Marquis James, later winner of the Pulitzer prize for his biography of Andrew Jackson, writing stories for the pulps between takes of copy while he was on the rim of the copy desk of the Chicago *Tribune;* he would read a take of copy, write heads and subheads for it, then turn to his story and write right along, as though he hadn't been interrupted, until another batch of copy was thrown into his slot, a demonstration of relaxation and concentration that amazed me; reading my way practically through the philosophical section at the University of Chicago library and yet never prepared for my lessons in philosophy class; listening enchantedly to Alfred Kreymborg recite his wistful, amusing, and touching little songs to his own accompaniment at the Dill Pickle Club, presided over by an ex-I.W.W., an extraordinary character named Jack Jones, his audience largely consisting of University of Chicago and Northwestern professors and students, with a large sprinkling of raggledy-taggledy soapbox radicals anxious to spiel to the crowd; listening to the sensible talk about life and art by Stanislaw Szukalski, whom I consider the greatest sculptor since Rodin and one of the greatest sculptors of all time, as he rubbed shoe polish into a figure he had cast in plaster of Paris because he could not afford bronze and wanted to attain a bronze or ebony effect.

Then there were other memories crowding swiftly upon the ones that came before: swimming in Lake Michigan before breakfast from what amounted to a private beach at the foot of our street in Rogers Park, swimming again before dinner with the family, and enjoying the lake breezes on the sands again after dinner; spending long hours on Sundays in the old Field Museum, a relic of the World's Columbian Exposition, in Jackson Park; interviewing Titta Ruffo and having him bid me come into his suite at the Congress Hotel with, "I am being driven crazy by that damned Irish tenor upstairs,"—the tenor being John McCormack—and my saying, "Why don't you practice when he is practicing? You can holler louder than he can"; dancing in the moonlight on the terrace of the Hyde Park Hotel, with the pounding of the waves of Lake Michigan mingling with the music from the orchestra and occasionally sending a fine spray up to bedew the dancers and make the waxed stone floor both slippery and sticky; listening to Marie and Ben Hecht play duets, she at the piano and he with the violin, drinking Marie's homemade beer and watching Ben chuckle as he made some cynical observation or spun some fantastic yarn, corruscating with farfetched similes and glittering with bizarre epithets and adjectives, while Marie would say, "He doesn't believe any of that stuff; he's just talking for effect"; enchanted at the singing of Nora Bayes and Jack Norworth of

"Shine on, Harvest Moon"; plowing through one of the worst snowstorms in Chicago in years to St. Elizabeth's Hospital to watch, in almost unendurable agony, the convulsions of the mother while my daughter was being born; eating breast of guinea hen on Virginia ham, sous cloche, at Schlogl's with Harry Hansen, Richard Atwater, Keith Preston, Carl Sandburg, Sherwood Anderson, J. P. McEvoy, Ben Hecht, Henry Justin Smith, and Lloyd Lewis, while we drew out and ribbed some visiting literary celebrity from New York or London; listening to the yodelers while devouring lentil soup, Sauerbraten, pickled pigs' knuckles, and Wienerschnitzel and drinking Pilsener at a Bierstube on North Avenue, south of Lincoln Park; restfully contemplating the inspiringly beautiful St. Gaudens statue of Lincoln in that park; attending the forums of Dr. Bernard Iddings Bell at his Episcopal church on South Wabash where he invited atheists and I.W.W. members, syndicalists, and other radicals to voice their views and air their grievances, winning many of them to moderating their opinions and attending church, not by preaching at them, but by showing them sympathy, understanding, and the true meaning of the brotherhood of man, which they had all talked loudly about but hadn't believed in or practiced; paying, with pangs of conscience at my extravagance and with bitterness over the high cost of living in wartime, sixteen dollars for a pair of Cordovan leather shoes at French, Shriner & Urner's; having only $112 in the bank but being so struck in admiration of a bronze statuette on display at McClurg's that I drew out $98 for it and took it home, fully expecting to be admonished by my wife for such foolishness but embraced by her fondly instead, she liking the statuette as much as I did; winning $100 in the office baseball pool the very next day, though I had never won in such a pool before, nor have I since; going with W. B. Yeats from the home of Harriet Monroe, founder-editor of *Poetry: A Magazine of Verse,* to the parlor of a spiritualist medium in whose powers Yeats at the time believed, for he was a disciple of Madame Blavatsky's; searching the town in

32

vain for a good bowl of chile con carne; reading aloud to my wife nearly the whole first book of John Masefield's poems, which had just then swept into my ken, and from Simeon Strunsky's *Belshazzar Court,* still one of my favorite books of essays; reporting the feats of a young swimmer named Johnny Weismuller in the pool of the Chicago Athletic Club; meeting the gracious, witty, and impeccable John Drew when he came into the city room of the *Tribune* for an interview—Captain Stott, the city day editor, had phoned him at the Blackstone Hotel and said he would like to send a reporter over for an interview, but Mr. Drew said he wouldn't put the reporter to that much trouble but would come over to the office instead; he was playing in Somerset Maugham's *The Circle* and he asked me more questions than I asked him; I never met an actor so utterly without pretense or side; reading and writing about Proust's *Du Côté de Chez Swann* and *Al'Ombre des Jeunes Filles en Fleurs,* the first two parts of *Remembrance of Things Past;* this was four years before Proust was translated into English and five years before a book of tributes to Proust was issued containing laudations by twenty British writers, including Arnold Bennett, Arthur Symonds, George Saintsbury, Compton MacKenzie, Alec Waugh, and Logan Pearsall Smith; Proust's monumental history of the Swanns and Guermantes, by the way, was brought out in America over a period of ten years, the separate parts issued first by Henry Holt, then by Thomas Seltzer, then by Albert & Charles Boni, and finally the plates of the complete work were acquired by Random House; touting W. Somerset Maugham's *Of Human Bondage* and Norman Douglas's *South Wind* eight years before these books were "discovered" and touted by Alexander Woollcott and Heywood Broun in New York (nearly the entire sale of the first editions of both novels had been confined to Chicago and its environs; *South Wind* had been imported in English sheets and when, on a visit to New York, I told Frank Dodd of Dodd, Mead & Co. that he had one very fine novel on his current list, *South Wind,* he said he had never heard of it, nor did his editor know Dodd, Mead had the book; a search of the records showed that sale of the novel had been almost entirely confined to Chicago bookstores; the novel had been imported in sheets from England and the second edition was not set and plated until the demand grew strong in the Middle West); reading with glee H. L. Mencken's pronouncement that Chicago is the literary capital of the country, the only city in which literature is a lively subject, considered worth fighting for, and being glad of my part in making it so, as implied in Mencken's essay.

These, then, were my thoughts, my reveries, as the train carried me toward Seminole and away from Chicago which had so successfully filled this period of my life.

I had wired an old high-school sweetheart that I would have an hour between trains at Kansas City and would like very much to see her, her husband, and their baby; and they were all at the station to meet me when I arrived. The baby was chubby, affectionate, and beautiful, and came to me from his mother's arms voluntarily when I held out my arms, and I carried him and held him in the taxi while we went to their apartment for a delightful half hour of chatter, coffee, and cake.

The next afternoon my father and my wife and two children (who had preceded me to the farm in Oklahoma, because my wife was recuperating from pneumonia) were at the station in Seminole to greet me. An hour later I had a swim in my father's artificial lake. Then I donned boots and riding clothes, and my wife and I took a long ride through the pasture land and wooded hills of my father's four hundred and fifty acres, returning to a dinner my mother had cooked that made my eyes bulge—Southern-fried chicken with dumplings and gravy, country-cured ham, broiled squirrel, roast spareribs, baked Irish and sweet potatoes, radishes, young onions, lettuce, sweet and sour pickles, piccalilli, corn bread with cracklings in it, fresh biscuits, deep-dish apple pie, and coffee. I did justice to it, taking a portion of everything; and after dinner we sat around in the living room, chatting, my father and I drinking a brandy wine my mother had distilled out of wild plums until he and I were a little tight. Then someone said my two brothers had fixed up the tree house for my wife and me to sleep in and toward midnight she and I climbed the ladder to that heavenly place in which on clear nights the canvas roof could be removed and the moon and stars could be seen through the limbs and leaves.

CHAPTER 3

Dirt Farmer to Oil Baron

FARM LIFE IN OKLAHOMA. LURE OF WAR WAGES.
EXODUS FROM THE LAND. BOURBON (COUNTRY
STYLE) AND JIMMY SHARPE, LAST OF THE BAD
MEN. OIL IN OUR BACK YARD. BACK TO CHICAGO.

Farm help was scarce and hard to get at any price in 1920, as it had been since 1915, and I was a welcome hand to a work crew which consisted of a tenant farmer and his son, who had a house on the land, my father, and my two brothers. Even before we got into the war there had been a mad rush to the cities, not only on the part of farmers' sons and farm hands but of tenant farmers, share croppers, and small landowners—all attracted by the high wages prevailing in the plants that were supplying the Allies with war materials. High wages in the war industries had also drained men away from their ordinary peacetime occupations, resulting in inflationary wages not only in unskilled labor but in work like that of driving a streetcar or trucking, and this situation had been intensified by the call to arms, with the resulting drain on civilian man power.

These high wages were illusory; housing shortages had developed as a result of the influx of farm laborers to the cities and rents were high, prices of food and clothing had rocketed upward since 1914; taking 100 as the norm for 1913, retail food prices had gone up 68.3 points in 1918 and had reached 203.4 by 1920; but the average man thinks of wages only in terms of figures and not in terms of the purchasing power of the dollar.

In vain had my father pleaded with his fellow farmers, tenant farmers, and share croppers to stay on the land in a time of rising costs, telling them they would not only have the shelter and food they could produce themselves but a larger net cash income than they would have by going to the city. All they could grasp was salaries of from $6 to $15 a day for unskilled labor; they couldn't grasp the fact that, with the rising living costs, their net on the week might not only be nothing but that costs might even eat into their savings.

My father told me, with saddened irony, that, when Allied purchasing agents had gone through the county seeking mules and horses and offering farmers two or three times what the farmers valued the animals at, he knew farmers who sold their only work teams for $300 cash, thinking they had hit a bonanza. My father asked, "How are you going to till your land?" This had not occurred to them; and when farm labor began to get scarce in 1917, many such farmers with no teams to work with and no able-bodied help abandoned their farms and joined the trek to the cities where they thought they would strike it rich because of the high wages being offered in almost any line of work.

I had seen the same thing happen in Chicago, but from the other end. Agents had gone through the South offering transportation to Negro farm hands for themselves and families and what seemed like fabulous wages; the Negro population of the "black belt" of Chicago (they segregate Negroes in the North as well as in the South) doubled between 1915 and 1919; housing for the newcomers was inadequate even in the slums at high rentals; the 150,000 new arrivals spilled over into other residential districts, creating friction with the whites who owned property that depreciated in value whenever the landlord of an adjacent tenement took advantage of the high rents he could squeeze out of the Negroes and filled his flats with them; the friction developed into the race riots of July 1919; and when the war boom collapsed early in 1920, about 100,000 Southern Negroes were stranded in the city, without jobs or means of getting back to the farms in the South. They turned (see Carl Sandburg's *The Chicago Race Riots,* 1919) to gambling, robbery, dope-peddling, prostitution, petty thievery, and menial work at bare-subsistence pay, which of course lowered the general standards of wages for that kind of work, thereby creating further racial animosities which broke out sporadically into dynamitings, killings, arson, and terror.

My father and mother had always considered their farm primarily as a subsistence one, whereon they could grow all the food they needed, including beef, pork, and poultry, and only secondarily as a source of income. They had cows, pigs, chickens, guineas; and my father had stocked his lake with bass and perch from the government hatcheries. He had created the lake by building a concrete dam to hold the water that washed down from the higher terrain during rains and that came from two springs. This not only provided him a diversion—because he liked to fish —and fish for the table to vary the diet, but in summer it provided him a source of income.

He had not thought of this at first; but when my brothers had constructed two diving boards and began inviting their friends to come for a swim, others passing by on the highway asked if they might swim there also; Dad gladly granted them permission and they would go away to return in their bathing suits. Then some of them began to ask him why he didn't provide bathhouses with towels and lockers and charge a fee.

So Dad, being a good carpenter, erected model bathhouses, laid in a supply of towels, soap, and combs, and turned the running of the enterprise over to my brothers. There was an overflow outlet in the dam, which was always flowing because of the supply of fresh water from the springs, even in droughts of short duration. This kept the lake water clean and fresh and thereby attracted many, because the only other swimming places in that part of the country were muddy rivers and ponds without outlets which tended to become stagnant and covered with green scum.

38

My father also so channeled the overflow that it irrigated his whole section of bottom land, on which he raised sugar cane, watermelons, cantaloupes, and peanuts. These products he did not sell; prices did not justify it; he fattened his hogs on the surplus after taking the family needs. The cane would be made into sorghum at a mill nearby where the fee for the milling was a share in the molasses; there would be several barrels for Dad and only half a barrel would last the family for a year. He mixed portions of the rest with his hog swill which consisted of watermelons, cantaloupes, buttermilk, peanuts, sorghum molasses, corn shorts, corn, and barley. His pens were clean and his pigs and hogs and sows were fat and healthy.

So also did he feed his horses and the horses of others which he pastured for a fee on a 100-acre strip of grazing land. Nearly all the other farmers in the region—except an intelligent Seminole Indian named Billy Bowlegs (descendant of the famous Seminole chief of that name) who was Dad's friend and took his advice— were unshakeable one-crop farmers. That is, they would plant their entire arable acreage in cotton for sale, neglecting not only to plant enough corn for their own needs but being so cash-greedy they had no vegetable gardens, planting their cotton right up to their doors. Then they would have to buy corn in town usually on a rising market for corn and a falling market for their one product—cotton.

Dad was terracing and cross-furrowing his land twenty-five years before the catastrophe of the long drought in the "Dust Bowl" showed the imperative need for such soil conservation; and he grew nearly everything imaginable on his farm besides his two major crops, cotton and corn. He grew alfalfa, milo maise, popcorn, wheat, barley, sugar cane, watermelons, cantaloupes, Irish potatoes, sweet potatoes, muskmelons, blue-stem grass (on the pastureland), sage for his sausage, and even experimented successfully in growing tobacco, but just for the fun of it and to give away, because he loathed tobacco.

39

Mother's private domain included the vegetable garden and her flower garden, in the former of which she grew radishes, onions, leek, tomatoes, parsley, lettuce, beets, turnips, cabbage, cauliflower, peppers, cucumbers, okra, squash, and eggplant, much of which she preserved against the months when they would be out of season. On the land there were wild plum, apple, persimmon, walnut, and hickory trees, all bearing. We stored the hickory nuts and walnuts for cracking around the base-burner stove on cold winter nights.

I built a tent house on the farm. There was plenty of room for us in the house, but I thought my wife, my children, and I should try living entirely on our own. And, besides, I wanted to see what sort of Robinson Crusoe or Admirable Crichton I was capable of being. I had seen single tents; I didn't see why a two-room or even a three-room or larger house could not be built by joining these single tents together. I learned that the county had a surplus of tents, used by road-construction gangs during the war, and that these could be purchased at two dollars each. I bought two of the double-roof kind.

Then with the help of my brothers I laid a wooden floor for the living room and scraped the hard clay of the other room down to where it had the surface of linoleum, over which we spread a straw carpet and then laid several cheap rugs over the carpet. I dug trenches around the house to drain off the water which came from the canvas eaves during rain. With a post-hole digger I set a series of posts on the north and south sides of the tents and notched them so that the ropes attached to the canvas roof could be tightened after rain or heavy wind, providing a smooth and even super-roof. I set the entrances of the tents four feet apart, facing each other, and over that passageway I overlapped the super-roofs, making the passageway weatherproof, and joined the two tents together on one side by cutting out the fronts of one of them and using the spare canvas as a wall on the north side and as the wall of an elbow entrance on the south side. This was to keep the wind from sweeping in between the two tents; the elbow entrance, which had a canvas door which I devised with reinforcing strips of wood, was in effect a vestibule. Also I did what my brothers said couldn't be done: I devised weatherproof windows for the tent, cutting holes for the windows, leaving two inches of canvas from the wall to be split at the four corners and thus be tacked down on the wooden frames of the windows. I supported the windowframes from the bottom with two-by-four planks set deep into the ground. I further weatherproofed the windows by using bicycle tape around the edges. Heavy rains and heavy snows came and high winds, but we were always snug, dry, and secure inside the tent, the main room of which was warmed by a tiny stove which needed only a few pine knots and a handful of coal to keep the room warm throughout the day and night even in sub-zero weather.

In the barn I had found an old kitchen range with its stovepipes, which Mother had discarded when she bought an oil-burning range. It was a magnificent old contraption, remarkably efficient not only for cooking and baking but for warming up the second room, which served us as kitchen and dining room. The children preferred to sleep in the big house and so we had no need for a second bedroom. I found a section of a tin-covered wooden flue of the kind used on threshing machines through which to blow the chaff. It was on a dump heap a mile out from Seminole. I spied it as I was driving home from town. It served my purpose precisely; I made a sort of refrigerator out of it, to keep out butter from melting and our milk and cream from turning sour. I tacked a wire screen over the opening to be exposed on the outside of the tent and made a door, with leather hinges, for the opening that would be inside the tent, cut a square hole in the canvas for the "refrigerator" to pass through, propped it up, and weatherproofed it as I had done with the windows. Thus in cool or cold weather it was not necessary to go outside the tent to the cooling place for milk and butter that I had made by digging a hole near a spring, flooring and walling it with planks, making a door for it, and insulating it with wet sawdust.

I built open-shelf bookcases for my small library. I shopped around in secondhand stores in Oklahoma City and bought a small upright piano for $75, got it tuned for two dollars and shipped it down so we could have music in our tent house. My wife played beautifully and I liked to hear her play while I read.

With team and wagon I foraged through the woods for dead timber, which I sawed and corded against the winter's cold. I learned to manage a long, two-handed crosscut saw by keeping it balanced properly when there was no one to hold the other handle of it. I cut and stacked several cords of kindling and laid in a five-gallon can of kerosene to aid in starting a fire. We used acetylene lamps to light the tent house. When winter came, with winds howling over the prairie and snow beating against the windowpanes collecting on the roof, and drifting up against the north side of the tents, we were warm, happy, and extremely healthy. Through strenuous but relaxed physical labor in the fields and with the saw and ax, swimming and horseback riding, eating well and sleeping soundly, I had gained, by early fall, nearly twenty-five pounds, and it was all sinew.

I did no writing until the fall, when all the crops were in and there remained only hog-killing day, after the cold weather had set in. Even then I wrote only two short stories and two magazine articles, which I sold to the first magazines I sent them to. Evenings I would read Greek and Latin in the Loeb texts and translations, Anatole France and Remy de Gourmont in French (I got through the forty-odd volumes I had of these two writers), and current magazines, such as the *New Republic,* the *Nation, Harper's,* the *Atlantic Monthly,* and the *Saturday Evening Post.*

Another publication which gave me hours of fascinated delight and instruction was the Montgomery Ward mail-order catalogue. I wish I had a complete set of them, going back to the first issue, for I know of no better source of information about the needs, styles, implements, and luxuries of rural and sparsely populated districts at any given period since the founding of the company than that contained in these catalogues of articles for sale. They should be invaluable to the social historian, recording, as they do, the development and improvement of farm implements, the changes in styles of clothing, the prices obtaining in any given year, and the accessories offered, from fringe-topped buggies to parts for Fords, from a hunter and fisherman's supplies to pre-fabricated houses, from ladies' corsets to girdles.

Mother and Dad had some old Montgomery Ward catalogues and it was interesting to compare those of 1910 with those of 1920. The latest one was a book of useful knowledge to me as well as a pictorial display of varieties of merchandise. I ordered a number of items from the catalogue, one of which I had not hitherto known existed—a sanitary chemical toilet for indoor use, compact and odorless and so designed that it did not call attention to itself. I had already dug a deep cesspool over which my father had set a pretty privy, which he had carpentered in expert fashion and I had given a coat of paint. I had laid in a keg of lime to keep it sanitary. It was all right for clear, warm days and nights, but a nuisance in rainy or cold weather. This chemical toilet was a blessing in bad weather.

Reading the Oklahoma City *Daily Oklahoman* was a concession I made to the demands of the outside world upon my attention. The paper was delivered every morning by the R.F.D. carrier to our box at the outer gate of the farm. I never read it until evening, because I disliked the intrusion upon my health-giving rural quiet of the reports of violence and unrest crowding the pages.

Oklahoma has always been a dry state; it was admitted to the Union only on the provision that prohibition would be enforced within its borders. The reason for this was that Oklahoma was made a state by the combination of Oklahoma Territory and Indian Territory. Oklahoma Territory had been "wet" (although it was against the law to sell liquor to minors and Indians), and Indian Territory had been "dry," because Indians, not having had the long racial experience of the whites in developing a relative immunity to the more horrifying effects of alcohol, were (or at least alleged to be) easily crazed by alcohol and converted into a warlike and murderous mood.

But in 1920 good, well-distilled moonshine liquor (unaged and uncolored bourbon) was fairly easy to get at three or four dollars a gallon; and even today the best bonded rye and bourbon in the country is to be had in Oklahoma City at prices considerably under those of Texas, which enjoys local option but is predominately "wet." The reason for this is that Oklahoma bootleggers do not have to pay state taxes or license fees.

Very little hard liquor was brought into our house, because Mother strenuously objected to it; but she distilled an excellent wild-plum brandy of high potency and gooseberry wine for family use; and Dad made a vile-tasting brew, called Choctaw beer, from milo maize, according to an Indian recipe, and called "chock" for short. Cooled in an icebox, or in a bucket of ice in the fields, it was an acceptable refresher after a long morning's session of picking cotton or cutting sugar cane or at the end of the day—but for others, not me.

The most horrible experience I had with alcohol during my stay on the farm occurred one day when I caught a ride home from Seminole in the horse-drawn buggy of a deputy sheriff. He was driving past my father's farm to run down a tip about a moonshine still which a farmer was alleged to be running in the hills of the southern part of the county. I had gone into town with Dad in his model-T Ford and I had finished my business in town before he had finished his, so I had welcomed the chance to catch a ride home with the deputy sheriff, especially since that arm of the law was always good for a yarn or two about his experiences and had a congressman's or a prohibition agent's flexible moral sense about the necessity of rigid enforcement of prohibition;

privately he drank like a fish. Enforcement officers always had a large private supply of confiscated liquor on hand.

After we had driven a short distance from town, the deputy asked me if I would like a snort. I said it was just about time for one. He pulled a half-pint bottle out of his inside coat pocket and handed it to me. I took a swig, swallowed it, and jumped out of the moving buggy all in the space of five seconds. After I landed on the ground I kept jumping up and down and flinging my arms. I felt as though I were on fire inside; the roof of my mouth and my tongue burned as if I had eaten live coals. I was ashamed of my performance and when the tortures subsided, I apologized. I was still holding the bottle, and I handed it to the deputy and climbed back into the buggy. He had neither laughed nor been particularly concerned, merely puzzled. He took a hefty swig of the stuff and said he guessed I wasn't used to it. I asked him what it was. He said it was "jake." That meant nothing to me.

When Dad got home I told him about the incident and asked him what the liquor was. He said it was a concoction of alcohol and Jamaica ginger, sold in drugstores as medicine, but was poisonous and, if taken in considerable quantities, caused paralysis or death; that a number of Negroes in Seminole had died of it. He said he couldn't understand why the deputy drank that stuff when the sheriff always had a plentiful supply of good bonded liquor seized and held as "evidence," unless the deputy's stomach lining had been so thoroughly tanned by raw alcohol that he got no kick out of anything that wouldn't burn through the leather of his insides.

It reminded him, he said, of the remark of a stranger who had stopped off in Seminole. The stranger had struck up an acquaintance with a couple of farmers who took a shine to him and invited him to come with them to a livery barn and have a drink with them. Out of sight of disapproving citizens, one of the farmers took a pint bottle out of his pocket, pulled the stopper, and handed it to the stranger. He took a swallow, gulped, made a wry face, wiped his mouth, handed the bottle back, and said, "That's just right!" The host, seeing the expression on his face, asked, "What do you mean, just right?" "Well," said the stranger, "iffen it had been any better, you wouldn't have give me none, and iffen it had been any worse, it woulda kilt me."

Dad, George, and I often practiced pistol shooting. George had won a marksmanship medal at West Point but was no better at it than Dad was, though after practice and learning about the action of a revolver I got to be pretty good myself. I was already a good shot with a rifle, though never a good shot with a shotgun on quail hunts. Dad, George, and Henry often talked about a former "bad man" in the county who had killed six men, in (so he said, and the juries believed him) self-defense. He had served one short term in the penitentiary as a participant in a bank robbery, but was now a reformed man. They said he was the quickest man on the draw old-timers had ever seen and the best marksman with pistol or rifle. Dad said he had often seen this former bad man give exhibitions of shooting at county fairs and that he could drive a tenpenny nail into a tree at twenty-five yards with a rifle and do the same thing with a pistol at ten yards; that he was a dead shot in fancy, free-play shooting, and shooting from the hip.

I asked my father if it would be possible to meet this man. Dad answered, "Certainly. We'll invite him and his wife to dinner this coming Sunday."

When Sunday arrived, I could hardly wait for noon to come. Dinner is at noon on the farm. Supper is the evening meal. Sunday dinners are usually served around one o'clock. I had pictured our guest, of course, as one of those tall, strong, silent men, steely-eyed, leathery-faced, and with a look of cool calculation on his countenance. I had seen a lot of Bill Hart "Westerns" in the movies. He would be, I thought, a man of few words, but one

46

who would make his presence felt by the sheer force of something desperate yet marvellously efficient in his make-up.

While I was standing on the porch, looking toward the highway gate about a quarter of a mile away, for the twentieth time in an hour, I saw a roadster draw up, someone alight from it, and hold the gate open while the car went through, close the gate, and get back into the car. Presently the car reached the driveway alongside the house and I could see nothing except an enormous woman at the wheel. When the car stopped, there emerged from the far side of the car a skinny, insignificant-looking chap, about five feet six inches in height, carrying a baby. He trailed his tall, buxom and very jolly wife to the porch where we were all waiting to greet them. The family knew our visitors, but my wife and I were introduced. I was gape-mouthed. This was Jimmy Sharpe, the dead shot and former outlaw, now, as Dad said, policing a convict gang on the county roads.

Mother had cooked up one of her enormous Sunday dinners at which there was a superfluity of everything; but first, as soon as the baby was nursed and tucked away, Dad brought out glasses and cold well water and poured about six fingers each of bonded bourbon for Mrs. Sharpe, Jimmy, George, Henry, and myself. Mrs. Sharpe tossed hers off with relish and took a refill with Dad, while Jimmy drank his in relays, alternating with large draughts of water.

About halfway through the dinner Jimmy turned white and then a sickly green, got up, and rushed out of the house. Dad and I followed him in time to hold his head while he retched. He had to lie down while the rest of us ate our dinner; he didn't want any more. Mrs. Sharpe drank whisky straight throughout the meal and had some wild-plum brandy afterward and wasn't any the worse for it.

Jimmy and I got to be quite pally after he recovered; and thereafter he would often drop by at our tent house for a chat on his way to Seminole from his home in Wewoka.

47

Once I asked Jimmy if he had any notches on his gun. He said, "What would I want notches on my gun for?" I said, "To mark the number of men you have killed." He said, "I don't need no notches on a gun to know how many men I killed." He wasn't acquainted with Wild West fiction or the movies apparently, so I had to explain this business about notches. He said he had known a lot of outlaws and sheriffs and he had never heard of anyone carving or filing a notch for any such purpose. "Besides," he said, "why would a outlaw want plain evidence like that that he is a killer? When a outlaw is arrested, he tries to prove he is a law-abiding citizen who never harmed a fly. Why would he want to ask for the rope with a damned lot of notches on his gun bragging about how many men he had killed?"

I found that one of the reasons Jimmy liked to visit us on his trips to and from home was that he liked to hear my wife play the piano. He especially liked Bach and Chopin. He didn't know the names of the composers or the titles of the music he liked but he could identify the opening bars. My wife would play a few bars and he'd say, "No; that's not the one." When she hit upon the right one, after several tries, he would say, "That's it."

It turned out that what he liked best were Bach's *Chromatic Fantasia* and *Fugue in B Minor* and Chopin's *Minuet in G*. Every time he came to the house he wanted to hear those two pieces. He did not like syncopated or jazz music, and was frank in saying so. He had joined a church and was so thoroughly reformed about the matter of killing people that it proved to be his undoing on one occasion. A convict gang mutinied when he was on a road-construction job with them and he refused to use his rifle when they rushed him. They beat him into bloody unconsciousness, took his rifle, filed off their chains, and took to the hills, leaving Jimmy for dead. He staggered to a farmhouse when he recovered consciousness and phoned the sheriff at the county seat in Wewoka to tell what happened. A posse was dispatched and the men ultimately recaptured. But Jimmy resigned his office and devoted himself thereafter to his little farm.

As I said before, my father's campaign among the farmers of the county to get them to rotate their crops and each year to plant at least a third of their acreage in corn and the rest in cotton was fruitless. In the spring of 1920 cotton was planted in the South at costs demanding a price, after ginning, of at least twenty-five cents a pound. It had reached a high of forty cents a pound in 1919. Before the 1920 crop was harvested cotton began to drop on the cotton exchange and the first bales into the Seminole market brought only nineteen or twenty cents.

Many farmers had mortgaged their crops for loans at the banks. When the price fell far under harvesting costs—cotton pickers were still scarce and demanded high wages—many of these farmers refused to pick the cotton, forfeiting the crops to the banks, which couldn't afford to pick the cotton and market it either. This started a series of bank failures in Oklahoma, which ran into an epidemic throughout the South and spread to the North. The district Federal Reserve banks were unable to stem the tide of bankruptcies, because the small banks had loaned beyond their assets and reserves on uncollectible loans and had therefore defaulted on their obligations to larger banks. So the banks toppled over like a stack of cards falling against one another. There were thirty-three bank failures in Oklahoma in one month, November 1920.

A small town bank in Oklahoma, and in the South and Southwest generally, was, properly speaking, not a bank at all. It was primarily a firm engaged in real-estate speculation, horse-trading, and mortgage foreclosing on defaulted notes bearing usurious rates of interest. The farmers were not depositors; they had nothing to deposit, most of them; they were borrowers at the banks, in which the officers put their own money as working capital. The state usury law in Oklahoma limited the interest rate at 7 per cent.

But this is the way it worked in 1920. Farmer Brown, say, has a span of mules worth $350 in the inflated 1919 market and farm implements worth a couple of hundred dollars more. He needs $200 for food and for the salary of farm hands to tide him over until he has finished bringing in his crop. Early in the season he has already mortgaged his crop at the bank for the money necessary to live on while he is planting his crop. He applies for a loan of $200, giving as security a mortgage on his mules and implements. He receives $175 in cash and signs a note promising to pay back $200 at 7 per cent.

In other words, $25 in interest is collected before he gets his money. The amount subtracted from the loan varied in 1920 according to the urgency of the farmer's needs and the readily liquiding value of the collateral. Sometimes the amount deducted from a $100 loan was as much as $30. If the farmer invoked the usury law (as some poor devils did to their sorrow), he would be blacklisted by every bank in the state and thereafter could not borrow a cent, no matter what security he had to offer.

Bank-deposit insurance and other reforms later were designed under the New Deal administration to protect the depositors, which is to say the bankers with individual accounts in their own banks, the merchantmen, professional men, owners of small industries, and the men who buy cotton, grain, and tobacco (in the South) for the large operators, who speculate in those commodities and buy for large individual corporations.

Depositor insurance has only an academic interest to the farmer in the South. It merely protects the credit deposited to his account after he has negotiated a loan at the bank. Farm subsidies under the regime of Henry Wallace as Secretary of Agriculture, as I learned from tours of the South, did not decrease production in times of surplus; it increased it. A farmer would be paid a subsidy for every acre he did not till. He would put in a demand for cash reimbursement (and would get it) for not tilling land he owned *that was not arable;* and then he would practice intensive agriculture on his best land.

The ultimate effect of this was good, however, in as much as it taught many farmers, who had hitherto farmed haphazardly and inefficiently, to practice intensive cultivation; but it didn't reduce farm surpluses. This trick of turning in claims for cash reimbursement for not tilling land which was not arable wasn't practiced by small farmers only: it was also practiced by big syndicates and insurance companies owning thousands of acres of land in certain cotton-growing regions of the South. Syndicate ownership of land in Oklahoma, by the way, is not possible, in spite of Steinbeck's *Grapes of Wrath,* which erroneously attributed to land syndicates in Oklahoma the practices of land syndicates in his native California; the Homestead Law of Oklahoma makes non-resident ownership of large tracks of land impossible by an annual increase of taxes on assessed valuation and final confiscation by the state after fourteen years. But in other states, which have no such law, I know of large land-owning syndicates which drew more money annually from the government for not cultivating non-arable acres than they derived from the net profit on the sale of their products.

I learned to have no sentimental illusions about the average farmer in Oklahoma in 1920 be he a small landowner, tenant farmer, or share cropper. Individually all those—or nearly all those I met—were kindly, hospitable, generous with what they had, companionable, and eager to help one another out at harvesting time or in times of trouble, from childbirth to prairie fires.

But the average farmer, of the Southwest, at least, is woefully ignorant, clannishly mistrustful of townfolks, independent to the point of brutish pigheadedness and unenlightened selfishness. He is narrow and bigoted. Field workers from the Department of Agriculture stand ready to help him, instruct him in scientific farming, in the conservation of his resources; but most farmers will have none of this, even though it is free of charge; they refuse to change their ancient and wasteful ways of doing things, saying, "No city dude or college kid is going to tell me how to farm my land."

51

My father gave me an example of the way the average farmer's mind works. In the early spring of 1920, before planting time, he had some handbills printed at his own expense and distributed them to all the farmers in the county (he was a state-employed cattle inspector seeing to it that tick-infested cattle were dipped—and what opposition he ran up against in that job!—and he reached them all in the rounds of his duties in his Ford), asking them to meet on a certain Sunday evening in a district schoolhouse for purposes of discussing farm conditions and a farm program. Nearly all of the farmers came to the meeting—largely, Dad said, to get away from their wives and drink corn liquor.

Dad addressed them. Most of them were one-crop farmers, raising cotton year after year on the same land, thereby making it less and less fertile every year. He showed them that by not raising enough corn for their own needs they had to buy shorts in town at two dollars a bushel to feed their cattle. He explained the economic foolishness of this. Then he told them there were signs of deflation in cotton prices and that by fall they would no longer be getting forty cents a pound for cotton but probably less than half that. He called upon them all to pledge themselves to plant at least a third of their acreage in corn, reserve a small plot for vegetables for home consumption, and plant the rest in cotton, if they regarded that as their cash crop. There were resounding cheers and some spoke my father's argument. Then every farmer present raised his hand in the pledge.

"But," my father told me, "something in the way they acted told me that every farmer there except me said to himself as he drove away from the meeting, 'All these other sonsabitches will cut down their cotton acreage and produce a short crop. The price then will go up. I'll play smart and plant my whole damn farm in cotton and clean up.' And, as it turned out, that's just what every one of them did at planting time. I have been all over the county and seen their farms. Every inch of arable land in cotton and cotton prices down so low they can't pick and sell it without a loss. A lot of them have forfeited their crops to the banks, which can't afford to pick it either. A lot of them have lost their horses, mules, and implements through foreclosure and have nothing but sowbelly and black-eyed peas and corn pone to live on all winter and they will have to borrow most of that from neighbors who kept pigs and grew a little corn. Their kids will get rickets and pellagra and next year the whole family of a lot of them will be hiring out at farm wages, if they can get work. They are so ignorant they don't see the world outside of the county. Each thought the others would produce a shortage of cotton and shoot up the price, not realizing that there are millions of acres in cotton in the South every year and the only things that produce a cotton shortage are an unusually large mill demand, too much rain, or prolonged droughts."

I got to know these farmers well; I rode with them on their wagons, visited with them in the evenings, went to their country dances and church suppers, talked with them in town. They were gullible bait for demagogic politicians. In the radical magazines of the East there was much talk about recruiting the downtrodden agricultural proletarian for the radical movement. It would have been just as easy to persuade J. P. Morgan to dynamite the Stock Exchange as to persuade an Oklahoma dirt farmer to attend even a moderate socialist meeting.

Such farmers recognized only two parties, the Democratic and the Republican, and they lumped all others—Socialists, Syndicalists, the I.W.W., Communists (or Bolshevik) as they were called then) into one category, "Reds." They were ready to do violence upon anyone who did not identify himself as either a Democrat or a Republican. In the fall campaign of 1920, a national election year, the Republican demagogues had their Democratic opponents licked from the start with the farmers on the issue of the price of cotton. Republican candidates, for offices high and low, blamed the price of cotton (it had fallen to eleven cents a pound just before election) on the Democratic administration.

The state went resoundingly Republican for the first time since its admission to the Union in 1907. If a new election had been held within a week, the newly elected Republicans would have been thrown out by the farmer vote and the Democrats reinstated, because cotton dropped to nine cents within a week after the Republican triumph.

Residents in cities, particularly those of liberal leanings, have, I think, an exaggerated idea of the class-consciousness of the proletarian, at all events of the agricultural proletarian. In the first place, the agricultural proletarian doesn't know what a proletarian is, and if he did know he would be the last to acknowledge himself one.

Toward the end of summer land-owing farmers who had abandoned their small tracts to move to the city with their families to take wartime jobs began to straggle back to their old homesteads—weatherbeaten shacks mainly, with yards overgrown with weeds and farm land that had to be cleared of underbrush—pale, haggard, undernourished, and practically penniless. In one way their desertion of the land was a good thing, for the soil had lain fallow throughout that period and had been enriched with decaying vegetation, which it would not have been if they had kept on planting cotton on the same ground year after year.

In some instances, to be sure, where they had farmed on hillsides without terracing and with plow furrows running not crosswise but from the tops of the hills to the bottom, all the topsoil had been washed off by heavy rains and deep gullies had been eroded into the red-clay soil underneath. Those whom I chanced to know who had the money to return and were not forced upon the charities of the city, were disillusioned but grimly resolute and not discouraged; they set about renewing their agricultural pursuits, chastened in spirit and somewhat less prejudiced and superstitious as the result of their contacts with industrial workers and the ways of city folk.

Within three years, many of these who had returned to the land or had stuck to it through drought and excessive rain, with boll weevils and potato bugs ravaging their crops, ticks and Texas fever killing their cows, malaria and pellagra attacking their children, were suddenly, and often quite catastrophically, to become wealthy almost overnight; for in March 1924 the Cromwell pool was dis-covered in the northern part of Seminole County, and the first big well, yielding 4,600 barrels of high-gravity oil a day, was com-pleted. Land values, even on untested sections in the area, shot up to $10,000 an acre, where it had hitherto been overpriced at two dollars. With oil at two dollars and fifty cents a barrel at the well, farmers whose families for years had worked barefoot in the fields and lived on less than $300 a year cash income, found themselves with incomes in oil royalties amounting to anywhere from $300 to $15,000 a day. Then——

In the spring of 1926 the Amerada Petroleum Corporation, having secured an oil lease on my father's and adjoining lands, sank a well almost in the exact center of Dad's artificial lake. It was a gusher, producing an income of over $3,000 a day seven days a week to my father (this gusher soon played out; but eight wells were sunk altogether on his land; two of them are still pro-ducing a trickle of about 400 barrels a month). This was the opening of the famous Seminole Oil Pool, which in 1927 yielded 136,000,000 barrels of crude oil, or 10 per cent of the national production. This oil strike converted sleepy Seminole into an oil-boom town, the countryside into a jungle of derricks, pipe lines, drum reservoirs, and the highways into a madhouse of tractor-drawn trucks, clanking machinery, donkey engines, and drillers' shocks.

Underneath the very room of the tent house in which I sat reading such books as the *Dialogues of the Gods* of Lucian, *Livres des Masques* of Remy de Gourmont, and *Le petit Pierre* of

Anatole France, on cool and placid evenings, one of my fathers'
eight wells was to be sunk six years later. That alone was to
produce a small fortune and contribute its share to the world's
supply of motor oil, lubricants, gasoline, kerosene, and natural
gas. The crossroads which my father had named Bowlegs City in
jest, because of the old nestor who had a merchandising shack
there, was to become one of the wildest and most fantastic oil-
boom towns in the Southwest, romanticized out of all proportion
to reality by Edna Ferber in *Cimarron*. Today it is a ghost town,
with only a few of its wooden stores remaining, its wild and
raucous night life replaced by the monotonous metronomic sound
of oil pumps mingling with the howl of coyotes on the bleak and
denuded prairies, forever to remain a wasteland because of the
deep seepage into the soil of oil from overflowing and ignited
wells.

The reason Bowlegs City was chosen as a town site was that
for a half mile or more in each direction, from the crossroads as
a center, geologists had agreed there was no oil beneath the surface; and Wewoka and Seminole were too far away from the
center of operations of the pool. But with oil-crew roustabouts
drawing twenty-five dollars a day and experts and technicians
drawing seventy-five dollars a day or better and with lease scouts
and speculators bringing scads of cash swarming into the town,
town lots soared in price; and I am happy to report that our old
nestor was paid $40,000 for his little plot and that he took it and
retired to a boardinghouse in Oklahoma City. (As examples of
prices in Bowlegs City during the boom, drinking water was
twenty-five cents a glass because there were no water wells in the
town and drinking water had to be hauled a long distance; ice
was three dollars a pound, coffee fifty cents a cup, and hamburger
sandwiches two dollars each.

Incidentally, my parents cleared out as soon as they could
arrange their affairs with the oil companies, lawyers, and bankers,
and moved to Burlingame, California, where they bought a home

56

to live in and other property out of their oil royalties, after they had bestowed munificent gifts, out of their first months' certified checks, on a host of relatives on both sides of the family. They gave $20,000 out of their first royalties to each of their three sons and $2,000 to each of their three daughters-in-law, and were even more generous later. Dad on a visit to New York said he and Mother had derived a gross revenue of $850,000 from the wells in less than a year and that was piled up in the banks. Mother and Dad split the income half and half, each to do what he or she pleased with it. I never inquired about their finances; didn't care to know; but Dad seems to have had a grand time with his share —including trips to the Orient and South America—because he had only about $70,000 worth of property left when he died, at seventy, in 1932.

But, my mother said, she never had a more miserable time than during those hectic days before they could get away. The farm was soon turned into a shambles; her beautiful shade trees were cut down, her gardens were crushed under heavy trucks, the roadways and highways were ground, by tractors and mule teams drawing heavy machinery, into layers of powdered dust two or three feet deep which filled the air with clouds of it when the high winds blew and converted the roads and her lawn into vast muddy bogs when the rain fell; the drillers on hundreds of wells in the immediate vicinity worked all night long, making sleep almost impossible, and during the day it was even worse, with the clanking of machinery, the noise of motors, of shouting workmen, of the tearing down of fences, of the sawing down of trees, of the whine of timber being sawed into boards by electric saws, and of the hammering together of these planks and boards to make toolrooms and engine shacks.

Moreover, their income from the eight oil wells was not all velvet and their fortune was accompanied by many headaches; for no sooner is a rich oil pool opened up than swarms of title-clouding lawyers descend upon the area, with alleged claims of

Indian clients of title to the land. Before purchasing the land, nearly twenty years before, my father had gone to considerable expense to get clear title to the property, even getting quit-claim deeds from all the living descendants of the Harjos, Seminole Indian original owners of the land under government allotment, who were permitted to sell their land after Indian Territory was incorporated with Oklahoma Territory as a state. But he had to pay out $98,400 in out-of-court settlements of claims to his land besides heavy fees for attorneys and title searches. The court dockets were crowded with such suits and that's what made out-of-court settlements imperative; for the claimants could not only impound all royalties derived from a well, pending the outcome of a suit (which might take three years or even five years, involving legal expenses the landowner was not able to bear), but also stop production at a well, pending such outcome in the courts— a serious matter to an oil company in a newly exploited field, because offset wells might draw off all the oil on a property the company had leased while the case was in the process of litigation; and thus an oil-company investment of from $125,000 to $150,-000 for each well drilled might be a total loss.

The harassed landowner who had leased his mineral rights to a producing company in a rich pool could not afford to sit tight until a verdict was reached, because by the time the case was settled, even if he won, the wells might be drained dry by offset wells and he might derive nothing from the wells on his property and go heavily in debt for legal expenses.

All this sudden fortune of my parents was in the unforeseen future, however, when my family and I were with them on the farm in 1920. We were poor in purse then but living was serene, idyllic, health-giving, and conducive to expansion of spirit, at least on that little empire that comprised my father's land. Years before, when he was looking for a farm to buy, after years of running restaurants, hotels, and saloons in towns and never caring for town life—for he had been born and reared on a farm and was an expert agriculturist, horticulturist, and stockman—he had driven all over three counties and had found just the place he wanted, with all the potentialities of good soil, some black bottom land, pasturage, a ravine over which he could construct a dam for a fresh-water lake, and a hill studded with oak, walnut, and hickory trees, where he could set his house, and two two-room log cabins in which he and Mother and my younger brothers (I remained in town and worked my way through high school) could live until his model house and model barn were built.

There was a well near the log cabins, but this was a half mile from the spot where Dad wanted to build his house. Before deciding where to build his home he called in some "experts" to get their opinion as to whether water could be found at a reasonable depth near the spot where he wanted to build. One after another had shaken their heads. Then he hired a water witch, paying him twenty-five dollars.

I had come down from Shawnee on the early-morning train to spend Sunday with my parents (and stock up on some of Mother's home cooking) on the day the water witch came to perform his rites. His water finder was a willow branch with two prongs which he held in his hands, the main stem of which projected about a foot and a half from the jointure of the prongs. On the way to the hilltop, the serious little man held the instrument in front of him. At several spots he stopped and said, "There is water here but there is oil here too." Dad laughed skeptically and said he wasn't looking for oil or for water, either, down there in a ravine.

Afterward I was to recall that one of these spots where the water witch said there was oil underneath was where the first oil well of the great Seminole Pool was sunk after the ravine had long been converted into a lake. At the time, I thought the man was a fake and I didn't believe in his ability to locate a place for a water well much less for an oil well, and I deplored my father's paying him twenty-five dollars. Besides, I had watched the water finder and I hadn't seen the third prong bend and dip down as I heard it was supposed to do when water was present. I had seen the whole pronged stick slant down, but he could cause that with his hands. And yet, when he reached the hill and Dad showed him where he wanted to locate his house, the water witch stopped at one point and said, "There is a spring here. You will find an abundance of excellent water about seventeen feet down. It will never run dry. There is no oil on this hilltop."

The witch proved to be right on all counts, whether by sheer luck or coincidence I don't know. Dad believed him about the water—after the well driller had struck water at about seventeen feet; but he never took any stock in the witch's talk about oil. If he had, he would not have sold one hundred and twenty acres of his land; instead, he would have added to his holdings.

I have related in *Before I Forget* how I played Santa Claus for the neighboring farmers' children at the district schoolhouse and how my cotton whiskers caught fire when I reached under the tree for the last toy and how I ran out of the building so the children would not see it was I and not a real Santa Claus.

But I did not tell of the bitterness that entered my soul over the profiteering of Seminole merchants at the expense of the poor share croppers and poverty-stricken small-farm owners whose children had been brought to the schoolhouse to see what Santa Claus had for them. There were no dime stores in the town and the only places that handled toys were a drugstore and a notion store. These toys were shoddy and priced at ten and twenty times their retail value. Well-to-do residents of the town, of course, didn't depend upon the local stores for their Christmas gifts, including toys; they went to Oklahoma City for them.

I could have bought the town's whole stock of toys at retail in Oklahoma City for twenty-five dollars; and I would have made the trip just to get some decent cheap toys for the kids if I hadn't learned about the price-jacking too late. I paid ten dollars for some of this miserable junk; what I bought wasn't worth a dollar over any Woolworth or Kress counter. Tiny lead locomotives, dented and paint-scratched, were priced at a dollar; paper horns were fifty cents; drums worth a quarter at most, retail, were priced at two dollars; and poor farmers paid these ridiculous prices out of their meager cash earnings (from eggs they had sold at ten cents a dozen, milk they had sold at ten cents a gallon, chickens they had sold at a quarter apiece, and watermelons they had sold for as low as two for a nickel), so each of their kids would have at least one toy at Christmastime.

Mother, my wife, and a neighbor across the highway made candied popcorn balls and molasses candy and wrapped them in tissue paper; they candied apples and put them on sticks and popped many bags full of popcorn for the Christmas event at the schoolhouse. As I called out the names on the shoddy toys for the children to come forward, I would hand each an armload of candy, popcorn, and candied apples, especially loading up the rickety children of share croppers whose "boughten" toy might be only a lead whistle worth a dime but had cost the parents one dollar. Our own children remained home with Mother and went to bed early because we had a Christmas tree well laden with presents, including a bee-bee gun for my young son and a handsome doll for our small daughter, all of which I had purchased a month earlier on a trip to Oklahoma City, before I knew of the price-jacking of toys in the Seminole stores.

Just as I was beginning to get restless and desirous of getting back into harness as a newspaperman again, a letter reached me from a man whose name I did not know, the letter proclaiming him as the head of an organization I knew only vaguely about, asking me to come to Cleveland, Ohio, to see him. He said he had a proposition to talk over with me and if we did not come to terms he would set me and my family down, all expenses paid, wherever I wanted to go—New York, Chicago, or back to Oklahoma. Inclosed was a certified check for $300.

The letter was signed Earle Martin, president of the Newspaper Enterprise Association, a subsidiary of the Scripps-McRae (later the Scripps-Howard) newspaper organization.

Within twenty-four hours we were packed and on our way to Chicago, where my wife and children stayed with my aunt Ada Burton pending the outcome of my trip to Cleveland.

CHAPTER 4

Chicago Revisited

I REJECT AN EXECUTIVE POSITION. FREE LANCING
IN CHICAGO. I BECOME MANAGER OF CHICAGO
BUREAU OF NEA. RED TAPE AND BUREAUCRACY.
NEXT STOP NEW YORK.

Mr. Martin, on learning of the date of my arrival in Cleveland, had wired me that a suite had been reserved for me at the Hotel Roosevelt and to take my time about coming in to see him; there was no hurry, he said. When I did go in to see him, late in the morning after a night at the hotel, I met one of the most cultivated, gracious, and understanding gentlemen I have ever encountered in newspaper work. He was slim, tall, handsome, blue-eyed, thin-faced, with regular features, with a stoop and slouch that men over six feet in height sometimes acquire in an effort not to be conspicuous among smaller men. He was soft-spoken and utterly relaxed, the opposite of the temperament of the restless and excitable newspaper executive of fiction and the movies.

After he had inquired about my trip, my health, and the comfortableness of my quarters at the hotel, he said, "I don't want to talk over with you the proposition I have in mind for three or four days, maybe longer. First I want you and your wife to look around the town and see if you like it here or not. I'll get you tickets to the theater; I'll give you a map of the better residential sections and you can take a taxicab to inspect them and put it on an expense account. If you need any information, call on us. Later on one of the men here who has a car will drive you through

63

the parks. But for a few days I want you and your wife to be alone in sizing up Cleveland. I don't want to sell it to you."

I had not understood, until then, why he had asked me to bring my wife; and I had to tell him that my wife had thought there was no necessity for her to come with me and had stayed in Chicago with the children. He asked me if I wanted to wire her to come on and I said I thought she would be content to live in Cleveland if I was.

What happened within the next four days may or may not have been a rationalization of a subconscious desire to hasten the fulfillment of my firm conviction that I would soon be living and working in New York without any effort on my part to bring this consummation about; or it may have been an instinctive fear of rooting myself into an executive (that is, non-writing) job. But if either of these was a causative factor in my rejecting Cleveland as a place of residence and the job that Mr. Martin was to offer me, I was not conscious of it at the time. My reasons seemed very real to me.

First, it was raining when I arrived in the town and it rained almost steadily for three days. I had already associated Cleveland with rain, because on the three previous occasions when I had stopped off there on my way to or from New York to browse through Cleveland's excellent bookstores (Cleveland has always been a city in which cultural interests are fostered and a city of very lively and civilized newspapers, with brilliant local columnists and drama critics) it had always rained. The rain had never been a precipitous one but a cold, foggy drizzle with the skies darkened because of so much factory smoke in the air. It reminded me of Pittsburgh in that respect; both cities had, by mere coincidence, of course (because both cities have their share of clear days), become associated in my mind with dismal, murky, soot-filled skies and rain.

Until I was past forty I was abnormally sensitive to barometric pressure; several days of continued rain not only depressed me but lowered my vitality. For that reason I declined to visit London even when I had an excellent opportunity to do so; I had a sentimental regard for the city; I knew its streets and the tradition of those streets and I was familiar with the more important aspects of the history and literature of that cradle of Anglo-Saxon culture; but London was, and is, associated in my mind with murky fogs and rain and I didn't want any of my illusions about it spoiled for me by my sensitiveness to the weather.

So it was with Cleveland during those three days when I wandered about the city with raincoat, rubbers, and umbrella. The whole city seemed characterized by the dismal gray veil in which the somber Rockefeller mansion was enveloped when I looked at it. As I stared through the mists at that relic of the architecture of the heyday of the industrial barons, the whole atmosphere of the city took on a bleak, macabre quality.

It was my imagination (or perhaps my subconscious), of course, because the hotel where I stayed and the restaurants where I ate were cheerful, modern, and in every way agreeable; the stores were as up to date as those in New York (though at that time I would not have said they were as up to date as Marshall Field's in Chicago) ; and the newspapers were a pleasure to read. I ignored Mr. Martin's suggestion that he would get me tickets to the theater if I let him know which plays I wanted to see, because I was familiar with the plays then showing; and, besides, nearly two years of reviewing plays in Chicago—four out of five of which seemed puerile or shoddy to me—had given me a temporary phobia against all theatrical productions except the *Ziegfeld Follies* and the Raymond Hitchcock production. I chose Cleveland's vaudeville and burlesque shows on my own, and enjoyed myself very much at each.

On the afternoon of the third day I dropped in to see Mr. Martin, but still he was not ready to talk business with me. He took me through the plant, introducing me to various members of his staff, and told me to stick around for a while and observe the operations. He had a chair brought up where I could watch the functioning of the two chief sub-editors.

The Newspaper Enterprise Association supplies a "canned" news and feature service to a great number of newspapers. The service goes out in two forms. First there is a daily sheaf of proofs printed on glazed paper which look like the page proofs of a newspaper, with streamer headlines, photographic reproductions, comic strips, line drawings, and all. There is a solid front page of "news" of a staple character, an editorial page, with a "political" cartoon (unbiased enough to be used by a Democratic paper, a Republican paper, or an independent one), science features, and health articles; there is a woman's page filled with hints, a sports page with signed articles and a cartoon, and comic strips, besides human-interest stories and stories and pictures sent in by special correspondents. Printed up with a newspaper title and masthead, it would make an acceptable adless newspaper— with no spot news in it which would be stale news two or three days later. The other form of the service was that of mats for stereotyping plates of photographs, cartoons, comic strips, and line drawings.

I studied these pages as I sat there, eying the sub-editors from time to time to see how they performed. The first or "news" pages fascinated me, because I could see at once how these could be immensely improved, so that more editors would use, rather than discard, them. There was also a box on the first page offering five dollars to news editors of the papers, which NEA serviced, for hints to other news and city editors for popular news features. And the editorial page was especially interesting to me, also because it contained five daily editorials, each about four inches or less in length and two columns wide; and every one of them was on a timeless, non-controversial subject. I knew I could turn out editorials like that by the yard without the least demand on my creative faculties.

As yet I did not know what sort of job Mr. Martin had in

mind for me—a writing job or an editorial executive job; but I suspected it was the latter when he had me seated near the two men who were directing operations.

These two men had desks jammed together so that they faced each other. They had several phones each on their desks, radiograph, Postal and Western Union pads, pencils, paste pots, stacks of copy paper, and baskets for incoming and outgoing dispatches and memoranda. Both men were working as excitedly as if a great catastrophe had just occurred. I had never seen newsmen work at such tension since the first flash had come into the city room of the Chicago *Tribune* announcing the sinking of the *Lusitania*. They were both either feverishly writing out wires or radiograms, calling for copy boys, reading dispatches hurriedly, and marking them or making brief, crisp calls over the phone.

I didn't see any reason for all this hectic activity. There wasn't that much tension on a Hearst afternoon paper news deck in the process of replating hourly extras while a big story was breaking. These men had only one edition to get out and they had twenty-four hours between deadlines.

Then it dawned on me. Nine tenths of their activity is waste motion, I said to myself; it is the old system of giving two top executives practically equal power, the theory being that each will try to outdo the other, and so keep them on their toes every second—until one cuts the throat of the other by showing more fertility of ideas or more show of enterprise and someone else is moved in opposite him, whereat the high-pressure act starts all over again.

On my way to the washroom I stopped at the desk of an oldish chap in the sports department to whom I had been introduced. After we had exchanged some small talk I casually asked him how long the two managing editors had been with the organization. One of them had started in as copy boy fifteen years ago; the other was a comparative newcomer, having come over from the Press only a year or so ago.

That was all I wanted to know. If it was an executive job Mr. Martin was going to offer me it meant that I was going to be placed in competition with a man who had grown up in the organization and who knew all the ropes, angles, and weapons. He would cut my throat a damned sight quicker than I could cut his, even if I had the stomach for that sort of thing, which I didn't.

I went in to see Mr. Martin and it developed that that was it: the job was that of working with the chap who had grown up in the organization; both of us were to be accountable for originating ideas, giving out assignments, editing, and developing features for Mr. Martin's O.K. The salary, to start, was munificent for those days, $150 a week. I swallowed hard. That was tough to refuse, especially in as much as I did not know where or when I would get another offer. Jobs were getting scarce; unemployment was still widespread in January 1921. But I told Mr. Martin that I liked Cleveland well enough (which was a white lie) but that I had been on both sides of the fence of newspaper work— on the executive side as an editor and on the writing side—and that I preferred the writing side; I didn't want to give out assignments or handle copy any more, I wanted to write it, although on the *Tribune* I had done both contemporaneously for several years.

"You have quite made up your mind, then?" he asked very gently. "You don't want the job?"

"I am afraid not," I answered, "but I deeply appreciate the compliment you have paid me in offering it to me. And I regret that you have been to all this expense and trouble to no purpose."

"That's all right," he said. "I had a sort of hunch you wouldn't want the job. I have long been familiar with your work on the *Tribune* and I have read a lot of your signed stuff. I offered to set your family down wherever you wanted to go if our negotiations fell through. Where are you going?"

"I am going back to Chicago, at least for the present. I have an apartment, furnished, there. I sub-leased it, but the tenant defaulted on the rent for two months and then skipped out. It is waiting for us until I want to go elsewhere."

"Well," he said, "I have another proposition to make to you. When you get back to Chicago, will you write for us? I'll pay you triple our regular space rates for news and features and double our pay for editorials. Besides, you may have some editorial suggestions for which I will pay you extra."

He told me how much I would be paid per column for news and features and how much for editorials. He said he would get me some sample NEA pages so I could see the sort of thing they used. I told him I already knew what he wanted and that I would be happy to write for him. I also told him that I felt confident that I could improve on some of the feature stuff he was in the habit of sending out.

Privately I already knew of sources, which NEA had never tapped, of sensational "news" stuff; and I could write three NEA editorials in an hour every morning. He told me not to bother about drawing up an expense account; that if I had anything left over from the $300 I could keep it; that he would pay the hotel bill and my Pullman fare to Chicago and have my tickets ready for me when I checked out. I told him I'd like to go back to Chicago that night.

We shook hands and I told him, frankly and honestly, that I had never met a man for whom I would rather work than him, and that I was sorry that I had to turn down the job he offered me.

Back in Chicago the next morning, I told my wife and my aunt the result of the negotiations and said I wanted to get to work right away. So the four of us—my wife, the two children, and I—piled into a taxi with our bags and were in our old apartment on Sherwin Avenue on the North Side before eleven o'clock. Never have I forgiven anybody so readily as I forgave the defaulting tenant. Four months before he had written me a letter saying his sales commissions had fallen off and that he couldn't meet the rent unless I reduced it twenty dollars a month.

I had rented to him furnished at precisely what it cost me, unfurnished, under my lease, which did not expire until June 1. That meant I would take a loss on the apartment, but it might cost me more in the long run to sublet it to someone else. And besides, he touched my chicken heart with his tale of woe. So I wrote him a letter agreeing to the cut. He sent me a check for the arrears, deducting twenty dollars.

Later he wrote me that in cashing the check I had invalidated the lease and that he was not obliged to pay me anything. Legally he was right; but ethically I thought he was a scoundrel. He moved elsewhere on January 1, the superintendent of the building said, leaving no forwarding address. I was out four months' rent, but I had a home. The janitor let us in with a passkey. Our next-door neighbors, old friends, welcomed us. They said the tenant had left our keys with them.

That afternoon I took note pads and pencils and went down to the Crerar Library, which is devoted to scholarship and the advancement of the sciences. Its current periodicals then included, and probably still do, every scientific and medical journal, every journal devoted to theses and works of research in sociology, philosophy, archaeology, paleontology, and philosophy available in any language.

I had remembered that, when I was a campus correspondent for the *Tribune* at the University of Chicago, I made more money on space rates than any previous correspondent ever had, simply by digging through such publications. Chemists, medicos, bacteriologists, and physicists are forever burying sensational stuff in these esoteric journals, which are read almost exclusively by workers in their own fields. Besides the professional taboo against self-exploitation in research and scholarship there is the natural timidity of such men about disclosing to the layman the results of experiment or research until they have been fully discussed and approved by the most hidebound and reactionary of their co-workers in the field.

Moreover, such men are, generally speaking, notoriously bad writers, who hesitate to say the sun rises in the east without appending four footnotes of previous scholars to support the statement; like lawyers, they don't think the way other people do. Milliken's paper, giving the results of his tests concerning the rigidity of the earth, I had dug out of the heavy professional journal for physicists and had made the first page of the *Tribune* with an eight-column streamer with it, giving me two columns of space and a ten-dollar bonus.

My first afternoon at the Crerar netted me an eight-column streamer-head news story for NEA and two shorter items that were displayed on the front page. I wrote them and mailed them that night to Mr. Martin. Next day he sent me a wire of congratulation. I had already worked out a routine: breakfast at seven; seven-thirty to eight, scanning the morning papers for items that might be followed up and for editorial suggestions; eight to nine, writing editorials and typing out suggestions for feature ideas for NEA editor-subscribers; nine to twelve, writing up stuff from notes gathered the previous afternoon at the Crerar Library; lunch; to the library by two and there until four-thirty or five, going through the tables of contents of such periodicals as the *Astro-physical Journal,* the *Journal of Philology, Lancet,* the *Journal of Semitic Languages and Literature,* the *American Journal of Sociology,* the *Archaeological Journal,* the London *Economist,* the *Yale Review,* the *Urologic and Cutaneous Review,* the *Classical Journal,* and the *Philosophical Review* for story possibilities. *Iron Age* and other trade publications also yielded me spot news stories.

My first eight-column first-page streamer story for NEA had come out of the *Yale Review.* It was an article on longevity by the head of the Life Extension Institute. It explained how the life expectancy since birth had steadily risen during the past twenty years owing to better sanitation and the advancing knowledge of dietetics, hygiene, and medical care. He said—and this was the clincher which gave me my lead—that if the life-expectancy chart continued to rise as it had done during the past twenty years, owing to the progress in hygiene and sanitation, within fifty years the average man might expect to live one hundred years and Methuselahs would be common.

Thereafter, for several weeks, I wrote practically every story that appeared on the front page, all unsigned, of course, along with one or two "tips to city editors" every day for the box featuring that service; and I wrote from three to five editorials every morning. Twice all five of the daily canned editorials were mine, all of them innocuous and platitudinous but irrefutable and readable—homilies on the seasons, the first groundhog, the first robin, the anniversary of some historical event, the pleasures of walking, famous fallacies, the future of aviation—and often I was the author of three of the day's quota of five editorials. In order that most of my stories might not appear from obscure journals, I would take leads from articles and then call up specialists in the same line and draw interviews out of them concerning the theory or argument advanced in the articles.

My first week's string(that is newspaper slang for the number of agate lines of type occupied by the writings of one who is paid at space rates—6oo agate lines to the column) amounted to $314; the second week's, to $268; and then it began to taper off gradually until it was stabilized at around $175 a week, because I was more than satisfied with that income and saw no reason to exert myself to earn more. I slackened my strenuous schedule and began to devote more time to reading, music, and other recreations.

Even that weekly payment to a mere writer (as distinguished from a top-flight executive) seemed immoral, or something, to Mr. Martin, or to someone else in the organization. Either that, or because of the executive mind which figures that if a writer is worth that much to a newspaper on space he is worth more to the organization on a regular salary as an executive, even if he isn't paid any more, for Mr. Martin phoned me one night and said he wanted me to take over the management of the Chicago bureau of the NEA.

I didn't even know there was such a bureau. He said the bureau was located in the city room of the Chicago *Evening Post;* that the former incumbent of the office had "resigned" and would show me my duties the next morning; that he was sending me $1,000 to deposit to the NEA account, for running expenses, together with a letter of identification authorizing me to open the account in the NEA's name and sign checks as manager, and that I would be paid $150 a week, plus extras for features, editorials, and suggestions not in line with my regular duties as manager, which included paying all the bills of the office and covering assignments originating in the Cleveland office.

My predecessor kindly explained the routine. I saw at once that I who had been a very valuable member of the writing staff of NEA had been given what Mr. Martin or some other head man had considered a promotion. I was now a bureau manager, which means, actually, that I had been converted into a bookkeeper, a man who makes out checks for the monthly bills for wire service, radiogram service, rent, telephone, postage, messengers, and pictures bought from local news photographers, and a leg man and picture chaser.

I saw at once that they could get someone to do the work I was expected to do for thirty-five dollars a week and he would do it just as well or better than I, because keeping accounts is something I detest. I am accurate with accounts because I sweat over them; but it takes me five times as long to tot up figures and enter them into books as it does someone who has a talent for it.

After I got back from lunch Mr. Martin phoned to ask if I was on the job and everything was going all right. His letter containing the check and bank papers had arrived by special delivery. I did no writing that day; I was too busy being a big executive; i.e., a messenger boy with an imposing salary and title.

Not long after Mr. Martin's call I got a foretaste of what was to come. Three radiograms came in, two from the editor I was invited to share honors with and one from the chap I was to succeed. All three were idiotic, but one was typical of the rat race those two men were running. It ran:

"Rush picture and interview Wheaton society girl arrested for speeding." The unimportant incident had been briefly recorded in the back pages of the Chicago papers and I had difficulty finding it. I figured it would take at least four hours to get to Wheaton, a suburban town, and back even if I made close train connections, which was unlikely. I wired back, "Fire could destroy Loop while I was chasing Wheaton picture. Am ignoring other two assignments also as stuff you wouldn't or shouldn't use after I got it."

Next day there was a stack of radiograms and Postal wires on my desk when I got to the office. They were all silly except one— and it was silly, too, but in a different way from the others. It was a request that I go to Milwaukee and get pictures and story on two third-rate pugilists who were scheduled to fight there. I thought it was a gag, but decided to pretend to take it seriously. It would give me a chance to run up to Milwaukee and spend an evening with my old pal and college classmate, Larry Lawrence, of the Milwaukee *Journal*. So I wired Cleveland I was catching the next train for Milwaukee and had to pass up the other assignments. Larry got me pictures and helped me fix up a story in a few minutes from morgue clips, which I mailed special delivery to Cleveland, and then he showed me the town—a town where good draught beer still flowed freely.

Back in Chicago the next day, I found still another pile of radiograms. Glancing through them, I saw that the two editors were showing how much on their toes they were by seeing who could send out the most senseless radiograms to bureau managers, so I wired Mr. Martin: "Going home to read bale of wires and radiograms from —— and ——. At desk tomorrow if I recover."

Mr. Martin phoned me at my home that night and asked me what the trouble was. I said there wasn't an assignment in the whole mess of wires I had received that would net a story any sensible NEA subscriber would use even if NEA sent it out. And I read some of them to him. He said the wires and radiograms were suggestions, not assignments, and that I was to pay attention to only those I thought were worth it. I told him there wasn't one in the three days' lot that was worth following up. He said he would speak to the boys and ask them to use more care in the suggestions they sent me.

The wires and radiograms stopped almost altogether for more than a week, and I was thereby able to dig up some newsy and interesting stuff, with pictures, which NEA could use, and also write a few editorials.

Meanwhile Julian Mason, editor of the *Evening Post,* who had made that paper one of high literary and cultural standards, had introduced himself the first day I was in the office and we had become quite pally. An advance copy of Wilson's Secretary of State Lansing's book on the Versailles Peace Conferences had come to me and I had read it. I told Mason it was newsworthy, because of Lansing's wounded-vanity, personal attacks on his chief, and because of Lansing's alibiing of his own mistakes, and that I would write a news story on the book for him if he wanted it, for release on date of publication.

Mason was eager for it, so I turned out a two-and-a-half-column news story on the book which ran, with my signature, at the upper left-hand column of the first page, with runover on page two. He occasionally sought my opinion about features for the paper and I did one or two other writing chores for him.

Then, suddenly, "B.L.T.," the famous conductor of the "Line-o'-Type or Two" column in the *Tribune,* died. I had had lunch with Taylor at the Cliff-Dwellers less than a week before. We had talked about James Huneker and had agreed that it was foolish of Huneker to go to his office when he had a high fever, especially when going there meant commuting from Flatbush to Philadelphia; for that overconscientiousness had resulted in the pneumonia which killed him. Taylor had done the same thing, gone to the *Tribune* with a temperature of 102; he was dead the next day.

That morning I told Mason that now he had his chance. Patterson of the *Tribune* would be trying desperately to get someone to fill Taylor's place and that the first one he would try to get was the man who had been Taylor's wittiest contributor, Keith Preston. Henry Blackman Sell had given Keith a once-a-week column of his own on the Wednesday book page of the Chicago *Daily News*. Preston was teaching Greek and Latin at Northwestern but I knew he would jump at a chance to do a daily column, at a good salary, even if it meant sacrificing his academic career.

I told Mason that, if he agreed, I would offer Preston a daily column on the *Post* at the salary Mason was willing to pay and try to clinch the deal before Patterson got to him; but I told Mason to get Vincent Starrett, Samuel Putnam, and others on the staff to knock together a column for the *Post's* editorial page for the very next day and for every day until we got a permanent conductor. Mason was enthusiastic and he and his staff got up a column of verse and paragraphs, quips and digs, leading off with a tribute to "B.L.T." At my suggestion the column was called "The Pillar."

I phoned Keith and made him the offer. He was pleased and excited but said he would have to speak to Mr. Lawson (Victor Lawson, publisher of the *Daily News*) about it. I said to myself, "Oh! Oh! That means the tight-fisted Lawson will loosen up and better the *Post's* offer." But I told Keith okay and to phone me back; I asked him to speak to Lawson at once. An hour or so later Keith phoned to say Lawson had offered him a daily column on the same terms as the *Post* offer and he felt obliged to Lawson for giving him the regular space on Sell's book column (a strange sense of obligation, in as much as Lawson had never paid him anything for one of the best circulation features in the paper).

But that was that; and I knew the next man Patterson would try to get was Richard Atwater, known as "Riquarius" to B.L.T.'s readers. Patterson wouldn't know how to get in touch with Riq; I did, for he had just gone to the University of Minnesota as an instructor in Greek. I told Mason that Atwater was his second-best bet; that Patterson would be after him when he found Preston was tied up, and that I'd try to pry Atwater out of Minnesota. Mason gave me his blessing and told me to go ahead.

I wired Atwater. He said he would take the train down to Chicago on Saturday night and talk over the proposition with Mason and me on Sunday and then see if he could get out of his job at the university. That evening Preston came to my house with his wife, Etta, to tell me the developments. Patterson had got in touch with him by phone, offered him the "Line-o'-Type" column, named the salary, and sent a man out to Evanston to try to clinch the deal. But when Preston told Lawson about it, the old skinflint met Patterson's offer and reminded Preston of the loyalty he owed the *News*. Preston liked the *News* and he was not a dickering man, so he agreed to sign with Lawson.

So the day after Taylor's death both the *Post* and the *News* had wit-and-humor columns and the *Tribune* had none and continued to have none until, failing to land Atwater also (because the *Post* had signed him up), Patterson tried out a succession of possible successors to Taylor, including Percy Hammond and Fred Pasley, and finally turned over the column to the former press agent and music critic Frederick Donaghey. At first the *Post's* column was unsigned, each contributor signing his own initials at the bottom of his contribution. Then Vincent Starrett assumed temporary responsibility, signing his name at the close. When Atwater took over, the column title was changed to "From Pillar to Post" and signed "Riq." Thereafter, until Preston's death and the demise of the *Post*, Preston and Atwater were the two brightest and most eagerly read wit-and-humor features in the Chicago newspapers.

I had enjoyed putting ants into Patterson's pants in revenge for dismissing me, just as Walter Howey had enjoyed planting hoaxes which the *Tribune* fell for, advertising movie serials and Sunday-supplement stories which were presently to appear in the Hearst paper of which Howey had become managing editor the very day Patterson had fired him as city editor. But while all this enlivened the routine of keeping accounts and digging up feature ideas for NEA, that kind of a desk job began to bore me.

Besides, after a lull of a week the telegrams and radiograms from the two on-their-toes boys began to pour in again; first only four or five a day, then ten or fifteen. I read them all, with a certain morbid fascination; rarely did one have any validity as suggestions, and those were concerned with items that had already appeared in the wire service dispatches and required only a phone call for me to bring them up to date, which the Associated Press or the United Press would do themselves. But I'd duly write these follow-ups and file them by Radiogram or Postal, trying to give them an angle that would make them sound newsworthy three days hence.

(Let it not be supposed that these two men who were trying to show they were high-powered executives were acting unwisely. Long experience has taught me that many American businessmen honor and reward men who are capable of conspicuous waste. Bedazzled by the notion that the way to make money is to spend money, they often judge the worth of a man by the amount of the firm's money he can manage to spend, without regard to whether the money is spent wisely or profitably. The mere fact of spending money recklessly on long-distance telephone calls, wires, graphs, research, business trips, and expensive luncheons on expense accounts is evidence enough to some businessmen that the executive who indulges in this is a live wire, and therefore entitled to rapid promotion and higher and still higher salary. If the sub-executive can demand three secretaries, when all he needs is a stenographer to correct his grammar and put his letters into sound English, he is on his way to the top, especially if he is shrewd enough to claim credit for ideas and accounts originating in the minds of his subordinates, who dare not go over his head for fear of losing their jobs. Besides being capable and trained newspapermen, these two I speak of were realists enough to play up to this totem of conspicuous waste. One of them was able to impress a Detroit automobile manufacturer and so to land an important executive job in which he rapidly became a millionaire, and the other went on to conspicuous heights of salary and title in newspaper work. I might have been as rich as they in a few years if I had had their special talents and had accepted the Cleveland job which Mr. Martin had offered me.)

I was being given no chance to leave my desk to dig up stuff at the Crerar Library or snoop out feature stories around town or even to write NEA editorials, because of these queries and "suggestions" that kept pouring in every fifteen minutes all day long. Fed up with such play-editing, I wired Earle Martin: "If I receive one more telegram or radiogram from —— or —— I quit the job." Mr. Martin wired back he would stop them altogether and for me to conduct the bureau without any suggestions except from him.

That evening I had a long-distance call at home from Harry Payne Burton, editor of *McCall's*. He asked me if I would take the Century to New York on Saturday at *McCall's* expense and breakfast with him at the Plaza on Sunday morning. He said I could return on the Century on Sunday and be back on the job Monday morning. He said he had a proposition to talk over with me but to say nothing to Earle Martin about it. I told him I

79

would be there. Then it dawned upon me that it was he who was responsible for Martin's seeking me out and knowing my Oklahoma address. I had never met Harry and hadn't heard from him in six years. The last I had heard of him he was on the NEA and, I recalled, had asked me to write an article about the Sunday *Tribune's* features for a little magazine NEA got out for circulation among newspaper editors who subscribed for the service.

When I boarded the Century at Grand Central Station in New York the following Sunday afternoon after breakfast with Harry at the Plaza, I had agreed to come to New York on April 1 as associate editor of *McCall's* magazine. The company was to pay all expenses of moving my family and household goods to New York. The salary was less than I was making on NEA, but here was fulfillment of one part, at least, of what I had foreseen three years before; namely, that I would be working in New York within three years without any effort on my part to bring this about. I specified April 1 as the date for my starting to work, because I wanted to give Mr. Martin time to find my successor and also because my lease expired on April 1. Mother came up from Oklahoma to take the children down on the farm until we could get settled in New York, and we arranged to have our furniture packed and stored on March 20, which was the day we left, until such time as we could find a New York apartment.

A succession of parties was given for us and there were a few hardy souls who survived these gayeties well enough to see us off. The last one to leave our compartment was Gene Markey. He opened a topcoat and took a bottle of rare Johannisberger out of the pocket of his jacket. Handing it to me, he said, "I swiped this out of my father's cellar to cheer you on your way to New York. Father will raise hell when he finds the bottle gone, because it is his favorite wine and he has only three bottles left. But I told Mother about my crime and she said she would pacify him. So it is *her* parting gift to you as well as mine. Good luck!"

That evening we had dinner in our compartment, because I also had some rye and brandy and, since prohibition was in effect, we could not drink in the diner. My wife, I am happy to report, drank the whole bottle of Johannisberger (because I don't care for wines) and got very happily exhilarated. I had never known her to take more than a glass or two of Rhine wine and seltzer or a glass of beer at meals since we had been married.

CHAPTER 5

The Reader's Taste

"MCCALL'S" AND HARRY BURTON. WHAT AMER-
ICA READS. KATHLEEN NORRIS. BOOTH TARKING-
TON. KRAFFT-EBBING WITH SUGAR COATING. THE
NEW YORK LITERARY SCENE AND THE INTELLI-
GENTSIA.

There was an acute housing shortage in New York in 1921, because building construction had been halted by the war and had not been resumed. Harry Burton, with some difficulty, had secured a large room with bath for us at the Woodstock Hotel and there we remained for two weeks before my wife located a furnished apartment in West Sixteenth Street, between Fifth and Sixth avenues, for which we paid $135 a month for one large room, almost bare of furniture and with only one old, cheap, and dingy rug and a fireplace (useless in summertime), an ancient and untidy bathroom which admitted no light or ventilation, a two-burner electric cooker installed in a converted clothes closet, and a bedroom so narrow that we had to slide in sideways in order to get into bed.

We had liked the comfort, the homelike atmosphere of the Woodstock, and the excellent food, at reasonable prices, served in its restaurant. The dump on West Sixteenth Street was simply an unmitigated hellhole, in which we had to remain until fall when we located a room "railroad" apartment in a remodeled slum building on East Eighty-first Street, just off Park Avenue, where we had to climb five flights of stairs but had plenty of light and air and sufficient room for my large library as well as for ourselves, including a workroom for me.

But my wife hated New York during the first five weeks in the Sixteenth Street place and cried nearly every day, with some reason. That was one of the hottest summers I ever have encountered in New York. Sleep was difficult enough in the heat of that cramped bedroom, but across the street was a Spanish singing society whose members made loud and gaudy music until nearly every midnight; there was an electric powerhouse only five doors down the street, which roared all day and all night; there was a firehouse on the street, where engines and hook-and-ladder wagons seemed to be going to, or arriving from, a fire every hour of the day and night, with sirens and bells at full clamor; and, finally, at five or six in the morning the garbage collectors were about their chores, which seemed to consist largely of hurling empty cans from the tops of trucks to see how much noise they could make as they hit the sidewalk and bounded and rattled about.

We had hardly got to our room at the Woodstock on the first morning of our residence in New York before the telephone started ringing. This was a surprise to me because we had notified no one except Harry Burton of the day of our arrival; but I was soon to find that New York is a much more social town, in a villagy way, than Chicago. Chicagoans (at least among those engaged in the arts and journalism) were not so gregarious as New Yorkers and in Chicago a dinner or party at a friend's house was comparatively a rare event, because Chicago spreads out so that one's most companionable friends may live two hours away. Manhattan Island is narrow and compact, friends are usually only a few minutes' subway or taxi ride away or within easy walking distance.

Our first call was from Henry Blackman Sell, then editor of *Harper's Bazaar,* who lived only three blocks away, in an apartment on Fortieth Street overlooking Bryant Park. Henry (or Hank, as we had called him in Chicago) invited us to dinner that very evening and we accepted.

83

The only other guests besides my wife and myself were Johnny Weaver and some girl from the editorial department of *Harper's Bazaar,* and the dinner was in a small apartment. So I was surprised to find all four of them in formal dress. My wife and I were not. I did not know, at the time, that dressing-for-dinner business even at an intimate dinner party in his small apartment was not typical of New York but only a part of the routine Hank had had to adopt as William Randolph Hearst's social ambassador and *Harper's Bazaar* representative at the opening of the seasons at Bar Harbor, Newport, Asheville, White Sulphur Springs, Palm Beach, Bermuda, Nassau, and Southampton, and at all local semi-public social events where "everybody who mattered" was present.

The evening passed pleasantly, even if I was determined to remind Hank that he was once only a poor working stiff like myself. Thereafter, when I met Hank, he assumed a pose of being more Midwestern, lowbrow, and rough-and-ready than the occasion required; but his early cultivation of chi-chi cosmopolitanism paid off in dividends as it led to "contacts" with very wealthy and sometimes socially insecure people who were impressed by his urbanity; and, as he is a resourceful and talented man, he eventually became the head of a highly successful advertising agency after leaving *Harper's Bazaar,* and is now a very wealthy producer of canned foods. Ben Hecht once described Hank as being "as beautiful as a Neapolitan street boy," and age has not marred his swarthy handsomeness, with his full shock of wavy gray-streaked black hair and his slim build which is always set off to advantage by suits, shoes, and haberdashery from Bond and Regency streets, London.

Harry Burton, possibly because he was the editor of a woman's magazine whose circulation was almost exclusively among young suburban or small-town housewives whose husbands were young salaried employees and who did their own housework, and possibly because his was a different temperament from that of Sell's, was not like that. Social affairs were anathema to him and he probably never wore a dinner jacket throughout his editorship of *McCall's* and of the *Cosmopolitan*.

Harry was one of the most brilliant mass-circulation geniuses I have ever known and one of the most peculiar in his make-up. Ray Long established a reputation as a builder of mass-circulation magazines because he rarely bought a story or a serial that he himself did not like. Long's taste was for stuff like the Tarzan stories of Edgar Rice Burroughs and the Jack Londonish stories of the Northwest Woods by James Oliver Curwood; he was the discoverer of these two writers (and quite a few others of similar caliber) and by indulging his own tastes in fiction made a great fortune for the Eckstein Brothers, in Chicago, restaurateurs and art patrons who were the first owners of the *Red Book* magazine.

Harry Burton, on the other hand, achieved the remarkable feat of building the circulation of *McCall's* magazine within a year's time from 600,000 to more than 2,000,000—without ever reading, so far as I could ascertain, more than a few of the manuscripts that went into the magazine. His private tastes in literature were what a typical *McCall's* reader would consider very highbrow. He owned a vast library and read by preference Gibbon, Lecky, Saintsbury, Strachey, Henry Adams, Henry James, Joseph Conrad, W. H. Hudson, Clive Bell, Virginia Woolf, and Aldous Huxley. He eagerly followed all the advance-guard literary magazines and bought or subscribed to dozens of publications on post-impressionism and other schools of modern painting.

He had an acute journalistic instinct as well as an understanding of the kind of fiction, articles, and features that appeals to the broad mass of women readers. This he had developed during his years as a newspaperman and feature editor for the Scripps newspaper enterprises. As a magazine editor, he read the newspapers assiduously, looking for indications of trends in public interest which he could foresee would develop within six months or a year. He kept close tab, by questioning rental libraries, on what the mass of women, particularly young women, were reading, believing that rental-library patrons were better indicators of taste for a fifteen-cent monthly magazine for women than were the bookstores which cater to book buyers able to pay from two to five dollars for a current book.

He knew that the name of Kathleen Norris, Booth Tarkington, Mary Roberts Rinehart, or Robert W. Chambers on the cover of the magazine was good for an extra 150,000 or 200,000 newsstand sale, and he set out to woo these writers away from their established markets, the *Saturday Evening Post, Ladies' Home Journal,* and *Woman's Home Companion,* by offering much higher prices than they were accustomed to receive from these magazines. This was a profitable thing for *McCall's,* because it resulted in increased circulation and higher advertising rates. After Harry Burton wooed Robert W. Chambers away from the Hearst magazines, at a big jump over Chambers's highest word rate, with rich rewards in circulation, Ray Long of *Cosmopolitan,* imitating H. P. B., began to raid Lorimer's stable of pet writers on the *Saturday Evening Post* with prices which Lorimer refused to pay—snaring Irvin S. Cobb, Mary Roberts Rinehart, and others whom Lorimer considered his private property and whose departure he considered an act of disloyalty to him, forgetting that he had won these writers away from Robert H. Davis of *Munsey's,* who had "discovered" and encouraged them, with offers of payment higher than Davis could afford to meet.

From my own research as to what women—of the class that is now addicted to the soap operas of radio—were reading I brought into the *McCall* fold two extraordinary circulation builders, one of them a best seller whose work had never been serialized, and another practically unknown in this country at that time, but widely read in England. The first was Temple Bailey, a writer of sentimental, romantic novels which appealed to women

86

who could identify themselves with the middle-class and lower-middle-class characters who were involved in ordinary domestic problems and who remained cheerful or hopeful in depressing circumstances and triumphed gloriously in the end. The other was Ethel M. Dell. I read two Ethel M. Dell novels—which had fallen flat as book properties in this country—before I discovered the secret of their appeal to Englishwomen and of their potential appeal to American women. When I found that five more Dell novels had this same appeal ingredient, I persuaded Harry to sign a contract for her future output, when, as, and if delivered.

After reading the first two Ethel M. Dell novels, I was convinced that the spinsterish Miss Dell did not know what she was writing—or did not understand the plain sexual implications of them—and that her readers read them with titillation and sexual excitement without being aware of this, either, imagining themselves to be reading sweet, sentimental, pure love romances with happy endings after tear-jerking episodes in which the heroine was sadly put upon.

The Dell stories were straight out of Krafft-Ebbing with elaborate sugar coating. Homosexuality, fetishism, sadism, masochism, even incestuous love were their themes, but in stories so innocently and sentimentally narrated that readers did not suspect the morbid basis of their appeal.

A typical Dell novel, which we serialized, with romantic art (double-truck spreads covering three fourths of two pages), told of an orphan girl who disguised herself and shipped as a cabin boy to the captain of a four-masted trading vessel. The captain was a brutal and drunken bully who lashed the "boy" unmercifully for minor infractions of the rules or for disobedience of degrading commands. A stalwart and handsome young sailor took the "boy's" part and tried to shield "him" from the sadistic fury of the master of the ship, thus arousing the enmity of the master, who was cruel to the sailor also. There was a shipwreck in which all hands were lost except the cabin "boy" and the seaman. The

87

boy was nearly drowned when the sailor rescued "him," towing "him" into dry land. With the unconscious "boy" in his arms, carrying "him" ashore, the seaman glanced down at his burden to discover to his horror that the "boy's" shirt had become disarranged and that two beautiful virginal breasts proclaimed "him" a girl. Of course he was a gentleman; he rearranged her clothing and declared his honorable love for the girl whom he loved all along, with a guilty feeling because the object of his passion was (he thought) a fine and gentle boy.

Harry read none of this stuff, nor any of the fiction recommended to him by the first and second readers; he would read brief reports on the recommended manuscripts, and, if they met his conception of the mass-mind's taste in reading, especially the mass minds of the small, isolated towns, he would buy them. He figured that *McCall's* readers were a quarter of a century behind the tastes of the sophisticated readers of New York and he was right in this.

I remember I was somehow aghast when he asked me to run up to see Howard Chandler Christy and propose a contract for twelve covers in color for *McCall's* at $750 apiece. I knew they would be like all other Howard Chandler Christy "cover girls" I had ever seen, and that his vogue, even with Hearst Sunday-supplement editors, was waning. But Harry had just got confirmation that, by and large, Christy was still considered the greatest artist living by great numbers of Americans; Christy had just returned from Tulsa, Oklahoma, where he had painted portraits twelve feet in height of the wives of Tulsa oil millionaires, charging $25,000 each for them.

I went up to Christy's studio in the Beaux-Arts Apartments off Central Park West and met a ribald old boy, somewhat incoherent, but still a magnificent master of the technique of the sweeping and voluptuous line and of the romantic brush stroke. He showed me some portraits of the wives of Tulsa oil millionaires which he had not finished, or, having finished, was getting ready for an exhibition at the Rheinhardt galleries. They all looked just like Howard Chandler Christy girls of 1910 and I could hardly distinguish one from the other; but that was obviously just what the sitters wanted and had paid so handsomely for; so I didn't feel there had been any harm done, but on the contrary, only good, giving worthy ladies a lovely conception of themselves, which by sheer contemplation might enable them to grow to look like their portraits. And Christy women, say what you will, were always handsome, buxom, full-blooded, as sensual and fleshly as Rubens's nudes and yet very wholesomely dawn-of-the-century American women of the heyday of Charles Dana Gibson and Harrison Fisher.

The old boy agreed to do the series of twelve covers at the specified fancy price, he to retain the originals, which he could sell to Christy collectors. And he did a series which helped *Mc-Call's* circulation soar. Then Harry, through his own efforts, signed up Neysa McMein for a series of covers of "typical" American girls. Again the pictures all looked so much alike that, when a new magazine came out, I wondered how the newsstand purchaser could distinguish a new issue from one she had already read. But it turned out that McMein covers were definite newsstand "pulls." There was that McMein touch—an individualizing stamp like that which makes a Petty drawing of a pretty girl much more appealing than a Vargas drawing, even if all Petty drawings seem to be very much alike and all Vargas drawings differ only in the coloring of the hair and in the lingerie accessories.

Harry indulged his own tastes occasionally without any harm to circulation. Thus he gave commissions to Arthur Dove, the very modernistic painter, cautioning him to be as conventional as his conscience permitted him, and sent me to negotiate with Dean Cornwell, John J. A. Murphy (in my opinion the best woodcut artist America has ever produced), Henry Morton Stoops, all superb technicians in magazine illustration.

Cornwell, while illustrating magazine stories for Ray Long's

Redbook, his first work as an illustrator, had discovered, accidentally, that paintings in full color reproduced better in black and white than if drawn in black and white. He discovered this when Long reproduced a series of his paintings in one issue of the magazine, which contained an article about Cornwell; most of the paintings were reproduced in full color but several were reproduced in black and white. The reproductions in black and white showed values he had never been able to get out of simple black.

Right after the success of Hendrick Willem van Loon's *Story of Mankind* I learned from Horace Liveright, Van Loon's publisher, that Hendrick was at work on the *Story of the Bible.* I phoned Harry in Los Angeles, telling him of this and suggesting that we ought to buy it sight unseen before someone else grabbed it, because Van Loon (after long hardship) was the raging best seller of the moment in non-fiction. Harry told me to try to clinch the first serial rights to the book and offer up to $50,000 for it.

I went over to see Liveright and made light conversation and shop talk with him for a while. The *Story of Mankind* was Liveright's first big financial success as publisher, and this success was entirely due to Liveright's tenacity of belief in his hunches. He had published a series of children's books, in which Van Loon had retold the story of the development of civilization in simple language and had illustrated them himself. They had all been costly failures, but Liveright kept on bringing them out because he, personally, liked them and they had taught him what he did not know about the origin, evolution, history, and progress of civilization, and also because his two young children liked them. He got the idea of printing and binding them in one volume for the general trade under the title *The Story of Mankind.* And the rest is book-selling history; it became a sensational best seller; it paid Liveright's overhead for the year and put Van Loon into the high-income brackets—hitherto a poverty-stricken ex-professor of history at Cornell who had been kicked out of that post by super-patriots because his views on World War I did not coincide with those of the "Hundred Per Cent American" patrioteers.

I told Liveright, after some dawdling about, that I was interested in the possible serialization of the *Story of the Bible* in *Mc-Call's* and asked him how much Van Loon wanted for it. He said he was Van Loon's agent and he was setting the price. He said, "The price for first serial rights is $30,000," in such an emphatic tone that I knew that if I chose to haggle he would cut it to $20,000 or less; but Harry had given me a limit of $50,000 and I knew the subject would be a sure-fire circulation builder worth more to the company than the price asked, and so I said, "Sold, $30,000!"

The reason Harry was in Los Angeles was this: he was out there to try to persuade Gene Stratton-Porter, whose extraordinarily popular novels had never previously been serialized, to sell the first serial rights to her next novel to *McCall's*. Her publishers, Doubleday, Page & Co., were opposed to serialization, fearing (unwarrantably, as it turned out) that serialization would lessen the book sales; they had persuaded her that she would make more money by not appearing in magazines. It was a tough nut for Harry to crack. Ray Long had visited her and had thrown a certified check for $75,000 on her desk as advance payment for the serial rights, sight unseen, to her next book. She had coolly refused it, saying she would not write for Hearst, and was adamant against all of Long's arts of suave persuasion.

Harry took a different tack. He had never read a line she had ever written, but he knew what her work was about and the secret of her appeal—she was genuinely interested in outdoor life for young women as compensation for her own semi-invalidism and that of several of her numerous dependents; she wrote from the heart; there was no fakery about her, however sentimental her work may have been. Harry first cultivated her as a sympathetic admirer of the great good she was doing toward promoting the health and happiness of the young women of America and of the whole world.

He first proposed that she should write a monthly signed editorial addressed to the young women of America. He said she owed that to her vast public who should not have to wait a year or two for inspiring words from her pen. He offered her $1,000 each for a 500-word message and a long-time contract. She was so captivated by Harry's sympathetic appreciation of her work that he came away not only with a contract for the messages but also with a contract for the serial rights to her next novel, price, $75,000. As it proved, this was not only an editorial coup but an excellent bargain.

Mrs. Porter's monthly editorials always came in on exactly one sheet of disintegrating yellow typewriter "seconds." They began an eighth of an inch from the top and ran to the bottom of the page, with practically no margins and without paragraphing. The typing was blurred and the sentences were often run together. The grammar and spelling were atrocious and the syntax often so puzzling that it would take me two or three days of concentrated study to figure the thing out and put it into understandable English. These editorials were obviously dictated to one of her many dependents who was innocent of grammar and didn't know how to operate a typewriter, because the letters she wrote by hand were clear and grammatical. These were always pleading letters for advances against future earnings. She had one of the highest writing incomes in the world and yet she seemed always to be genuinely in need of money. Once she listed sixty-two persons who were dependent upon her, giving the ages, ailments, and general circumstances of each—a pathetic tabulation—in extenuation for her requests for money not yet due her. These requests were always granted, for she was a fine property for the magazine; but it did seem to me that she had a pretty heavy cross to bear, because she was such a generous and charitable woman, and apparently such an easy touch.

I had got a fine romantic story from Scott Fitzgerald and a promise from Paul Reynolds, the literary agent, of the next six stories Booth Tarkington turned out (Tarkington worked as he pleased and would make no commitments beyond when and if). Another author Harry allowed me to go after was Joseph Hergesheimer, after the success of *Cytherea,* but with a request for stories more along the line of *Linda Condon* and *Java Head.* I visited Hergesheimer for a week end at Dower House, West Chester, Pennsylvania. Dower House was an ancient Pennsylvania Dutch house built of local boulder stones, with all the original timber still intact. He had made almost enough money to pay for the house and modernize it by writing about it in the *Saturday Evening Post;* he was especially proud of the Dutch-oven fireplaces, five feet tall, six feet wide, and about four feet deep, which had been walled up when he bought the place and behind the sealing walls of which he had found ancient hand-wrought iron hooks, cranes, cooking utensils, fire prongs, and lighters.

Joe was an epicure and an exponent of charming living; he delighted in glassware, fabrics, and fine wines; he had become a collector of book rarities and first editions and he pored over the new collectors' catalogues that had been delivered in the morning's mail while we ate a fine breakfast of fruit, scrapple, sausages, eggs, toast, and coffee served on antique Dutch china. He was an entertaining monologuist and his lovely wife, Dorothy, was a pretty and gracious hostess. He promised me some stories at my rather fancy price and, while appreciating the nature of the *McCall* audience, he turned out for us some of his most exquisite work.

Harry sent Dean Cornwell to the Holy Land to paint a series of scenes of that sacred ground for which he engaged William Lyon Phelps to write the text. Cornwell wanted to paint in oils on the spot, but when he got to Palestine the terrific heat melted all his tubes of paint; he had to bring back water-color sketches and paint from them. Cornwell, whom I had known back in the days

93

when he was making layouts, drawing pen-and-ink sketches for tailpieces and illustrating Sunday-magazine stories for me on the Chicago *Tribune,* was a terrific worker, conscientious and painstaking, who was, and is, always learning. He studied under Frank Brangwyn in London (in Brangwyn's will he designated Cornwell to finish any of his unfinished work) to learn the technique of mural painting (which art won him many prizes and commissions in the United States for murals in public edifices), and yet he was just as painstaking with an ephemeral illustration for a magazine as he was, for instance, in his murals for the Los Angeles Public Library or the Missouri state capitol. When he wishes to relax from painting or work out a painting problem at his studio he gets out his traps and drums and whangs away to the accompaniment of a phonograph. In his early days, in order to lay by enough money for art studies, he had been a one-man band, playing a jungle-like assortment of musical instruments affixed to his body in vaudeville houses and on Ohio River showboats; and at artists' and illustrators' shows he has often demonstrated his ability as a multiple musician, burlesquing his act and using very corny tunes.

Harry Burton once told he how he got the editorship of *McCall's*. He was looking for a job as editor of a magazine and it was his custom to buy up an armload of magazines from a newsstand and study them critically while he was eating dinner at the uptown Mouquin's (killed by prohibition, alas!) then in the Herald Square district. One night while going through several of the magazines very carefully, marking them with criticisms, he had come to *McCall's*. While drinking his coffee (he drank pots of it) he marked up critical comments on nearly every feature of the magazine—fiction, articles, and art layouts.

When he had finished and was taking up another magazine to study, a man came over from a nearby table and said he and the two other men at his table had been watching him and wondering why he was going through the magazines and what he was writing in them. Harry said he was just amusing himself with remarks on how he could improve them. The man then introduced himself as the president of the *McCall* company and said he would like to see Harry's comments on the current issue. He invited Harry over to his table.

The others there were the business manager and the head of *McCall's* pattern service. They all studied Harry's comments, asking him for elaborations, and inquired into his background. Harry's chief criticism was that the magazine then edited by Bessie Beatty, who was an intellectual and a leader of the Feminist movement, was all right for readers of the *New Republic* or the *Nation* but, except for the fashion service, all wrong for a mass-circulation magazine. He said a young married woman living on Main Street in a small town, making ends meet on her husband's salary, wasn't a Carol Kennicott (the crusader heroine of Sinclair Lewis's *Main Street,* then a widely discussed and vigorously denounced best seller) interested in woman's suffrage or interested in raising the cultural level of her town; she was interested in how to save money, pretty up her rented house, and hold her husband, and that her tastes were for romantic fiction in which she could identify herself as the heroine; she was strictly a Kathleen Norris or Gene Stratton-Porter reader, not a reader of May Sinclair or Virginia Wolfe. He was offered the job on the spot.

By the time I got on the staff of *McCall's* as Harry's associate editor, the newsstand circulation of the magazine was already going up by leaps and bounds under the complete transmogrification Harry had accomplished; and a survey had shown that the typical new *McCall* reader was a young married woman, twenty-six years of age, with two children, living in a four-room rented bungalow in a town of 10,000, her husband a bright young garage mechanic earning $40 a week and owning a Ford, both engaged in instalment buying for the greater beauty and comfort of their home, and both reading little except current magazines. Promotion was built around the idea that McCall Street was a highway from coast to coast touching all the Main Streets in between —a reservoir of tremendous potential buying power among women with money to spend but not for high-priced luxury merchandise.

Harry was a thin, swarthy, hatchet-faced dynamo of energy who talked (when he talked) a blue streak, gesturing with hands and arms. Sinclair Lewis once said that during all the time he was a manuscript reader for George H. Doran, the book publisher, he had found no evidence that Doran had ever read a book; but that Doran had an instinct about the potential sales value of a book even if he had never heard of the author; moreover, he trusted the judgment of the editors he hired; hence he nearly cornered the American market of such British authors as Wells, Bennett, Walpole, Beresford, Maugham, Belloc-Lowndes, Drinkwater, Arlen, Huxley, McKenna, Lucas, Hichens, Mackenzie, Onions, Doyle, Swinnerton, Thomas Burke, Margot Asquith, and controlled the early book output of such popular American writers as Mary Roberts Rinehart, Edna Ferber, James Oliver Curwood, Robert W. Chambers, Albert Payson Terhune, Frank L. Packard, Stewart Edward White, Irvin S. Cobb, Sophie Kerr, Oliver Herford, Nina Wilcox Putnam, and Margaret Culkin Banning—as well as such new writers as John Dos Passos, Elinor Wylie, and Donald Ogden Stewart.

Harry Burton had read plenty of books but he did much the same as Mr. Doran. He would read the slips containing brief summaries of the text and the readers' opinions of the scripts, sift out what seemed possibilities to him, and pass them on to me. If I agreed with the first readers he would buy the script without reading it. But without reading it he seemed to know what was in it and the right artist to illustrate it. It was my duty, as art editor as well as associate editor, to take copies of the story to an artist Harry selected and arrange for the number and kind of illustrations I wanted. Harry and I made up the schedule each month for the "front of the book," leaving the "back of the book" to the women in charge of fashions, household hints, recipes, and beauty secrets.

The first reader weeds out the possibilities of the score or more of unsolicited manuscripts that come in every day to a magazine office, rejecting the rest with a printed slip bearing nicely worded regrets. The possibilities then pass through the hands of other readers for a consensus before they are passed on to the editor. On *McCall's* we had a democratic procedure in regard to all unsolicited manuscripts. The majority vote on any such scripts won. This sometimes resulted in the rejection of manuscripts which Harry and I were eager to buy. Usually such manuscripts were from well-known and highly esteemed authors, whose work was submitted to us by agents who had learned of the high rates Harry was paying for circulation-building names. Manuscripts from agents, especially when they were from established writers, were passed on to me, even when the first reader was violently opposed to them. Often these scripts bore, besides a brief summary of the text, the words "Excellent, but not for *McCall's.*" Occasionally I read the manuscript of such a story and got so excited about it that I wanted it very badly for the magazine. I would urge Harry to read it. He would be enthusiastic about it too. Then we would have a staff conference on the story, with heated arguments; but the first reader always won: the other manuscript readers, all women, would line up solidly with her, saying the manuscript was "too sophisticated," or "too daring," or "to subtle" for *McCall* readers. We lost Fitzgerald's *The Diamond as Big as the Ritz* and Ferber's *The Afternoon of a Faun* that way, the girls ganging up on the former as being over the heads of our readers and on the latter as being too daring. Other magazines apparently felt that way about the Fitzgerald story, because it finally landed in *The Smart Set* like Maugham's *Miss Thompson* (*Rain*) which had also gone the rounds of the higher paying magazines.

One day I got a large envelope addressed to me. Inside it was a letter and the manuscript of six short stories. The sender's name was Sarah Haardt; her address Montgomery, Alabama. She wrote that she had subscribed to the Chicago *Tribune* just to get my book reviews and comments and had always read my stuff when it appeared in other periodicals. She had learned I was an editor of *McCall's* and was sending me six stories which she considered the best she had written. She had submitted none of them elsewhere, she said, and would appreciate my opinion of them even if I rejected them.

I read all of these six stories at a sitting. They were little more than sketches involving character and incident; but they were excellent, moving, impressive, the skillful work of a keen observer of life. But they were definitely "not for *McCall's*." I knew that the first and second readers would reject them, even if they personally liked them, because the stories had no plots and were not romantic or sentimental; there was sentiment in them but it was in the overtones of the realistic narratives.

I wrote Miss Haardt that her stories were little literary gems but not suited to our requirements. I said, however, I was taking the liberty of sending all of them to H. L. Mencken with my urgent recommendation of them as possibilities for the *Smart Set*. Mencken bought four of the stories, he wrote me, and thereafter Miss Haardt became one of the most distinctive contributors to *Smart Set* and later of the *American Mercury* under the editorship of Mencken and Nathan. She and Mencken met when she was a patient in Johns Hopkins Hospital and they were married in 1930. She died of tuberculosis in 1935, leaving behind her a small body of first-rate sketches which gave promise of high achievement in the field of the novel if she had lived.

One of the most amusing visitors to our offices in *McCall* was Everett Shinn, the painter and illustrator, examples of whose more serious work hang in the Metropolitan Museum and many other museums and who was one of the most-sought-after illustrators from about 1900 to 1925. As a boy I had been fascinated by Shinn's illustrations in which the men always seemed to be about seven feet tall and dressed in full evening dress, accentuating their slim height, and the women only slightly shorter. Shinn himself was as good-looking as any of his men but was only about five feet six inches in height. He had the charm of the leprechaun and all the women of the staff fell in love with him—in a maternal sort of way—on sight. He was at once gallant and utterly irresponsible. When he came in, it was always to tell us why he hadn't finished on time the drawings we had commissioned him to do. He told us the most hilariously outrageous stories about himself; about how and why he had been locked out of the house by his wife (one of quite a succession of wives), sparing no absurd details, and how Texas Guinan had gummed up a motion picture he had written, directed, and produced with her as the star, costing him about $100,000. All work was suspended whenever Shinn came in; we all gathered around him to hear him relate his woes, which seemed real enough, but related in such a way as to provoke howls of laughter.

When Joseph Hergesheimer dropped in to deliver a three-part serial I had ordered of him one day, he was ushered into my office in a great state of agitation. Depositing his hat and the manuscript on my desk, he took a chair, leaned toward me, his eyes flashing, and said, "Burton, Cabell [James Branch Cabell] has lost his mind! He has gone stark crazy! He believes in the immortality of the soul! Night before last he sat up nearly almost all night in my room at the Jefferson Hotel in Richmond arguing with Mencken and me. Henry and I had gone to Richmond to visit him. Henry and I tried to convince him by simple reason and scientific arguments that the immortality of the soul is poppycock which no intelligent man could accept, but the more we argued the more preposterous were James's reasons for believing the soul is immortal. James is in a bad way, poor fellow!"

I sensed at once what had happened, and a letter from Cabell afterward confirmed my hunch. Mencken, who even now has not progressed beyond the nineteenth-century materialism of Thomas

Henry Huxley and is the Dean Wilberforce of our time, had probably cited as an example of the "superstitions of the booboisie"
the common belief in a life after death—and Cabell, in his droll
way, and just to draw him and Hergesheimer out, had said that,
in the absence of any evidence, for or against the theory of the
immortality of the soul, he was on the side of those who believe
in existence after death. And the more excited Mencken and
Hergesheimer grew in trying to batter his opinion down the more
fun Cabell had demolishing the premises on which they based
their belief. Of course when Cabell argued rightly that there is
nothing to disprove the contention that there are hell fires awaiting all sinners and harps and glory awaiting all righteous persons
in heaven, he had Mencken almost apoplectic and Hergesheimer
thinking he had lost his mind. I was sorry I missed that show.

The happy time I had at *McCall's* was twice marred, not seriously, but annoying enough to Harry and me to make us wonder
at the mental make-up of highly successful men of business. First,
I had been at work not more than a week when Harry, with a
gesture of disgust, came into my office and handed me a memorandum slip from one of the officials of the company. I forget the
exact words, but it advised H. P. B. that Mr. Rascoe had been
observed wearing a blue shirt to work; that this was incompatible
to the dignity of my position as an editor of *McCall's;* and that
whereas a white starched collar and white shirt were preferable
for executives, a soft collar would be permissible if the shirt were
white.

Harry said, "I don't own a blue shirt but I am going out immediately and buy a dozen." Thereafter he and I wore nothing
but blue shirts to the office, even though it meant that I had to
buy some more.

The president of the company, a quietly forceful and intelligent
gentleman, had brought to the conduct of a magazine the ways
of thinking he had acquired as president of a highly successful
department store. He had brought in an efficiency expert, who at

great cost had introduced regulations which saved about three dollars a year on ink erasers and so on, and a check system of percentages which allegedly reflected the weekly average of efficiency in each department. These percentages were arrived at by a daily check of the time-clock tabs. A clerk who was five minutes late because of some unavoidable transportation delay or who remained out to lunch three minutes beyond the allotted time brought the efficiency rating of his whole department down a notch or two.

The president and all the other officials of the company punched the clock and, naturally, they expected Harry and me to do so also—in at nine, an hour for lunch, out at five. Of course an editor does very little work in the office, except routine; he is working nearly all of his waking hours; he is working while he shaves and bathes, while he reads his newspaper or goes through rival magazines; he is forever looking for ideas, trends, new ways of building the circulation of the magazine.

For a while Harry and I ignored the time clock. We were reminded by memoranda that this was as oversight which it was to be hoped we would amend in the future. Harry and I rarely came in until ten in the morning, but also we rarely left at five. When he and I were at lunch with authors, talking over themes for articles or listening to a novelist's outline of a story he wanted to sell us, we would be gone two or three hours. We would punch the clock. Then at the end of the week there would come a memorandum stating the number of work hours we were absent and showing by chart how our delinquencies brought down the efficiency average for the whole department.

The chart showed that the efficiency of the editorial department, because of the irregular habits of Harry and me, was 60 per cent lower than that of the filing department. We were requested, in a nice way, to bring our efficiency up, so as not to lower the morale of the more conscientious employees by our bad example.

At first Harry's reaction and mine was simply to arrive at eleven or eleven-thirty instead of ten, lunch together, and talk over ideas for the magazine for three hours and check out at four. When the head office became dismayed and alarmed at this and requested an explanation, Harry went in to the president and very thoroughly explained to him that creative editors do not work on a piece-time basis and told him some other facts of editorial and creative life. That gentleman understood and thereupon exempted Harry and me from punching the clock.

Much of Harry's work was done, curiously enough, in auction rooms, where he would sometimes spend hours at a time. He would come back with ideas for the magazine, but also sometimes he would come back with an overdrawn bank account. He would have to borrow from me to get himself out of hock. Once I had to get $300 worth of Liberty bonds out of my safety-deposit box and sacrifice them at seventy-six cents on the dollar so that Harry's checks for junk would he honored at the bank.

For junk was what he mostly bought, filling his house in the country and his apartment with it. He bought two crystal chandeliers that had hung in a razed hotel ballroom of a gaudy era. If he had hung them up in any of his places of residence you couldn't have gotten into the room even if the ceiling would have sustained them. They were on the floor of the front room of his country place until he found room to store them in a barn. He bought an Italian Renaissance chest so large that a wall had to be knocked out to get it into his house and, once there, it filled a full third of the dining room. He bought an Italian marble mantel for a fireplace. He had no fireplace; the object was installed against a blank wall in the vestibule of his house. He bought whole truckloads of stuff for which he had no possible use, even as adornments of the home; they just cluttered up the rooms, driving his wife frantic. I suspect that he often bid in an item up for auction without knowing what it was and while thinking of a cover series for the magazine. Certainly there can be other explanation for the purchase of two hotel chandeliers, each ten feet in diameter, five feet in height, and weighing half a ton.

Harry did not drink or smoke and had no other extravagance I know of except that of eating in the most expensive restaurants and patronizing Hicks's soda fountain where ice-cream sodas were sixty cents apiece. He was soon able to indulge his taste for chandeliers and Renaissance cabinets to his heart's content, however, because as the circulation of the magazine rose from 600,000 to over 2,000,000. Hearst and other magazine owners sought him with high-salary offers, which he declined when the *McCall* management met the offers and gave him bonuses of stock in the company.

Ray Long was editorial director in charge of all Hearst's magazines at a reputed salary of $300,000 a year. Harry and Ray had worked together on the Cleveland *Press* and Ray had not only observed Harry's success with *McCall's,* but had emulated Harry's example in raising his rates to "name authors." He sought Harry out and offered him twice as much as he was getting at *McCall's.* Harry turned him down, telling me that he wouldn't play second fiddle to Ray, whom he considered less a rival than a lightweight who had bluffed his way into editorial splendor on the strength of his success with *Red Book,* which he had largely achieved with two authors, Edgar Rice Burroughs and James Oliver Curwood. His opinion was that Ray was out of his depth running *Cosmopolitan, Hearst's International, Harper's Bazaar, House and Garden, International Studio,* and the Cosmopolitan Book Corporation; but Ray lasted quite a long time as the tenure of office of Hearst executives goes. When Harry succeeded Ray as editor of *Cosmopolitan,* his term of office was much shorter than Ray's, probably for the reason that Harry, an exceedingly nervous and high-strung person, had no taste for "office politics" and no talent for the intrigue that goes on within a great journalistic empire like Hearst's.

It was Harry's frequent reiteration to me that either he or I could edit *McCall's* successfully "with one lobe of our brains," just as Theodore Dreiser had edited the *Delineator* and Arnold

Bennett had edited *Woman.* This was in a measure true; for while working for *McCall's* I found time to contribute critical essays, articles, personality sketches, and book reviews to the *New Republic,* the *Nation,* the *Reviewer,* the *Bookman,* the *New Freeman,* the *Double-Dealer* (a little *Tendenz* magazine then published in New Orleans and edited by John McClure, a poet), the *Literary Review* of the New York *Evening Post,* and the New York *Tribune.* My subjects included essays on George Santayana, Max Beerbohm, Stendhal, Clive Bell, Emile Zola, Remy de Gourmont, Théophile Gautier, the poetry of Conrad Aiken, character studies of Sherwood Anderson, H. L. Mencken, Joseph Hergesheimer, Henry Blake Fuller, and Carl Sandburg; on the biblical style; on farmers and bank loans in Oklahoma; and reviews of many current books; a short story for the *Smart Set,* and a piece in the *Bookman* that caused a great deal of consternation among motion-picture producers and distributors. It was called "The Motion Pictures: An Industry, Not an Art."

That critical appraisal of the movies of the period which led the November 1, 1921, issue of the *Bookman* contained nothing that was not later said over and over again by others, often in a more scathing tone than I had employed. Nowadays Louis B. Mayer, Samuel Goldwyn, and all other powerful figures in the movies are proud to speak of film making as "the second largest industry"; but the movie-makers, and especially the writers who provided the scenarios, of those days were self-conscious and (with the exception of men like David Wark Griffith, Charles Spencer Chaplin, Harold Lloyd, and Mack Sennett) rather unaccountably ashamed of what they were doing.

My good and admired friend, Rupert Hughes, had just been given $250,000 by Mr. Goldwin to write and direct an original story for the movies. That amount would be considered paltry now, for it not only included all costs of production, but Mr. Hughes's salary; yet it was a large sum in those days. Moreover, Mr. Hughes had just been converted to the belief that the movies were a distinct art medium, differing from that of all other arts, and he was of the conviction that the finest pictures of the future would not be adapted from the novel, short story, or the drama, but created entirely in terms of the camera. It is probable that no one else in the industry would have seen or heard of my article (for the *Bookman's* circulation was small and largely among the "literary") if Mr. Hughes had not read it and made an issue of it. He was greatly incensed at what I wrote, and at a large banquet of motion-picture people, magazine editors, and newspapermen given in Hughes's honor by Mr. Goldwyn, attacked me furiously and proclaimed the movies to be one of the highest of art forms.

The substance of Hughes's address was reported in the newspapers with the result that the *Bookman* was sold out at the newsstands and bookstores for the first time in its history, editorial writers and movie critics leaped into the controversy and the mild and rather academic piece became a journalistic sensation. The brilliant and scholarly Ralph Block, in a letter to the New York *Times* (alone, as I recall), not only took my side with vigor and point but went to great length in specifically sustaining my charges, ending up by saying that if the movie industry was to grow up out of its drooling infancy it should heed all criticism that was honest, however trenchant. (Mr. Block left Mr. Hughes and my other critics somewhat abashed, for he was important in the industry himself; he was then story editor for The Goldwyn Picture Corporation.)

That piece had had a curious history. Harold Stearns, an editor and political oracle of the *Dial* and self-proclaimed "young intellectual," had persuaded Joel E. Spingarn, editor and vice-president of Harcourt, Brace & Co., that the time was ripe for a devastating attack to be called *Civilization in the United States,* to which experts in various fields would contribute and he would edit. He had rounded up Elsie Parsons, Katherine Anthony, Lewis Mumford, Van Wyck Brooks, Walter Pach, Albert J.

Nock, George Soule, Robert Lowie, John Macy, Paul Rosenfeld, Clarance Britten, Ernest Boyd, Thorne Smith, H. L. Mencken, George Jean Nathan, and myself to write on different aspects of American culture: I was chosen to treat of the movies and I got Frank Moore Colby to write a chapter on humor and Ring Lardner to write a chapter on Americanese.

In the spring of 1921 meetings were held once a week for a while in Stearns's squalid quarters in Barrow Street. (Stearns had a Murger complex and, whatever his circumstances, seemed to wish to outdo *La vie de Bohème* in the dinginess of his surroundings.) Mencken, Nathan, and Boyd considered the whole thing a practical joke designed to rouse the ire of the patrioteers, go-getters, and the booboisie and make them squeal. They sent in their pieces and attended no meetings. That was as it should have been. But Stearns and a few of the others took the matter with lugubrious seriousness. Smith, and I attended the meetings out of morbid curiosity, inwardly chuckling over the dreary and profitless discussions, so like the meetings of a high-school debating society, and amused at the ease with which we could break the proceedings up by sending out for a jug of chianti or suggesting a party.

At length all the contributions were in and the book was ready to go to press. Spingarn invited me to lunch at the Biltmore and there told me that he thought my attack on the movies was intemperate and asked me if I wouldn't tone it down. As long ago as 1917 I had wounded Spingarn by ridiculing his basic assumption in *Creative Criticism* (that it was the critic's duty to judge the writer's intention *at the moment of the creative act*—an assumption easy to explode for the reason that the intention of an author at any given moment of the act of creation is not only difficult to arrive at, hence the arguments over *Hamlet*, but even when the author's intention is known; as in the case of Edgar Allan Poe's essays on the composition of certain of his poems, the intention has no relation to the effect upon the reader; the intention of novelist or playwright may be very noble throughout the composition and yet the novel or play may be trash), and I knew this criticism was still rankling in his breast, because he referred to it when we first sat down. I suspected that that was the reason he was rejecting my piece. But I told him it was all right with me if he left the article out, but I wouldn't revise it, because I didn't expect to get paid for it even if it were used and that I would peddle it elsewhere. That night at dinner at Eugene Saxton's house (Saxton was editor of the George H. Doran Co., publisher of the *Bookman*) I told Gene about the article; he asked to see it, and, after he had read it, strongly recommended it to John Farrar, editor of the *Bookman,* and Farrar was so enthusiastic about it that he rearranged the schedule of his forthcoming issue in order to lead off the magazine with it.

I have written about Stearns in *Before I Forget,* but inasmuch as nearly everyone who knew him seems to have his own "Stearns story" about his apparent inner conviction that people ought to pay for the privilege of knowing him, I must relate one incident. Waldo Frank has this story about how he once outwitted Stearns, and he is the only one I know who ever did this except myself, and mine was a discomforting victory, whereas Frank's was a real triumph.

It was Stearns's habit to rotate among his friends in asking them to dinner, usually at some fairly expensive place like the Lafayette or the Brevoort and always on the urgent plea that he had something important to discuss with them, usually hinting that it was to the guest's financial advantage. He had been a brilliant, if erratic, student at Harvard where he was considered a sort of boy wonder in political economy, as Walter Lippmann was when he published *A Preface to Politics* at the age of twenty-four; and he had written quite a great deal of awesome and ponderous stuff for the *Dial* and the *New Republic*. He had a forehead as high as Arthur Brisbane's or as the caricatures of Little Johnny Boston Beans, sad brown eyes that made women want to mother him, and he cultivated a preoccupied and rather dopey manner, as though his thoughts were always on profound problems.

I liked him and he amused me so much with the act he put on that I didn't mind his sticking me pretty regularly for the drinks or for a dinner. It entertained me to have him tell me just what varied European chancelleries were up to at any given moment and explain why the United States would be bankrupt in five years if the Treasury Department didn't pay attention to him and alter its gold policy. I was privately of the opinion that he knew less about any given subject than anybody I knew, and I found it amazing that he was seriously considered an intellectual by editors of highbrow magazines and Greenwich Villagers.

I think Waldo Frank, Paul Rosenfeld, Albert Boni, Lewis Galantière, and others who had their "Stearns stories" also didn't mind being the patsies to Stearns's forgetfulness that a host is expected to pay the reckoning because of the amusement Stearns afforded them.

But I was the prize patsy of them all and my wife didn't like it a little bit, and had insisted that I be as smart in my next encounter with Stearns. Stearns's trick was to invite you to dinner and either ignore the check when it came and talk on and on until you picked up the bill and paid it in sheer anxiety to get away, or, after ordering a half-dozen postprandial brandies to aid in his pontifications, he would suddenly glance at his watch, say excitedly that he was half an hour late for an important appointment, grab his hat, and dash out of the restaurant, leaving you with the check. One time Waldo Frank (so he gleefully related) beat Stearns to the "appointment" stunt, looked at his watch, and dashed out, leaving Stearns dumfounded. Waldo said he hoped Harold had to wash dishes and scrub the floor to pay the tab.

One day in June 1921 I ran into Stearns on the street and he told me George Doran had given him an advance on a book about the plight of the artist and the intelligentsia in this benighted country. It was to be called *America and the Young Intellectual*. He asked me if I would look over what he had written. I agreed. The next evening he came to my lodgings with two armloads of clippings from the *Dial*, the *New Freeman*, the *New Republic*, and the *Nation* of book reviews of already forgotten novels, outdated editorials, letters to editors, and some scattered pieces bearing on the subject of his proposed book. There was not a single sheet of new stuff. I told him he ought to weed out all the irrelevant material and confine himself to the subject of his book. He asked me if I would do the selecting and I, like a damned fool, said I would. Free, of course.

I spent hours every night for three weeks, reading, editing, pasting, discarding, until there emerged a fairly coherent book on what Stearns considered wrong with the country. I even got up a table of contents for him. He called for the stuff on July 3, neglected to thank me, and said he was sailing to France on July 5 and would write an introductory chapter and mail it to me from Paris. Then that night he phoned to ask me if I would have breakfast with him next morning at the Brevoort. He said he wanted to talk over some points about the book.

My wife said sternly, "You are not going to let him get away with it this time, are you?" I replied firmly that I wasn't. But next morning, just before I left the house, she said, "If you pay for that breakfast, I'll walk out of here and never speak to you again."

It was a blistering hot day. Stearns was on the steps of the Brevoort waiting for me and watching the Fourth of July parade that was being lined up off Washington Square. This was a holiday, mind you; the banks were closed; and Stearns was sailing at noon the next day. Nevertheless, after leading me through the first-floor dining room to a table that looked out over the street, he said, "By the way, have you any money on you? I have only French currency." I had more than $100 in my wallet but I said, "Harold, I haven't got a cent." Then he said, "We will have to go somewhere where I can cash a check," and we strode out. He walked me fourteen blocks through the sweltering heat to a foul saloon on the water front, which ostensibly sold only 2 per cent beer, and there, after whispered colloquy with the bartender (he wrote out no check, nor did I see any money pass into his hands), he returned, and said, "It's too hot to walk all the way back to the Brevoort. There is a nice place across the street where we can get breakfast."

The place was a one-arm lunchroom swarming with flies, and the floor, covered with dirty sawdust, didn't look as though it had been swept out in a week. The patrons were longshoremen. Stearns got a tray and ordered quite a substantial breakfast. My appetite fled, but I ordered a cup of coffee. He would pay for that, by God! And he did. The coffee was only a nickel, but he paid for it. He went back to the saloon and I had to walk some distance before I could find the Sixth Avenue Elevated. When I told my wife about my discomforting triumph, she said, "Just for that we will now go over to the Brevoort and have the sort of breakfast he meant to stick you for."

By the time Stearns's book came out, people were tired of hearing about the young intellectuals and calling them the young ineffectuals, so the book fell flat; it wasn't even attacked by the older and orthodox critics. But Stearns's wistful brown eyes and high dome and air of being an uncommonly wise and learned young man had wangled a $500 advance out of George Doran, which enabled him to go to Paris and join the literary ex-patriates who hung around the Dôme and the Rotonde, and talked about writing but did none.

This life proved too much for Stearns. He then earned a precarious living as a race-horse tout and returned at last to die at an early age in an America that had largely forgotten him. The promise he showed at Harvard (as I have heard attested, though I know nothing of it at firsthand) flickered out, perhaps because his instability of character made him reject his environment in

America with a Henry Jamesian distate without the compensating faculty James enjoyed of a definite drive to write and an inherited competence. He was a much too willing victim of Van Wyck Brooks's early fallacy that America does not nourish its thinkers and artists (Brooks altered his point of view in *The Flowering of New England* and in subsequent books and America nourished *him* very well, putting his books in the best-seller class).

We had hardly got settled in that hole in West Sixteenth Street (it had one redeeming feature: the living room was very large and the ceiling high) before it became a sort of gathering place (much to my delight) of writers who had followed my writings when I was in Chicago and who were individualistic and not connected with any self-conscious or dominant group, neither that of the "Algonquin crowd" nor of the plangently Bohemian set of Greenwich Village, nor of the old orthodox hierarchy of letters, whose hierarchs were Brander Matthews, Richard Watson Gilder, and Dr. Clifford Smythe, editor of the almost omnipotent New York *Times* book supplement, nor of the Lambsian disciples of whom Christopher Morley and Robert Cortes Holliday (both of whom I liked very much as persons and whom I later came, with some reservations, to admire as writers), nor the Ludwig Lewisohn-Joel E. Spingarn group of radical pedants.

Frequent callers at the flat during the five months we remained there were John Macy, Ernest and Madeleine Boyd, Thomas Beer, Ben Ray Redman, Robert Nathan, Guy Holt, Coburn Gilman, Alfred and Dorothy Kreymborg, Djuna Barnes, Willard Huntington Wright. Occasional visitors included Sinclair Lewis, Hendrik van Loon, Jerome and Florence Frank, Edmund Wilson, E. E. Paramore, John Farrar, Padraic and Mary Colum, Antonio de Sánchez, T. R. Smith, Albert and Charles Boni, and Horace Liveright.

The most entertaining conversationalist of these was Ernest Boyd, whose valid contention it was that few Americans even of intellectual pretensions had any fund of general ideas; they were fair at chit-chat and shop talk and gossip but they had no general fund of information. Redman, Holt, Gilman, and Nathan were not of this category, and Boyd was pleased to write at length that I was not; so the Boyds, who lived next door to us, were at our place two or three evenings a week. Boyd was a delight to listen to, even when the two of us were alone, for he had a beautiful, resonant Irish tenor voice, almost exactly of the same quality as that of Bernard Shaw and James Joyce. He was a linguist who read Greek and Latin and read and spoke five languages with ease and fluency. Born in Dublin of the generation of Joyce, Synge, "Æ," Yeats, Stephens, Dunsany, Moore, Lady Gregory, and Padraic Colum, he became the historian of the Irish Literary Renaissance; self-educated, he had passed the competitive examinations in the British consular service and had served as consul in Barcelona, Copenhagen, and Baltimore. In Baltimore he had been a crony of H. L. Mencken during the second decade of the century, coming to New York in 1920 as an editorial writer for the New York *Evening Post*. He was on the *Post* when I first knew him, and he lived next door. He had not yet become what he was destined to become—one of the most active participants in the literary and social life of the twenties, as critic, essayist, and man about town.

He was slim and of medium height with a copper-colored beard, and his expression, then, was gentle and benign. In his youth he had posed for the head of the Christus in the Stations of the Cross in Dublin cathedral, and the head of this Christus has been pronounced by many experts as the finest in existence, a matter in which Boyd, a professed agnostic, at least pretended to find a source of amusement. In 1921 he liked to come to our house, especially when Redman, Holt, Gilman, and Nathan were there, because, he said, it was one of the few places in town (except when Mencken came up from Baltimore) where he could find intelligent conversation. He wasn't given to small talk, and he found in this company eager young men who were seriously enough concerned with European as well as American literature to talk of it lightly and familiarly; and Redman, an ex-lieutenant of the Royal Flying Corps, was a poet and student of modern French literature, with a solid background of the classics; Holt, editor of McBride's publishing house, had published James Branch Cabell's earlier books in the face of general discouragement until Cabell scored a success with *The Cream of the Jest* and finally a triumph with *Jurgen*; Gilman was the droll editor of *Travel* magazine, whose complete freedom from all conventions especially appealed to Boyd. When Gilman was hauled up and questioned because he had failed to register for the draft, he was asked if he was a conscientious objector and he had replied No; and when they probed him further the only reason he would give for neglecting to register was "Just a caprice." Nathan, poet and budding novelist, who was a devotee of Anatole France, rarely spoke but was an enrapt listener.

Boyd's proper sphere in life, I always thought, was that of a librarian or curator of a museum with leisure to write, like Edward Garnett, critic, dramatist, and poet, who was curator of printed books in the British Museum. He would have been at home with Edward Eglinton and Edwyn Martin in the library of Trinity College, Dublin, or in the company of George Saintsbury, Sir Arthur Quiller-Couch, and Sir Edmund Gosse or of Salomon Reinach, Anatole France, and Marcel Schwob; but he found himself in New York in an atmosphere of jazz and wisecracking, of superficialities and logrolling. His mind was to be divided as the twenties progressed. Temperamentally he belonged in the ranks of W. C. Brownell, editor of *Scribner's*, who had written *French Traits* and has introduced Rodin to America; of William Lyon Phelps, who had first popularized the Russian authors in this country; and of Henry Seidel Canby, all of whom were scholarly and conservative. Boyd had such a distinguished appearance and was such an entertaining conversationalist that he was soon in demand at all literary gatherings, especially those in which there were journalists, playwrights, and editors who were in tune with the popular taste of the period and, indeed, set that taste; though he could awe and fascinate them socially and intellectually, he could not compete with them financially, for he was out of sympathy with the frivolous nature of their writings. He tried to bend his temperament to what he thought was editorially in demand and succeeded only in so agglutinating his prose that little of the sparkle and wit of his talk got into it.

CHAPTER 6

America Coming of Age

I BECOME LITERARY EDITOR OF THE NEW YORK
"TRIBUNE." TWO EXCITING YEARS FIGHTING THE
"GENTEEL TRADITION." THE "DAYBOOK" IS BORN.
THE ALGONQUIN CROWD. JOHN HELD AND THE
FLAPPER. OFF TO PARIS.

In January 1922 Julian Mason came on from Chicago to take
over the managing editorship of the New York *Tribune*. As I have
already related, he and I had become friends when I was with the
NEA and had my office in the *Post's* city room. He wrote me from
the Yale Club, saying he was a greenhorn about journalism in New
York and that if we could have a talk I might be able to give
him some tips which would save him a lot of grief. He invited
me to dinner, and, later, by phone, we set a date.

After dinner at the club we went to his room where he opened
a bottle of scotch and we talked until nearly two in the morning.
Among other things, I told him that local stories in the New York
newspapers, except for an occasional story in the *World,* were
either dull, factual, and ill-written, or, in Joe Patterson's *News*
and the Hearst papers, jazzed up but without any distinction in
the quality of the writing; that none of the less sensational newspapers apparently encouraged their reporters to rise above the
humdrum recording of local news; that local news in the *Times,
Herald, Sun, Post,* and *Tribune* was almost always relegated to
the back pages to which such stories had been assigned during
the war to make way for cable news from Europe and wire stuff
from Washington.

The war was over, and it was my opinion that Patterson's tabloid had fully demonstrated that people were more interested in local news than in the situation in the Balkans. The *World,* under Herbert Bayard Swope, I said, was beginning to show in all its columns the life, humor, and creative spirit set by the standards of Frank Cobb on the editorial page and by Franklin P. Adams and Heywood Broun, ex-*Tribune* men, on the opposite-editorial page. The *World,* I said, was proving to be a fine training ground for such a brilliant galaxy of young writers as Deems Taylor, Laurence Stallings, Dudley Nichols, Paul Palmer, Frank Sullivan, Elsie McCormick, and Louis Weitzenkorn. Stallings was made literary editor, followed by Harry Hansen; and Deems Taylor was made music critic, followed by Sigmund Spaeth; Maxwell Anderson, later to bloom as one of America's foremost dramatists, was then an anonymous editorial writer on the *World;* Broun was batting as drama critic and baseball reporter as well as columnist.

The *Tribune,* I told Mason, had the two best sports writers in active harness—William O. McGeehan and Grantland Rice; two of the most popular of all cartoonists—Clare Briggs and H. T. Webster; therefore the sports pages could hardly be improved, but that he had a great chance to buck up the local reportorial staff. The staff at present, I said, was largely made up of doubly disgruntled men: they were given no leeway in which to write news stories of character and color and they were getting the lowest salaries paid by any newspaper in the city, the old gag being worked (as I had heard) that there was "prestige" in working for the *Tribune* which compensated for the inadequate pay checks. I reminded him that George Horace Lorimer had worked that gag on the *Saturday Evening Post* very successfully until Harry Burton, and, later, Ray Long, showed such writers as Irvin S. Cobb and Mary Roberts Rinehart that there is exactly $1,750 more "prestige" in a check for $3,000 for a story than in a check for $1,250 for the same story.

I suggested to Mason that the first thing he ought to do was to give his men the same sort of encouragement to write well and with flavor and color as he had given Francis Hackett, Floyd Dell, Llewellyn, Charlie Collins, and Richard Atwater on the Chicago *Evening Post;* that Walter Howey had given his men when he was on the Chicago *Tribune;* and that Henry Justin Smith had given to such men on his staff on the Chicago *Daily News* as Carl Sandburg, Harry Hansen, Ben Hecht, Wallace Smith, Lloyd Lewis, and Keith Preston. I reminded him that you can get good men who will work for you at low salaries out of love of the game if you give them the means and authority to take pride in their work, but you cannot pay sensitive and talented men wretched salaries and also condemn them to colorless, unimaginative treatment of news. The *Tribune* by this policy of double neglect of talent, I told him, was constantly losing such men as Adams, Broun, Robert Benchley, Kenneth MacGowan, Frazier Hunt, and many lesser lights.

(Mason did, immediately, improve the news quality of the local coverage of the *Tribune* by the encouragement he was able to convey, through his city editors, Dwight Perrin and Stanley Walker, to such rewrite men as Forrest Davis, Boyden Sparkes, Ward Morehouse, and Robert Peck; such women reporters as Emma Bugbee and Florence Brobeck, and such cubs as John Lardner and Thomas Sugrue. But until the Newspaper Guild came along the *Tribune,* which became the *Herald Tribune* in 1924, lagged very badly in general staff salaries, while rewarding "sacred cows" very liberally, Percy Hammond drawing $33,000 a year as drama critic and Grantland Rice and other syndicated writers drawing $75,000 a year plus percentage of syndicate earnings. The *Herald Tribune,* now, in 1947, has granted the Newspaper Guild one of the most liberal contracts enjoyed by newspapermen anywhere.)

Mason asked about other features in the *Tribune.* I reminded him that H. E. Krehbiel, the music critic, and Royal Cortissoz, the art critic, were institutions like Carnegie Hall and the Metropolitan Museum; that Arthur Folwell, former editor of *Puck,* was doing an excellent job on the Sunday-magazine section; that the *Tribune* had scored a scoop by hiring Jack Binns, hero of the *Republic* disaster, as the first newspaper radio editor; that Jimmie Montague was a bright spot on the editorial page; and that Harriet Underhill had quite a following as movie critic.

I told him the weak spots in the *Tribune,* aside from its local news stories, were: it had no "column," like Adams's "Conning Tower" on the *World* or even like Karl Kitchens's on the *Evening World,* or like Don Marquis's "Sun Dial" on the *Sun;* the drama department needed strengthening; and, since Broun had left, the book-review pages were probably the worst in the country. While Broun was dominant in the book pages of the *Tribune,* I told him, it had the only book pages in the East for which we had any respect out in Chicago; but after Broun's departure, its standard fell.

I also suggested to Mason that he start a lively and vigorous "Letters to the Editor" column on the editorial page and inaugurate a full-page daily spread of news pictures. Patterson's tabloid, I said, as well as the Hearst papers, had demonstrated the immense value of pictures in daily black-and-white reproductions as circulation features, and the *Tribune's* Sunday rotogravure section plus the daily use of isolated pictures did not fulfill the need.

(Mason instituted both features, the correspondence column immediately and the picture page after months of argument with other executives of the paper; but the letters column did not, and never has, become the kind I suggested. Robert R. Patterson, father of Joseph Medill Patterson, made the "Voice of the People" department the most widely read text feature of the Chicago *Tribune,* and his successors, Keeley, Patterson, and McCormick, and Patterson in the New York *News,* carried on the tradition. That tradition is to select letters for their liveliness. Robert R.

Patterson had discovered the important psychological fact that nobody but confirmed letter writers, who have no other outlet for expression, habitually taken pen in hand to write the editor a letter congratulating him on his stand on this subject or that, and when he does so the letter is likely to be otiose and flabby. The average reader, however, does not trouble to write the editor unless he is burned up about something, particularly about something that has appeared as an editorial. Because the writer is angry his stuff has fire and readability. Moreover, if the paper prints his letter, two things are likely to occur: first, the writer becomes the paper's friend through the simple act of the paper's permitting him to have his say; second, the reader, even if he is in agreement with the letter writer and against the editor, honors the paper for visible evidence that it is honest enough and strong enough to "take it" as well as "dish it out." The more vituperative the letter of condemnation the more readable it is and the more it redounds to the paper's advantage, whereas the encouragement of soft soap from readers, which so many newspapers indulge in, is not only likely to be unread past the opening sentence but also considered so much hogwash even by those who read it.)

A few days later Mason invited me to lunch and said he had been studying the paper and wanted to know if I would take over the job as literary editor. I said my contract with *McCall's* had two months to go but I would be ready to come to the *Tribune* then, provided I should have an absolutely free hand to write and edit the pages as I saw best, without any interference from the business office and without any reference to the editorial policy of the paper. I told him that a wise newspaper publisher would regard book reviews as circulation features like sports, cartoons, and "colyums," and not as hooks for advertising; that book reviews, like drama reviews, should attract and hold the reader by the integrity and writing skill of the reviewer; that honest and well-written reviews enhance the prestige and circulation of a newspaper.

Mason agreed with me about this and promised me what I asked. I gave notice to *McCall's* and engaged to go to work for the *Tribune* on March 1.

When I became literary editor and chief book reviewer for the *Tribune,* my record as the champion of new writers of merit, as a fighter for the American literature then in being, as an opponent of the desiccated "genteel tradition" and of a too-restrictive censorship, together with the stuff I had written for Eastern magazines, had made me pretty well known in newspaper and book circles of New York, so my appointment received a considerable and very gracious press. Nevertheless, I thought it was highly necessary for me to make the readers of the newspaper plangently aware that a change had taken place. I wrote to Lewis Galantière in Paris, appointing him my Paris correspondent and asking him to send me a weekly letter of from five hundred to one thousand words of news and comment on the new books and literary affairs in France at a salary of twenty-five dollars a week. I wrote to Douglas Goldring, asking him to perform the same service at the same salary in London. I engaged Ernest Boyd, the multi-lingual litterateur and critic, to write on books from Ireland, Italy, Germany, Spain, and the Scandinavian countries. And I lined up a regular staff of reviewers consisting of Will Cuppy, Ben Ray Redman, Bruce Gould, A. Donald Douglas, Howard Irving Young, Stanton Coblentz, and Isabel Paterson. Soon my pages were dotted with names signed to special reviews, among which were Elinor Wylie, Thomas Beer, Henry Blake Fuller, Professor Paul Shorey, Edmund Wilson, Gilbert Seldes, Nicholas Roosevelt, Ben Hecht, Zelda Fitzgerald, and Carl Van Vechten.

Usually, when I first assigned a book to a new reviewer, he would ask, "How do you want this book treated and what length should the review be?"

My reply was invariably somewhat to this effect: "I don't want you to treat this book in any way except the way you hon-

estly feel about it. You may think it is worth no more than two
paragraphs of comment or you may think it is worth two columns.
My opinion of the book, if I were writing the review, might be
exactly the reverse of yours. But I am not writing the review of
that particular book; you are. I want you to write what *you* think
about it, with as much force and distinction as you can muster,
clearly and honestly. Please do not write the review *for me* or for
the *Tribune* or for any imaginary group of readers. Write it for
yourself. If you try to anticipate how others will take your review,
your review will be false and will show that falseness in every
line. If your review runs too long I may have to cut it for space,
but I guarantee not to alter your essential points or contentions
even if I thoroughly disagree with your point of view. Nor will I
change your vocabulary or alter your sentence structure thereby
substituting my rhythm for your own."

I was specially emphatic on that last point because of Menck-
en's habit on the *Smart Set* (and to some extent later on the
American Mercury) of substituting words from his own racy and
individual vocabulary for words his authors had used, thus making the authors seem like imitators of Mencken; several writers
in whose work I had found usages of words that were not natural
to them aggrievedly told me Mencken had changed their copy.

As a result of such admonitions and by the examples of
their results I got variety and individuality into the book pages.
Thus, also, I was able to remove from the book pages the stiffness,
formality, and pedestrianism which were characteristic of most
of the book-review sections of newspapers and of the more consciously literary magazines of the period (among which I did not
include the *New Republic* as it was in those days, with its staff of
contributors which included Frank Moore Colby, Clarence Day,
Jr., and Francis Hackett, whose writings, to me, were unmitigated delights, each so individual and each so free from pom-
posity or pretension and yet so soundly grounded in scholarship
and broad culture).

The *Tribune's* book pages were an integral part of a section of the Sunday paper entitled "A Weekly Review of the Arts." I was allotted two pages in this section for the issue of April 2. (There were only two columns of book advertising in this issue, or only a slight increase over the former average. The publishers were waiting to see how the book pages turned out under my editorship. Within three weeks the book department was allotted eight pages, equal to sixteen tabloid pages, with twenty-one and one half solid pages of a tabloid section. In September I was given a whole tabloid section entitled "Book News and Reviews.")

The leading article of my first issue was headed "The Bow and Blush," wherein I went to rather extraordinary lengths to define my conception of criticism, to show wherein I disagreed with Brunetière and agreed with Lemaître in the dispute over objective and subjective criticism—I holding with Lemaître and Anatole France that there can be no such thing as objective criticism—and to disparage the academic critics for failing to deal with the literature of their time and the type of critic who is ready enough to see merit in a contemporary European writer but reluctant to grant any merit to such American writers of fiction as Dreiser, Cabell, Lewis, Anderson, Cather, or such poets as Millay, Robinson, Sandburg, Wylie, Aiken, Lindsay and Masters. I ended up by saying:

"I should like to herald in these pages the work of the men and women whose writings are worthy in our own age and country. My belief in the American literature of the present and of the future is profound for the very simple reason that I do not share in certain disparagements of our literature of the past. Whitman, Poe, Hawthorne, Emerson, Thoreau, Holmes, Lanier, Parkman, Paine, Franklin, and Lowell are not names that are negligible in the world's literature. The first two were the fathers and grandfathers of two separate important literatures which have enriched the whole of Europe and three or four men in this list have not only profoundly influenced the thought of our own country but of other countries as well. And it is fatuous to despair of the future when the present is so full of promise."

When I took over the department I found that my predecessor (or somebody) had removed from the shelves every book that could possibly have a resale value at the secondhand stores and had left only a hodgepodge of queer oddments such as *Sales Talks: Being a Series of Man to Man Articles,* The *Glory of Going on, A Survey of Civic Improvements in Upstate New York,* and several treatises that had originally been prepared for doctorate degrees. Reminding my readers that no book is negligible, at least in the eyes of the author and his publisher, I reviewed this miscellany seriously, with the result that some readers considered the review amusing.

In the next issue, I emphasized my conception of criticism as fundamentally a subjective matter, depending upon the background and talents of the critic for whatever merit, or lack of it, the review displayed, by using as a precede to my leading article this quotation from Clarence Day, Jr.'s *The Crow's Nest:*

. . . "The great point is never to admit it's only you who are talking. The modern Jeremiah or Charlie Sniff accordingly rents a small office, and talks his opinions on to paper as fast as he can; and then instead of signing them C. Sniff, he signs them The Editor. The Editor is a self-bestowed title, yet people respect it. They observe that any man who is an editor takes himself seriously. And not only himself, but other editors—he takes them all seriously—they all pretend to take each other that way, same as Kings or High Priests. They quarrel, and they criticize each other, but that doesn't hurt—the main thing is for each of them to speak of himself by his title, and never allude to himself as 'I' or to his views as 'my' views but to call himself 'We,' so as to sound like a bishop or king."

I have never thought of myself as an agglomerate entitling me to speak of myself as "we," except when I wrote anonymous editorials for which the owners of the newspaper took responsibility; and the only requirement I made of my reviewers was that they not make this kingly confusion of pronouns, especially inasmuch as their names were signed to what they wrote and their names were singular proper nouns, not plural.

I frequently assigned books for review to men with whose general ideas I was in strong disagreement, because these men seemed to me the ones best qualified to write the reviews. Thus I assigned a new Murray translation of Euripides to Professor Paul Shorey, head of the department of Greek and Latin languages at the University of Chicago. Professor Shorey was such a confirmed "classicist" as opposed to a "romanticist" and he not only had a fixed idea that Sophocles was a classicist and Euripides a romanticist but spent much of his life denouncing Euripides and Gilbert Murray who, to Shorey's mind, corrupted thousands by translating Euripides. During World War I, Shorey went so far as to blame the Kaiser and German militarism on Euripides, being very sarcastic toward Irving Babbitt, who blamed Kaiserism on Jean Jacques Rousseau; toward Gilbert K. Chesterton, who blamed Kaiserism on Martin Luther; and toward William Archer, who blamed the war on Friedrich Nietzsche; all these were Johnny-come-latelies, according to Shorey; the real hyena who fathered Wilhelm II was Euripides, a Greek dramatist who flourished around 450 B.C. But Shorey knew his Greek. I was privately of the opinion that Murray was good Murray but bad Euripides, Shorey, it turned out, also held that opinion: he tore the translation to pieces.

I got John Macy to review Upton Sinclair's *The Goose-step,* which, on the face of it, was a doubly daring thing for me to do on a Republican newspaper, for Sinclair was the bête noire of all newspapers at the time because of his attack on the press in *The Brass Check,* and Macy was a socialist. Macy allegedly had lost his job on the Boston *Herald* because of his electioneering for Eugene V. Debs, and he was so badly in Dutch with the conservative press that he had a difficult time earning a living. I considered him one of the most brilliant and best-informed literary critics this country has ever produced. There was no kick on Macy's review, and so I gave him more work.

With the second issue of the *Tribune's* book pages under my editorship I instituted a feature which was to be very eagerly followed, often called "the most striking journalistic innovation of the past decade," and described by C. Hartley Grattan in this wise:

"In his 'Bookman's Daybook,' he [Rascoe] recorded what he did, what people he met, what he read, what they read, and what was being said. It is hardly necessary to point out that such a record is of considerable importance, for in it there was bound to be reflected the spirit of the times if nothing else. The quality of the record, which I believe to be high, is the product of Rascoe's peculiar ability to seize upon the significant statement, to say the incisive thing, and to record the crucial fact, a talent that is closely related to reporting. In one of its many aspects, the 'Daybook' is superlatively fine reporting. More importantly, however, it served as an outlet for a fine, alert, and discriminating intelligence. Into it for over two years Rascoe poured all that was best in him and the best is very fine indeed . . . One of the truly worth-while critics of the day, he seems more responsive to the literary currents of the time than any other single man whose vocation is literature. No man with whose writings I am acquainted quite so completely gives me a sense of the modern age while he is still dealing chiefly with literature."

An anonymous critic in the *Bookman* wrote: "He makes quite terrible gaffs occasionally by overshooting the mark, failing to distinguish between the thing that may be cried in the market place and that which must be murmured in confidence, among friends. Upon this colorable evidence there are those who charge him with malice. They are totally mistaken. He has no enduring grudges, and never bothers to pay off scores in cold blood. When he indulges in controversy, it is for an ulterior motive; and if he is accused of not fighting fair, so was Napoleon, for the same reason, because they aimed at victory and hit at the weakest point. Moreover, Burton Rascoe really does not perceive why any person should mind what he does to them, since he would not be put out if they did the same thing to him, and is not when they repay him sevenfold. To say the least this sounds improbable, but it has been proved. Some years since a man who stood on the footing of a friend endeavored to inflict upon him a grave injury, with no possible justification. Mr. Rascoe must have been annoyed, but contented himself with avoiding that person thereafter; and lately, when the false friend wrote a book, Burton hailed it as a minor masterpiece. 'How could you?' asked a third person who was acquainted with the circumstances. Burton looked surprised, and replied simply that the novel was a minor masterpiece . . . He gets on with the techiest of our young literati in spite of themselves; and there are a lot of violently inflammable egotists among them. One in particular has wasted as much nervous energy trying to pick a quarrel with him as would have sufficed to make an epic. This morbid poetaster writes Burton an insulting letter at least once a month, announcing a complete severance of diplomatic relations and comes around a few days later to find Burton unruffled and unchanged."

To this day I cannot understand why it should surprise the *Bookman* critic, or anybody else, that my personal regard for a writer, or lack of it, has anything whatever to do with my critical opinion of his literary ideas or work. I have known writers whom I loathed as persons and whose company I would always take the greatest pains to avoid and yet whose writings have given me either pleasure or instruction, or both; and so I have proclaimed their merits as writers, in print, whenever the opportunity arose. On the other hand, there are some writers whom I hold in great affection whose work I think is mediocre. I would not go out of my way to voice this opinion of their work, but also I would not lie about it if my job forced me to take notice of it.

Sometimes a writer and his work are almost identical; their

characters and their work are equally irreproachable. I could name dozens of such writers I have known, living and dead, of whom this is true, among them, to speak at random, Clarence Day, Jr., Frank Moore Colby, James Branch Cabell, Sherwood Anderson, Edwin Arlington Robinson, James Stephens, Padraic Colum, John Masefield. There are also some writers whose disagreeable personal characteristics are implicit in everything they write. But Wagner's music is not to be judged in terms of his personal scoundrelism nor is an author's personal attributes to be confused with the self which he displays on paper. George Moore was an unconscionable boor and jackanapes, but *Hail and Farewell* and *The Brook Kerith* are literature; George Bernard Shaw would not invite Frank Harris to his house but he repeatedly paid tribute to Harris as a writer of forceful English and as an intelligent editor up until Harris's death; Dunsany's woefully bad manners when he visited this country on a lecture tour should not blind one to Dunsany's gift for phantasy. For some reason Dreiser was always amiably, even affectionately, disposed toward me, and yet I saw him be intolerably rude, without cause, on several occasions, to persons he did not know at all; his work I would not judge in terms of his personal relations with me or with anybody else; indeed his *Sister Carrie* is no less a monumental work of American fiction for the fact that *Hey rub-a-dub-dub* is a literary quagmire, and the one book is not to be judged in terms of the other.

Quite a number of writers have written me abusive letters; but I suppose the poet the *Bookman* critic had in mind was Maxwell Bodenheim. The *Bookman* critic was mistaken, though; for a long while Bodenheim didn't write me abusive letters once a month; he wrote them once a week, or oftener. This was entirely my fault; I had brought it on myself; and, besides, however hard he might try to insult me, personally, I could not take offense with anyone who charmed me as much as he had with the poems in *Minna and Myself* and *The Sardonic Arm*.

I had brought Bodenheim's vituperative abuse of me upon

myself by an unguarded act while I was preoccupied with something else. I had "loaned" him two dollars. When I first met Bodenheim, back in Chicago in 1917, I had sized him up as the sort of person whom, if you do not wish him to become your mortal enemy, you must never give him a sense, that he dreaded, of being under obligation to you, intentionally or unintentionally. Therefore, over a period of years I occasionally bought poems from him only because I thought they were good, rejecting others, because Bodenheim would know it instantly if I bought a poem out of kindness of heart; I occasionally assigned books to him for review; I invited him to dinner quite often but never when I thought he was obviously in need of a meal; or, when he came to see me, I would take him out to lunch. But whenever he asked me to "lend" him money I steadfastly refused, even if he asked for no more than a dollar, because I felt sure he would turn on me if I did.

One afternoon, however, Bodenheim came to my office when I was behind in my work and desperately trying to make a deadline. He was unkempt, his face was as pale as whitewash, his eyes were haggard, he was gasping for breath. He staggered to a chair and collapsed in it. I asked him what was the matter. He gasped, "I am starving. I haven't had a bite to eat in three days." If I had not been so anxiety-ridden about the deadline, I would have grabbed my hat and said, "I am hungry too. Let's go get a bite to eat." Instead, I dug into my pocket and pulled out the contents—two one-dollar bills and a dime—handed it to him, and said, "Go get yourself something to eat."

Bodenheim pocketed the money. His act was over. He sat up in his chair, color came back into his face, he stopped gasping. And right away he began to lay me out. "You have become, my dear Mr. Rascoe, nothing but a literary prostitute," he began. "Like all the others in this gilded bordello of publishing parasites, ever since you came to New York you have kowtowed to nincompoops and well-dressed mediocrities. Once you had some promise but you have been corrupted by the Heywood Brouns, the Joseph Wood Krutches, the Carl Van Dorens, the Edmund Wilsons, and all the rest who undress and show their spiritual and intellectual nakedness in such bedizened sepulchers of the soul as the Algonquin and the Brevoort. You have sacrificed my respect; I have no use whatever for you."

I said, "All right, Bogey! Now, will you please go out and get a drink and let me get back to my prostitution. Poets may idle but whores must work."

He got up, filled his pipe, stuck the stem through the cavity of a missing front tooth, lighted his pipe, grinned maliciously, bowed from the waist, and said, "Adieu, M'sieu Rascoe. You will be hearing from me." And I did. Ben Hecht offered him a job on his Chicago *Literary Times* at ten dollars a week and board and lodgings at Ben's house. As long as the paper lasted, Bogey devoted most of his space to denunciations of me. He would carefully send me clippings and elaborate on their contents in private letters. He was later to break very violently with Hecht and Hecht was to caricature Bodenheim quite outrageously in *Count Bruga,* to which Bodenheim was to reply with an even more unflattering caricature of Hecht in *Duke Herring*. Of Bodenheim I have given other glimpses in "A Bookman's Daybook." I have dwelt with him here only to explain the point of view behind that feature I ran in the *Tribune's* book sections, a point of view which some people misunderstood.

In "A Bookman's Daybook" I tried to keep as faithful and as illuminating a record as is permissible in print, hoping, as Grattan said I did, to reflect the spirit of the times. Quite often I wrote about or quoted persons wholly unknown to, or affiliated with, the literary world. As a result, I would be asked why I mentioned the names of "nobodies" in the column. I reminded such interrogators that nobody is "nobody" to himself, and that if John Doe makes a remark or expresses an opinion which I think worth recording, the credit should go to John Doe just as readily as if what he said came from the lips of John Dewey. Also I often quoted people without comment when I thoroughly disagreed with what they said. Only thus, I thought, could I give a true report on ideas and impressions current and display the quality of the mind of the person quoted.

Diaries and intimate journals have always interested me, from Pepys's to Emerson's; from Saint-Simon's to *The Journal of a Disappointed Man;* from William Hickey's to Gouverneur Morris's; from those like "Fighting Bob" Evans, the brusk and earthy British admiral, to those of Maurice Paléologue, the subtle and witty French Ambassador to the court of the Czars, and I thought (rightly) that many others shared my interest. Moreover, inasmuch as an account of my reading was a part of my daily life, I could record briefly my impressions of many books which interested me to which I could not devote space in formal reviews.

While I was writing the "Daybook," I made an interesting psychological discovery. Many people were attracted to it because they thought it was a sort of thing that later became known as a "gossip column," because I recorded the names of those I had lunch or dinner with, of those whom I knew at parties, and of those who came to my house, and I often described these persons or quoted their opinions if I thought what they said had pertinence or general interest. As a matter of fact, what might be termed "gossip" comprised only a small fraction of the "Daybook." Nine tenths of the "Daybook" was either reflections of the ideas in the air at the time, as those ideas were expressed by persons I encountered or expressed in books and magazines of the period, or they were my own informal comments on what I read.

Besides the "Daybook," which usually occupied a whole page or two pages in the back of the book-review section, I nearly always wrote the lead review, which appeared on the first page. These bore my signature. But they were formal reviews, carefully

written, each a study not only of the content of the book but of
its significance and of its quality in relation to that of other work
by the same author. Most of them were of the sort which, bound
up into a book, might make a volume or several volumes of critical studies of the authors whose books were under review. But
just as books of essays or books of critical studies have a very
limited popular appeal, so also, I found, these critical studies were
read only as book reviews and quickly forgotten, whereas all
sorts of people, literary and nonliterary, could quote back to me
passages from the "Daybook" which had appeared weeks or
months before.

It was a disappointment to me to discover that a great number
of people, even among the so-called intellectuals, who read the
"Daybook" with avidity, omitted to read my formal reviews, because I was waging quite a number of battles in those reviews,
apropos of the books I was reviewing. Thus, eight or ten years
before Adolf Hitler was heard of I was exposing and denouncing
the pernicious and preposterous racial theories which Hitler and
his gang were later to adopt, and I was attacking what is now
called the "fascist" philosophy long before anyone heard of
Mussolini, who gave the name of "Fascismo" to his hoodlum
reign.

I attacked this doctrine time and time again; I took a whang
at it when another phase of the doctrine was propagated in 1924
by an eminent British scientist, F. G. Crookshank in *The Mongol
in Our Midst,* a horrible travesty on scientific thinking, which
attempted to prove that idiocy in the human race is derived from
the Mongolians, who, he said, were descendants of a species akin
to the orangutan, whereas the highest type of human being (that
is the purebred Englishman, of which he was one, to be sure) is
descended from a species akin to the chimpanzee. When the pure
blood of the Nordics is infected with Mongoloid blood, according
to Crookshank, either idiocy or something worse, such as Georges
Clemenceau, Premier of France, results.

This mongoloid nonsense of Crookshank's got into the alleged scientific writings of all sorts of treatises and was not only taken seriously by many medicos but propagated by popular writers on scientific subjects. Arthur Brisbane, himself a blue-eyed blond, was fascinated and convinced by the Stoddard-Grant-Gobineau bilge and, in column after column, alleged that all the great men of the world, from Alexander the Great to Arthur Brisbane, were Nordic and blond and that the inferior men were brunets from the Mediterranean seacoasts. Among many of my acquaintances who prided themselves upon keeping up to date with scientific progress a game developed, half in fun and half in earnest, in which they attempted to gauge whether people they knew were touched with Mongoloid or orangutan blood or not; for Crookshank had charts and pictures showing how to tell racial strains apart by postures.

A lone book reviewer, even if he had numerous allies among sociologists, physicists, biochemist, and biologists, could make no real headway against this mental-and-emotional-corrupting poison, because at the time such stuff was an "intellectual" fad, and as such was supported by irresponsible writers who had the power of disseminating these views through books and periodicals.

So, also, there were philosophical fads seized upon and propagated by "intellectuals" of the period which led directly to the deplorable vogue of Oswald Spengler and Vilfredo Pareto in the early thirties; these fads were such short-lived flare-ups as the "New Humanism," which basically was Gobineauism in literature, as also was the whole fundamental thesis of Stuart Pratt Sherman's reactionary, anti-alien books, *On Contemporary Literature* and *The Genius of America*. (I suggest, by the way, a thesis for some young student in search of a master's degree or in search of a theme for a book: let him dig up the reviews and essays in praise of Spengler and Pareto written by the band-wagon jumpers who would now be very much embarrassed to be con-

132

fronted by the evidence that they once touted "philosophers" whose fundamental political and social concepts were identical with those of Mussolini and Hitler.)

I was conscientious enough about the "Daybook," but it was dashed off at high speed and haphazardly, very often at the conclusion of a busy day, just as a diary should be written. I was very conscious of style in my lead book reviews, however, and more careful in composing them. I wanted to give them the polish and precision of permanent essays. Many of them have that value, I am immodest enough to think, even now; but I had plangent evidence that they did not make the impression the items in the "Daybook" did.

The "Daybook" was read, as I had ample evidence to show, by thousands of people who ordinarily do not pay any attention to the book-review sections of the newspapers. How they learned about the "Daybook"'was (1) by word of mouth, (2) by the way I dressed up the pages with caricatures instead of photographs. Among the caricaturists whom I got to do work for me were: Helen Hokinson, Ralph Barton, Djuna Barnes, Soriano, Dwight Taylor (son of Laurette Taylor), Gene Markey, and Hans Stengel. But the two men whose work I was proudest of were Miguel Covarrubias and Reginald Marsh, and I was proudest of them because I was the first editor ever to buy their work. For a year or so I provided them an income (meager, to be sure) and an opportunity to show other editors what they could do. They became famous later on.

When Covarrubias first came in to see me, he was only eighteen years old. He had come to New York on a government scholarship from Mexico City. He had the face of a very happy baby, with an olive skin, black hair, white even teeth forever displayed in a beatific smile, a way of giggling nervously. He said he had come to me because he had seen that I used caricatures. He showed me the contents of his portfolio, samples of his cartoons and caricatures, in full color, of Mexican bigwigs in that individual style that is now familiar to book and magazine readers. I thought Covarrubias's stuff was marvelous.

At once I dug out of my files a bunch of publicity photographs of authors of current and forthcoming books and engaged Miguel to make caricatures from them. But I was so impressed by his work that I phoned Frank Crowninshield of *Vanity Fair,* the foremost art-fashion-and-culture magazine of the time, for which I was writing the book reviews, and asked him if I could bring over a young artist who had some stuff I thought was good.

Frank asked us to come right over. When we got there I had another demonstration of Frank's suave, urbane, subtile, complex personality. He radiated old-world charm as he acknowledged the introduction to Covarrubias. He took Miguel's portfolio, put it on a table, opened it up with care, almost with reverence. As he glanced at each picture, he would rub his hands as though he were ecstatically washing them and mutter, "Nice lines! Nice color! Nice feeling!" He took an interminable time going through them. I thought anyone could see at a glance that Covarrubias was sensationally good.

Finally Frank selected three or four caricatures of Mexican politicians, looked at them carefully, and put them down. Then he said, pointing to a caricature of a Harlem "sporting man" in which the victim wore a coat whose shoulders curved up sharply where they joined the sleeve, *"C'est un peu exagéré, peut-être?"* with just the slightest rise in the inflection of *"peut-être."* His use of *"peut-être"* rather than *"non?"* or *"n'est-ce pas?"* was wholly in character with his reassuring air of false humility, of delicately polite deference. . . . I knew from those words that Covarrubias's goose was cooked as far as Crowninshield was concerned. He did not have to add, though he did, in an aside to me, *"C'est un peu sauvage."*

"Crowny" was a bit gun-shy at the moment, for Billie Burke had sued, or threatened to sue, the magazine for a poem written by Dorothy Parker, in one of her amusing series of "I Hate——"

verses telling why she "hated" Miss Burke. Mrs. Parker had been fired from the Nast publications for this offense; and on the day she was fired Robert Benchley, another member of the staff, went out to lunch with Mrs. Parker and never came back.

But if "Crowny" didn't trust his own judgment, he trusted the judgment of someone and I think it was Carl Van Vechten; for a few months later, after Covarrubias had been illustrating my book pages with delightful caricatures, *Vanity Fair* suddenly blossomed out with several reproductions of Covarrubias's work in full color, together with an article about the young artist; and Covarrubias thereafter became a regular monthly contributor to the magazine.

Marsh didn't do any caricatures for me; he did two- and three-column cartoon panels in charcoal of scenes of literary life. Djuna Barnes, who was as subtle and as individualistic in her caricatures as she was in her short stories and pseudo-Elizabethan stories of bawdry, was one of the handsomest women I have ever seen and one of the most amusing. I never saw her wear anything except a tailored black broadcloth suit with a white ruffled shirtwaist, a tight-fitting black hat, and high-heeled black shoes; and I rarely saw her without a long shepherd's crook which she carried like a Watteau figure in a *fête galante*. Her story of the "Odyssey of the King of the Ostermoors," in which she, Jane Heap, Margaret Anderson, and Georgette Leblanc, Maeterlinck's first wife, figured hilariously, as Djuna told it, is one of the classical anecdotes of New York literary life which, unfortunately, I am not privileged to relate.

John Held, Jr., of course, was the historian, in caricature, of the flappers of the twenties, with their rolled stockings, their low heels, their cigarettes with long holders, their flasks of gin, and their sloppy boy friends; and he had much more influence upon the fashions and the slang of the youngsters of the period than had Scott Fitzgerald or any of Fitzgerald's imitators. Life imitated John Held, Jr.'s, caricatures of the flappers and flapdoodlers so much that nearly all the kids, especially in the small towns, began to look as though they had stepped out of Held's pages.

Ralph Barton was a gentle, diffident, smallish man, who always wore gray pin-striped trousers with a blue or black double-breasted jacket and rather formal haberdashery. He was neat, intelligent-looking, rather sad-faced and extremely shy. Besides being a superb caricaturist, he was an amateur lexicographer whose hobby it was to find errors, type or otherwise, in standard dictionaries. When I knew him he had gone through the first three volumes of the monumental Oxford English Dictionary and had uncovered three errors, which the OED editors had admitted. The letter he wrote for the public just before he committed suicide is one the most moving documents I have ever read. Hans Stengel also committed suicide in grief over the loss of the woman he loved to another; he gave a large party at his flat in Greenwich Village and hanged himself in a closet while the festivities were going on. His, however, had been a tortured soul ever since he was interned as an enemy alien along with Karl Muck, the conductor of the Boston Symphony Orchestra, and thousands of others during World War I. As an artist on the famous German satirical magazine, *Simplicissimus,* he had devoted his talents to savage cartoons directed against Prussian Junkerism and militarism and had fled to America to avoid being jailed. He had taken out his citizenship papers but the probationary time had not expired when we were plunged into war with Germany. Stengel had felt no resentment about being interned; but after long imprisonment he had begun to feel that fate was against him and that, having lost nearly three years of his productive life, he could never be a success.

After the *Tribune* had moved uptown to its new building in West Fortieth Street, forsaking the old red-brick skyscraper in Nassau Street, a war veteran came to me with an elaborate letter of introduction from Ben Hecht, proclaiming the bearer an undiscovered genius, "civilized and eccentric," so Ben said. The bearer's name was John Armstrong. He had a silver plate in his head as a result of a shrapnel wound. After long hospitalization, he had been qualified for learning a trade at government expense. He specified newspaper work. Hecht had been his sponsor in Chicago and had let Armstrong do some writing chores on the Chicago *Literary Times*. Armstrong wanted me to be his sponsor in New York. This meant that he had to spend several hours each day in the office, in order to draw his allowance from the Veterans' Administration while he was supposed to be learning a trade.

All I could do was give him an occasional book to review. My correction of his copy, which did not need correction (he could write very well), fulfilled my function as sponsor, except that I had to fill out a printed report on him at regular intervals. I asked Mason if it was all right for me to act as Armstrong's sponsor. Mason said it was absolutely forbidden; that they had had several veterans cluttering up the office from the rehabilitation bureau and had had to get rid of them because they were a nuisance.

Whitelaw Reid had been Ambassador to the Court of Saint James's and the *Tribune* was strongly Anglophile; it had urged this country to get into the war on the side of England right from the first in World War I, so I thought the *Tribune* could not well afford to refuse to permit me to do this trifling service for an American soldier who had had a part of his brain shot out by shrapnel at the *Tribune's* bidding. I took John in, anyhow, never disclosing my action to the front office. He was there for nearly a year, but inasmuch as we were on the top floor and rarely visited by anyone from the management, Mason never learned he was there. I paid Armstrong for the book reviews he wrote.

Armstrong and Isabel Paterson, for some reason I never bothered to learn, didn't get along at all; and for about eight months they shared the outer office without ever speaking. They would glare at each other when Armstrong came in and that was all. Mrs. Paterson was my secretary and assistant and had considerable work to do, because she wrote reviews, kept records of books given out for review and of the space the reviews occupied, took care of payments to free-lance reviewers, and helped me with the make-up. She had a desk with a typewriter, but I did not see how I could wangle a desk and typewriter for Armstrong without disclosing the reason for his presence in my office. So he wrote his reviews at home and just sat there day after day, reading the newspapers. His agreement with the Veterans' Bureau required him to spend so many hours every day under the eye of his sponsor, and he was conscientious about that.

Whatever became of Armstrong I don't know. He was writing a novel while I was his sponsor, but he was cut adrift when I left the *Herald Tribune*. I heard from him from time to time, from Havana, Mexico, or California, until 1930; and I bought the only two articles he ever sent me, one for the *Bookman* in 1928 and one for *Plain Talk* in 1929. They were excellently written and very informative. One article was the by-product of a job he had at the Astor Hotel for a while as a headwaiter's assistant at large banquets; it gave details about the work of waiters and the caste system among them, with many amusing and sharply definitive sketches, much in the manner Ludwig Bemelmans was to employ years later in his accounts of his life among the waiters at the Waldorf-Astoria. The other article was an exposé of the glaring inefficiency of the veterans' hospitals—an inefficiency that developed into a great scandal—and it was not merely a criticism of the hospital staffs but of the dodges of the malingerers to remain as permanent guests of the government.

It seemed tragic to me that one of Armstrong's ability should become such a social waste. Some provision, I thought, should have been made to channel his energies and his talent into productive work. Certainly millions of the taxpayers' money had been provided for the rehabilitation of wounded and psychotic veterans; but, as the conviction of the administrator of the veterans bureau's funds for embezzlement showed, bureaucratic agencies are often used as the means of political patronage, with scoundrels and incompetents seizing the opportunity to get their feet into the public trough.

The people—all of us—owed a debt to Armstrong and his like who had been crippled or incapacitated in combat, although he would have been, when I knew him, the first to deny this vehemently. An excessively tenderhearted and idealistic fellow, his war experiences and the scrapheap onto which he had been thrown after the war had not enraged or embittered him; Armstrong's experiences had left him with the resigned conviction that all life was a tragic farce, with blackguards in the seats of power and under their rule a teeming mass of unprincipled and comical slaves. He considered the plight of humanity hopeless and his own case as hopeless as any. Yet I never knew a man who craved affection and sympathetic understanding as much as he did. He was reserved, even rather coldly stand-offish with me, but he adored my wife and children and seized every opportunity to be with them, because we treated him like one of the family.

Once there was a large party at our house in East Eighty-first Street. Armstrong had come to dinner *en famille* before the party because he liked to help serve canapés and the drinks at our parties. Ring Lardner and my wife played some duets on the piano; Tallulah Bankhead gave some of her imitations of theatrical stars; and there were some other exhibitions of talent by Charley MacArthur, Fania Marinoff, and Sidney Howard. Armstrong, who had overcome his reserve by getting very tight, brought three phonograph records into the living room and announced that he ate phonograph records. To our horror, he began chewing them up and swallowing them before my wife could persuade him to desist, insisting that the record of Gershwin's *Rhapsody in Blue* was very precious to her. Then he said he was an acrobat and called upon us to witness how he could dive down a flight of stairs. Before we could do anything to prevent it, he dashed into the hallway. Some of us got there just in time to see him dive and somersault down a whole flight and land in a sitting position. He came upstairs, apparently unharmed and quite sober. He was a model of decorum throughout the rest of the evening.

Isabel Paterson had become my secretary and assistant shortly after I became literary editor of the *Tribune*. Alta May Coleman, a young woman of means who devoted her life to furthering the interests and careers of her friends, never asking anything for herself, had brought Mrs. Paterson and me together when I was on *McCall's*. I had never heard of Mrs. Coleman at the time; but in her direct way she phoned me at the office, saying she knew some Chicago friends of mine and would like to meet me. She asked me if I would have lunch with her the next day. She said nothing about Mrs. Paterson. I assented, and Mrs. Coleman said she would pick me up at twelve-thirty. This sounded a little irregular to me; I thought it was the man's part to call for a woman when they had a lunch engagement, but I concluded that they did things differently in New York from the way we did them in Chicago.

At precisely twelve-thirty the next day the receptionist announced Mrs. Coleman. I went out to find a very smartly dressed young woman with the round, cherubic countenance of a Wisconsin dairymaid, who led me downstairs, chattering all the time, and opened the door of her Rolls-Royce roadster to the seat beside her at the wheel. As we shot through the traffic, she nodded her head toward the back, introducing me to Isabel Paterson, who had slunk so low in the seat I hadn't noticed her. When I looked back in acknowledgment of the introduction, Mrs. Paterson glowered at me malevolently.

At Pierre's I found that Mrs. Coleman had ordered an epicurean lunch, with champagne, in advance. Mrs. Coleman and I got along famously, but Mrs. Paterson kept on glowering at me until I was very uncomfortable. I decided to ignore her and talk of current plays and books with Mrs. Coleman, but nearly every time I opened my mouth to express an opinion Mrs. Paterson flatly and emphatically expressed a contrary opinion, in a way to imply that I was a little better than an idiot. I took (I think justifiably) a violent dislike to Mrs. Paterson and was very glad when the lunch was over.

Mrs. Coleman dropped Mrs. Paterson off some place and took me back to the office. On the way there the purpose of the luncheon became apparent. Mrs. Paterson had written a short story which Mrs. Coleman wanted me to consider for publication in *McCall's*. If one was ever pre-prejudiced against a manuscript I was against that one as I took it and told Mrs. Coleman I would report on it in a few days. She drove gaily away.

I turned the story over to one of the women first readers and to my annoyance, later, the story came to my desk with a memorandum earnestly recommending purchase of it. I gave it to another reader, with the same result. I turned the manuscript, with the memoranda of recommendations, over to Harry Burton. He bought it without reading it. I never did read it, although I arranged for its illustrating and saw it through the press.

Some months later, after I was on the *Tribune,* Mrs. Coleman took my wife and children for a drive in the country one Sunday and in the car was the, to me, very much detested Mrs. Paterson. Fortunately she was in the back seat and I in the front. Besides, I thought, she won't be rude to me with my wife present. Sometime during the course of the day I told Mrs. Coleman I was in need of a secretary and would be obliged if she would find me one. She said she would try.

Next day Mrs. Paterson came to see me at the office. She said bluntly that she wanted the job I had spoken about yesterday. She had done newspaper as well as secretarial work, she said, and had read her way through the public library; she was at present employed by Gutzon Borglum, the sculptor, but wanted a chance to work with me. I told her my budget would not allow me to pay what she was worth. She said she would work for whatever

I was prepared to pay. I said the pay was forty dollars a week. She said, "I'll work for that."

I was afraid not to hire her. But I was soon to learn that her rudeness to me on our first meeting arose out of her feeling that her short story should sell on its merits and that she had resented a condition of affairs (as Mrs. Coleman's expensive luncheon had suggested) whereby she had to meet and be agreeable to an editor in order to sell a story. I told her that Mrs. Coleman had thus brought the story to the attention of *McCall's* editors perhaps forty-eight hours earlier than it would have been if it had been mailed in, but that, in the circumstances, I was so violently prejudiced against the story that I wouldn't even read it.

Mrs. Paterson and I got along famously from the moment she started to work for me. In fact she became a devoted friend of myself and family. Our temperaments and our literary tastes and sympathies were at considerable variance; but we had common detestation of stuffed shirts, pretense, hypocrisy, and opportunism, and she respected, even applauded, the fight I was making for the literature that was the reaction to the genteel Victorian tradition.

With the exception of a few writers such as James Branch Cabell, Thomas Beer, Elinor Wylie, Ellen Glasgow, May Sinclair, and Willa Cather, she had little or no sympathy for the work of any of the contemporary writers whom I praised. Joyce was anathema to her and so, to a lesser extent, were Dreiser, Lewis, Anderson, O'Neill, Dos Passos, Cummings and Hemingway; she approved of Virginia Woolf and Ford Madox Ford but she was antipathetic to nearly the whole younger generation of British and American writers. To this extent she shared the point of view that was reflected in the editorial columns of the paper on which we worked, which was not merely Republican in politics but anxious to preserve the Tory traditions of decorum and respectability that had flowered so abundantly under the good Queen Victoria, whose favorite author was Marie Corelli. I was aware that, as Mrs. Paterson once said, the *Tribune* was nurturing a viper in its bosom by employing me, just as it had previously nourished such rebels as Margaret Fuller and Karl Marx; so I thought Mrs. Paterson, by expressing the conservative point of view in reviews in other columns of our pages, would be something of a counterbalance to my intransigent wars against such forces of reaction as Irving Babbitt, Paul Elmer Moore, and Stuart P. Sherman, whom I considered Ku Kluxers of criticism.

Will Cuppy, whom I had known in Chicago, was soon to become a regular contributor to the *Tribune's* book pages. He had written me a very amusing letter about Aldous Huxley's *Crome Yellow* when I first took the job and I had asked him to come in to see me. He lived like a hermit in a shack near a Coast Guard station where Jones Beach is now and he was supposed to be writing a play. Mrs. Paterson took him under her wing and coaxed and coddled him into writing reviews for us, otherwise we would never have got any work out of him.

Cuppy's stuff was such a delight to me that every time he brought in a review or a sheaf of reviews I would shove all other work aside for the pleasure of reading his copy. I would chuckle or laugh now and then as I read, while he stood there anxiously awaiting my verdict. He always wanted to know which sentence or phrase had amused me. All of them did, for he is a droll satirist, but some more than others. Once he brought in some copy when I was so busy laying out the schedule that I did not stop to read his contribution but put it aside. Later I learned from Mrs. Paterson that he had come out and told her, "Burton doesn't like my stuff any more," and had gone away very gloomy, despite her assurance that this was not the case. It was with considerable difficulty that I was able to persuade him to resume writing for me. (I doubt whether he would ever have written the humorous pieces for the *New Yorker*, the *Saturday Evening Post*, and other magazines which comprise his books, *How to be a Hermit, How to Tell Your Friends from the Apes*, and *The Great Bustard and*

143

Other People if Mrs. Paterson, Florence Brobeck, and other women had not acted like doting mothers to him, encouraging him to write.)

I had come to New York with an irreverence amounting to contempt for those who were dominant in literary affairs in the publishing center of the country. There were many admirable, wide-awake, broad-visioned critics in New York who were aware of what was going on in the world of ideas and were alive to contemporary literature, but their voices were lost in the metropolitan clatter. There was Francis Hackett on the *New Republic,* Floyd Dell on the *Masses,* Gilbert Seldes on the *Dial,* Carl Van Doren and later (for one year) John Macy on the *Nation,* all of them with lively brains and sensibility. Not a critic but an alertly sensitive editor, with an enthusiasm for whatever was fresh and vital in the literature of his time, John Farrar on the *Bookman* was valiantly promoting such brilliant newcomers as Stephen Vincent Benét, Thomas Beer, Sidney Howard, Hervey Allen, and John Dos Passos. There were also critics such as Van Wyck Brooks on the *New Freeman,* Ludwig Lewisohn on the *Nation,* and Joel E. Spingarn, a critic-at-large whose essays went into book form, who were sympathetic toward the new spirit in literature but aloof from it, writing so consciously with an eye to posterity that they were afraid to commit themselves on the contemporary scene except in generalities and so wrote in a sort of vacuum, which posterity may or may not some day exhume, in a spirit of idle curiosity.

But the circulation of all the media of all these men, who might have had an *immediate* and salutary influence upon the public taste, was small. They were not without influence but that influence was almost exclusively confined to the "literary" and was slow in percolating through to any considerable section of the reading public. The dead hand of the genteel tradition was still heavy upon the magazines of cultural pretensions and upon that "bible of the booksellers," the New York *Times* book section, under the editorship of Dr. Clifford K. Smythe. Whatever there was of "modernism" in New York, aside from that reflected in the subsidized magazines, found expression in the supercilious and consciously sophisticated pages of *Vanity Fair,* a magazine frankly aimed at making the Westchester and Long Island country-club set imagine they were in the swim of culture—and in the newspaper and magazines which featured the writings of a frivolous, complacent, and self-congratulating clique, known as the "Algonquin crowd," who were mainly bent upon trumpeting the second- and third-rate writers and making them prevail.

I was particularly annoyed and aggrieved at the "Algonquin crowd," because I thought they were making such ill use of their talents and of their power to influence the taste of a great many readers. Franklin P. Adams, Heywood Broun, Robert Benchley, and Alexander Woollcott, the chief figures of the group, were journalists who wrote with clarity, smoothness, and distinction. Adams was a genuine wit, with a sound background of purposeful learning, an excellent craftsman in light and satiric verse, and an alert capper of the more obvious outbursts of bunk and stupidity. Broun was yet to hitch his wagon to the fad of Communism, which did not become fashionable until the depression of the thirties; he was exploiting the vogue of Freud and trying to make up his mind whether to emulate Will Rogers as a folksy American homespun philosopher, write novels or plays, or run the vein already staked out by Gilbert Seldes. He had already written an essay in praise of Benny Leonard, a boxer, in which he said, "He stands up straight like a gentleman and a champion and is always ready to hit with either hand. . . . No performer in any art has ever been more correct than Leonard." Woollcott had given evidence that he had read Charles Dickens with a sort of proprietary interest which was curious in that he gave more ample evidence that he "dearly loved a lord" and was sycophantically worshipful toward commercial success, bestowing his fervors upon Kathleen Norris, Edna Ferber, A. S. M. Hutchinson, A. A. Milne, Neysa McMein, Irving Berlin, Mrs. Minnie Maddern Fiske, Lord Jeffrey Amherst, and Ferenc Molnár alike.

The chief occupation of the group seemed to be the manufacture of wisecracks, and their concerns seemed to be mah-jongg, poker, the exploitation of themselves and their friends, and the touting of whatever contributed to their own sense of self-satisfaction. They were so preoccupied with whatever was in vogue that they were not only proudly fiddling while Rome burned, as Woollcott proclaimed, but antagonistic toward anything that seemed to challenge their sense of arbitrating the taste of the period. Thus Broun could drop his celebration of boxers, baseball players, and high divers long enough to write mean-spirited paragraphs about new work by Willa Cather, Theodore Dreiser, Sinclair Lewis, Ben Hecht, Joseph Hergesheimer, and others who were just beginning to achieve wide audiences, apparently without reading them and often apparently only for the sake of using what he considered a blighting pun.

It was, of course, unreasonable of me to expect this group to perform a cultural service that their jobs did not require. Adams was a conductor of a column of wit and humor; Woollcott and Benchley were drama critics and contributors to *Vanity Fair;* and Broun had a column in the *World,* in which he wrote about anything that came into his head, and contributed to *Vanity Fair* and *College Humor.* But it was the very latitude of expression they enjoyed which gave me an acute sense of their abusing it, or at least not making the most of it. Neither Adams, nor Broun, nor Woollcott, nor Benchley gets so much as a footnote in such an exhaustive study of modern American prose literature as Alfred Kazin's *On Native Grounds* (1942), nor do they receive more than passing mention in Allen and Irene Cleaton's *Books and Battles of the Twenties* (1937). But at the time they not only exercised the function of critics of all the arts, literature included, but did so with a complacency which they never doubted their positions justified.

Their self-complacency had appalled me in a trivial demonstration of it on my visits to New York while I was still literary critic for the Chicago *Tribune*. It was one of those trivialities that looms large only because of its implications. They had permitted themselves to be exploited by a hotel manager as an advertisement for his hotel, without, apparently, being aware that they were being exploited and assuming only that they were being deferred to with all the honor due them.

What had happened was that Frank Case, manager of the Algonquin Hotel for twenty-five years before he bought it in 1927, had carefully built up the hotel's reputation as a rendezvous for theatrical stars and literary celebrities, and he had hit upon an idea that would enhance that reputation: he would persuade some local celebrities to sit at a round table in the center of the main dining room each day at lunch to be gawked at by celebrity hunters among the other patrons. His inducement was a large platter of free hors d'oeuvres. They paid for their lunches, individually, although it was worth the cost in advertising if Case had served lunches at the "Round Table" free.

The regulars at the "Round Table" were: Adams, Woollcott, Broun, and Benchley; George Kaufman, then a member of the drama staff of the New York *Times* and collaborator with Marc Connelly on a play called *Dulcy;* Connelly; Herman Manckiewicz, a member of the drama staff of the *Times;* John V. A. Weaver, poet and literary critic for the Brooklyn *Eagle;* and John Peter Toohey, Richard Wallace, and Murdock Pemberton, press agents. Occasionally they were joined by Hendrik Willem van Loon, Edna Ferber, Laurence Stallings, Dorothy Parker, or some guest of one of the regulars. On my visits to New York from Chicago I had occasionally been a "Round Table" guest of Adams (who, being an ex-Chicagoan, was hospitable to me and the others were cordial), much to my embarrassment and to my embarrassment for them; for it seemed to me that they were being unduly exhibitionistic and quite as vulgar as if they had consented to demonstrate fountain pens in drugstore windows free of charge, for the chance it gave them to be seen.

But they did not feel that way; sitting in the spotlight as the center of attraction obviously contributed to their feeling that they were directing the destinies of the stage and of literature. And the appalling thing was that, in a sense, they were; their connections were wide, socially, with publishers and producers and with men whose money financed magazines, newspapers, books, and plays. Their indirect influence upon the taste and ideas of the day was perhaps stronger than their direct influence. When criticism arose that the "Round Table" group were mutual back-scratchers, they made capital of it by denying it with ingratiating remarks such as "Yes, I have the scars on my back yet."

I considered the influence of the "Algonquin group" to be a pernicious one, unfortunate in its effect upon the standards of the period and, therefore, I determined to undermine it in so far as I was able to do so, not only by what I wrote myself but also by attracting to the *Tribune's* book pages writers who were part of the main stream of contemporary literature and could be counted upon to write with liveliness and effectiveness. Criticism, as I had already learned, is, as Alfred Kazin says, a luxury trade, in which one can scarcely indulge without subsidies, private income, or compromises in which one's energies are divided and channeled into other ways of making a living, such as teaching, editing, or engaging in some of the more popular and more remunerative forms of journalism.

I knew I could not compete with the "Algonquin group" for popular attention and influence even with the methods I had employed on the Chicago *Tribune* to "make literature *seem exciting*" (as Edmund Wilson was to say I did) ; because the stuff of Broun, Adams, and Woollcott appeared daily whereas the book section of the New York *Tribune* appeared only once a week. The thing, I decided then, was to become *apparently* as self-centered and personal as Broun, Adams, and Woollcott, and to be in the Algonquin crowd but not, precisely, of it; I would not only jest at their pretentions and their enthusiasms for trivial writers and trivial notions but beat drums for writers they disdained or ignored whom I considered more worthy of attention.

The continual plugging of A. S. M. Hutchinson, author of the best seller of 1921, *If Winter Comes,* by Broun, Woollcott, and Adams seemed to me the very bankruptcy of all critical standards in their ranks. In my opinion *If Winter Comes,* with its sentimentally masochistic cardboard hero, was on precisely the same literary level as *Just David* by Eleanor H. Porter, the author of the Pollyanna stories, no higher. Shortly after I began work on the *Tribune* a new novel by Hutchinson was published with a great deal of pre-publication fanfare. It was called *This Freedom.* It was about a woman whose children came to bad ends and whose own life ended in tragedy because she was self-supporting and had thereby deprived her children of proper maternal care in her pursuit of a career—a novel in which all the cards were stacked in support of a fallacious argument and very badly written in a stilted, pseudo-literary style. If it had not been a novel by an author whom Broun, Adams, and Woollcott had acclaimed as though he were a great literary artist, I should have had it reviewed along with other run-of-the-mill sentimental novels. Instead I analyzed it at length, showing just wherein Harold Bell Wright was a more capable and distinctive novelist; Wright, I said, at least did not resort to the puerile device of exclamation points, which Hutchinson did on nearly every page.

This Freedom was an anti-feminist novel and in as much as Broun was then married to a highly vocal member of the Lucy Stone League and was himself a champion of equal rights for women, I was anxious to see what sort of comment he would make on this new effort of one of his literary idols. He was silent concerning it, and Broun and Woollcott, after my review, apparently crossed Hutchinson off their list. . . . My review had reverberations; it caused the advertising manager of Hutchinson's American publisher to cancel a year's contract for advertising in the *Tribune* and to avow, in doing so, that I had "killed" Hutchinson as a property, which statement was not true, although appearances would give it validity: two months after *This Freedom* appeared, *If Winter Comes* still topped the national best-seller list two years after publication, but *This Freedom* did not appear in it. This may have been because, as some publishers claimed, reviewers in other cities tended to follow my verdict on new books; but I believe the public itself had got its fill of Hutchinson with the so-widely touted *If Winter Comes*.

How correct I had been in gauging the relative appeal of formal reviews and of the informal method I used to make discussions of books and ideas an integral part of my published diary, was long afterward to be seen in the comments of Alfred Kazin on my critical career on the *Tribune*—comments which show that he neglected to read or quickly forgot my formal, front-page, essay reviews, which ranged in subject from Santayana to Ernest Newman, from Freud to Pavlov, but that he retained a very definite impression of the "Daybook."

In my accounts of parties, personalities, and brief comments on new books in the "Daybook" I imbedded an extensive amount of comment on the classics, from Homer to Joyce and from Aristotle to Croce; I carried on in those columns the fight I had waged in Chicago against censorial restrictions upon the freedom of the artist, against the dangerous fallacies of psuedo-scientific doctrine of "Nordic" racial supremacy, and against the urge toward totalitarianism.

Kazin was to catch something of the spirit in which I considered myself a part, but to miss an essential, when he wrote: "It was in Chicago, where an astonishing group of literary-minded reporters revolted against the materialism of the 'hog butcher for the world,' that fighting young men like Francis

Hackett, Burton Rascoe, and Floyd Dell made out of their book-review columns a lyceum for all the new American and European books that were coming to mean so much to their literary generation. Dell soon left for New York and the *Masses;* Hackett for the *New Republic;* and Rascoe was later to champion his enthusiasms on the New York *Tribune,* but out of their warm belief in the young writers coming up in the Middle West and their contempt for the conservative forces that still seemed to dominate literature in the East, they made a few Chicago newspapers play host to the new spirit. All the famous energy of Chicago, the experience of that life, which Rascoe described as a 'huge hydro-electric plant,' seemed to go into their literary criticism, and they fought unceasingly for the 'moderns' with the proud consciousness that all around them, in forces like the 'new poetry' and men like Edgar Lee Masters, Carl Sandburg, Sherwood Anderson, a native literature was arising. Like Huneker, who had long since set the tone for the fighting journalists of the new spirit, they all had extraordinary enthusiasm, an appetite for every novelty, and the kind of bounciness, particularly marked in Rascoe's later career, that made a fetish of energy and could convert energy into the very substance of their criticism. Yet it is easy to understand why they all, Rascoe in particular, placed so much emphasis on vitality and were so anxious to stir up critical battles. They were evangels, missionaries for anything that seemed fresh and honest and new, and even if they drew their sympathies in chortling black and white and even ranted on occasion, it was because they were busy pointing out the differences between a Mr. Dostoevsky and Kate Douglas Wiggin, between Harold Bell Wright and a young man named Sherwood Anderson.

"Rascoe allowed himself to be carried along by his indignation and by his hot idealisms; tremendously absorbed in books, writers, careers, he had, properly speaking, no ideas. It was not that he lacked taste or humility, or even the necessary respect for scholarship; it was merely that his veneration of literature was at bottom so exclusively energetic, romantic, and boyish that he seemed always to be on the outside looking in. What Rascoe lacked, as the Socialist Floyd Dell lacked them, was the depth of conviction, the depth of understanding, that arise from something more than courage and enthusiasm."

When Kazin says I had no ideas, he means I had no fixed critical program, no intractable theory from which to proceed in a straight line, trying to make life and literature conform to that theory. I hadn't any such fixed idea and I haven't now. I was, and am, as C. Hartley Grattan was pleased to call me, an "eclectic," and when Kazin finds a lack of standards or a lack of theory when, as he put it, I welcomed "Dreiser and Cabell as equally serious artists." I can only say that I like potatoes *and* I also like caviar.

I have seen critics fall into a fixed idea or adopt a theory. And I have seen what happened to them when they did. I have seen Irving Babbitt adopt the fixed idea that Sophocles was the exponent of the highest ideal in art—that is, measure in all things, nothing in excess—and its contrary, the fixed idea that all evils of modern life proceed from Rousseau's *contrat social*. Babbitt was thus forced to the logical conclusion that not only was the French Revolution a deplorable event but that the establishment of the American republic was a regrettable consequence of the democratic process that he imagined was set in motion by Rousseau. Such a fixed idea led Babbitt into a cul-de-sac wherein his concept of good government for the insurance of the good life was, basically, reactionary. I saw Paul Elmer More, an erudite, scholarly, and religious man, adopt a socio-religio-aesthetic idea, an extension of Calvinism, and pursue it straight to the appalling conclusion, "The rights of property are more important than the right to life" (vide *More's Aristocracy and Justice*). I saw Van Wyck Brooks ride a fixed idea—that America does not nourish its artists but sterilizes them with moralistic repressions—to the point of exhaustion and then change mounts, during the last war, and denounce his juniors in contemporary literature as "rattle-snakes" with no moral responsibility.

I have seen Edmund Wilson, in *Axel's Castle,* adopt a fixed Freudian idea that all genius is traceable to an unhappy incident and then, later on, interpret nineteenth- and twentieth-century literature on the basis of economic determinism; he had imagined that the politico-economic evolution had reached a triumphant apogee with the arrival of Lenin at the Finland station of Moscow as the herald of the new dawn of Communism, only to discard that idea with disgust after a tour of Russia as a guest of the Soviet state, during which tour he had found Communism an illusion and that the reality is a police state, in which the ikons of the Greek Orthodox Church have been replaced by the less aesthetically appealing ikons of Lenin and Stalin.

I remember that Stuart Pratt Sherman asserted it impossible to criticize without a theory and denounced Wells, Bennett, Moore, Dreiser, and other realists and naturalists because the characters in their novels did not conform to his theory of the proper standards of conduct; and then, when he was released from the confinements of the campus, he threw his theory out of the window in order that he might embrace the very realists and naturalists (or their spiritual children) whom he had formerly condemned.

A fixed idea or an arbitrary theory in criticism demands a consistency that is foolish in an evolving world; it cuts one off from an infinite number of sources of pleasure. If, as it has been alleged, all criticism of contemporaries is conversation, the criticism of contemporaries by someone who adheres rigidly to a theory or to a fixed idea is a one-sided conversation in which you are apt to be asked to accept certain debatable premises before you receive what instruction the speaker is ready to impart. And the critic is likely, very shortly, to adopt an entirely contrary set of convictions.

Such criticism can be felicitous and instructive. A relentless foe of Paul Elmer More's basic concepts, I have read many of *Sherburne Essays* with a definite relish. My joy in the work of Anatole France is not lessened by my joy in the instructive and luminous essays of Thomas Kettle, the young Irish Catholic litterateur who was killed in World War I, particularly his temperately devastating essay entitled, "The Fatigue of Anatole France." I can allow W. J. Turner his preferences in music and enjoy his essays on composers and their work—so free from mumbo-jumbo and so commonsensical and witty—without accepting his contention that music reached its apogee in Mozart and that all other music suffers in comparison with it. The peripatetic Huneker had no one idea; he had a million of them; and he and the impressionistic Arthur Symons, who wrote *The Symbolist Movement in Literature* like an enchanted journalist, eager to share his enchantment with others, helped to fructify a British and American literature from which grew plants as diverse in texture and coloring as T. S. Eliot's *The Waste Land,* Sherwood Anderson's *Winesburg, Ohio,* the novels of William Faulkner, and the work of many a contemporary young writer who does not know who his literary grandfathers were.

It is interesting to note that both Kazin and Grattan bracket Dreiser and Cabell as symbolic of the work I championed and that Grattan should include T. S. Eliot; for, as it happened, I reviewed only one book by Cabell, only one poem by Eliot, and no book at all of Dreiser's during the two and a half years I was on the *Herald Tribune.* I published a small book on Dreiser in 1925; I wrote about him as he appeared to me, under various circumstances and on different occasions, in the "Daybook," but I, myself, did not review *A Book about Myself* (1922), *The Color of a Great City* (1923), and only mentioned *Moods Philosophical and Emotional, Cadenced and Declaimed* (1923) in reporting my first meeting with Dreiser. I had considered Dreiser and Cabell well enough established before I left Chicago, and, besides, Carl Van Doren, John Macy, Ben Ray Redman, John

Gunther, and numerous other critics in New York were writing in laudatory fashion about Cabell in 1922; Sinclair Lewis, Hugh Walpole, Lewis Galantière, H. L. Mencken, Wilson Follett, and innumerable others had taken over the work of insuring Cabell's enshrinement as a classic while I went about my duties of trying to protect budding new talents of promise from being smothered by a blanket of critical reactionaries who were still strong and powerful in the land. (I suspect that few of the writers of the present generation, who enjoy a relative freedom of expression, realize how tough the battle was and how long prolonged, twenty-odd years ago, that enabled them to present their vision of life with honesty and without fear.)

It would appear from a superficial reading of Kazin, the Cleatons, and other critics who surveyed the literature of the twenties and its immediate predecessors that I championed Dreiser's work unreservedly and that I welcomed the new writers of fresh and individual talent without distinguishing among them or distinguishing among their works. The records show that I was severe in my strictures on Dreiser's work when he turned away from fiction and imagined he was a thinker, and that I was very severe with the young writers when their work fell off in quality. Of F. Scott Fitzgerald's second book I wrote, "The trouble with *The Beautiful and Damned* is not that it is racy, shocking, or ill-mannered, but that it is blubberingly sentimental. . . . The charm of *This Side of Paradise* was precisely in its puerilities. There we had a young man setting down his adolescent notions about love, capitalism, and literature at the very time he was thinking them. Now that he is three years older we find that he has not matured at all and that he has taken himself seriously as a thinker. . . . No one of late years has appeared on the horizon with a happier verve than Fitzgerald or with a more promising narrative talent; and no one ever collapsed so easily into the banal and commonplace as he has in this novel. This comes from a refusal to subject his spontaneous outbursts to the

155

refining process of self-criticism and to the clarification of plan. . . . He is too richly endowed with ability not to turn that ability to permanent account."

T. S. Eliot's *The Waste Land* appeared in the November 1922 issue of the *Dial,* which was on the newsstands on October 26. I read the poem on that day and was so profoundly touched and shaken by it that, in recording my impression of it in my diary that night, I did not dare quite trust the adjectives I wished to use in praise of it for publication. I wrote that it was "perhaps" the finest poem of the generation but conceded that it was "the most significant in that it gives voice to the universal despair or resignation arising from the spiritual and economic consequences of the war, the cross-purposes of modern civilization . . ." et cetera.

After the first impact of the poem had subsided so that I could read it in a calmer and more analytical mood, I did not doubt that it was, without the reservation of "perhaps," the finest poem of the generation and one of the indubitable minor masterpieces of English poetry. It was something of what biologists call a sport; there is nothing like it in English literature; a synthesis of tag lines from great poems juxtaposed with anticlimactical images from modern life, it is a sardonic dirge, a requiem for heroic dreams and exalted ideals, bitter, beautiful, and bizarre.

Because *The Waste Land* expressed in music so much that the young men who had survived the war felt about the collapse of ideals at the greedy imperialistic poker game around the peace table at Versailles and its echoes in the war-profiteering scandals, the rise of the Ku Klux Klan, the lawlessness incident to Prohibition, and other manifestations of cynicism and inhumanity, I had imagined it would be celebrated on all sides as an exciting poem. Instead, my outburst of praise served only to provoke a nation-wide battle between those who were "for" the poem and those who were "against" it, a battle that waged for months. I found myself and the poem attacked by Louis Untermeyer, Lee Wilson

Dodd, Keith Preston, Christopher Morley, John Farrar, and many others, almost as if I were responsible for the poem. Edmund Wilson, G. Lowes Dickinson, Gilbert Seldes, and I were almost alone, at first, in according the poem high merit; it was denounced as obscure, as a farrago of nonsense, as a libel on the life of the times, as a pastiche of plagiarism—and, in a letter I had from Harry Leon Wilson from California, the gifted creator of *Merton of the Movies* and the immortal Ruggles, a hoax: he avowed he had overheard Eliot say at a dinner party in London that he wrote the poem with his tongue in his cheek and that he did not expect it to be taken seriously, an allegation which Eliot was quick and angrily to deny.

The battle over *The Waste Land* enlivened my pages in a way that of course delighted me; it was reminiscent of the time when I got laymen and writers stirred up in controversy over literature when I was out in Chicago. As late as January 7, 1923, I was devoting nearly three solid columns in the "Daybook" to an elucidation of the poem and to answering its critics. By that time the battle had become a serious matter to me, but I knew it would be a tactical error to betray this fact, so I opened my elucidation of the poem with an account of how Wilson, Seldes, and I lunched together and made merry over the abuse that had been heaped upon us as "arch-conspiritors in an alleged effort to palm off on the public an unintelligible poem by an obscure scribbler as the great poetic work of the year." In December Eliot had been awarded the *Dial's* annual $2,000 award for the most notable contribution to literature for the year; Clive Bell, the London critic, had written an essay on Eliot, apropos of *The Waste Land*, saying that Eliot was the finest poet living, which was a debatably extravagant statement when one remembers that W. B. Yeats, John Masefield, Thomas Hardy, and A. E. Housman were still alive; and the curiosity of the public had been aroused enough by the controversy to warrant Alfred A. Knopf's publishing it in a fairly large edition in book form.

But that was the only crusading I did in Eliot's behalf. Indeed, although I had thought all of Eliot's poems neat, deft, and amusing, though derivative, up to *The Waste Land* (which I considered an important contribution to the poetry of permanence) I was to find neither his verse nor his prose to my liking after that. From his embittered cynicism as an impious and talented young poet just out of Harvard, during his residence in England he leaped over the resplendent grand canyon of *The Waste Land* into Anglo-Catholicism and tory reactionarism. If he had found comfort therein for his troubled soul, I was glad for him, but thereafter I considered him an ally of the enemy. After the flare-up of the "New Humanist" movement in this country, which seemed symbolically to coincide with the pre-crash final upsurge in the stock market in August 1929, which ended in a debacle two months later, at the request of Paul Palmer, I wrote what I considered an epitaph for the movement for the Sunday-magazine section of the New York *World* for April 20, 1930.

Chronologically, any discussion of the New Humanist shindig belongs further along in this narrative, at the close of 1929, in fact; but inasmuch as it involved a weak, momentary attempt to revive the literary Ku Klux Klanism which I thought I had helped to extricate before I left the *Tribune* in October 1923, it is to the point to summarize what I wrote which turned out to be the obsequies over the corpse of the movement.

The leaders of the Old Guard of Reaction, who wished to restore the spirit of American literature of the days of McKinley and Mark Hanna, were getting so groggy by 1923 that their language was becoming hysterical, unguarded, and rather amusing. Paul Elmer More, having described John Dos Passos's *Manhattan Transfer* as "an explosion in a sewer," labeled Joyce's *Ulysses* an "obscene rigmarole," dismissed the poetry of Robinson Jeffers as "sadism," called John Dewey "a loquacious apostle of sweetness and darkness," Benedetto Croce "an epoptic hierophant of the demonic mysteries," bestowed upon me the simple, homely, and succinct epithet, "hoodlum." Babbitt had confessed quite candidly that he hadn't had a new idea in thirty years but that the likes of me were the bastard spawn of J. J. Rousseau. There was a lull in literary excitement in the years 1924–29; the wars seemed over; no new writers of brilliant promise were coming up, and the young ones who had arrived—Fitzgerald, Hemingway, Dos Passos, Beer, Stephen Benét, and Thomas Wolfe— were settling down to mature achievement. Then, in 1928, John Middleton Murry in London was asked to review a new English edition of Irving Babbitt's *Rousseau and Romanticism* which had originally appeared in 1919. From Murry's reviewing it was apparent that he had never heard of Babbitt before, although Babbitt's *The New Laokoön* had set the critical world by the ears when it appeared in 1910 and Babbitt had finally been set down by the judicious as a learned but somewhat daffy old gentleman who had delusions of being pursued by an imp with a forked tail called Jean Jacques Rousseau. Murry, feeling lost and alone after the death of his wife, the noted short-story writer, Katherine Mansfield, was seeking some faith which would give him consolation.

Babbitt seemed just the philosopher for him, and he immediately staked out his claim to Babbitt. But he had Eliot to contend with over that. Eliot, nearing forty, had ceased to write poetry and had embraced the career of critic and editor of the *Criterion,* a monthly magazine dedicated to literary and philosophical matters. Eliot and Murry had been disputing over neo-Thomism, neither of them agreeing as to precisely what the message was that Saint Thomas Aquinas had to give to the modern world to save it from destruction. Eliot had been a student at Harvard when Babbitt taught there, and, having rediscovered his old but once disregarded mentor, claimed Babbitt for himself. Then Eliot and Murry began tearing Babbitt's body between them. Eliot was the cleverer writer and the better writer, so he emerged victorious. Promptly he set forth his articles on faith:

(1) Catholicism in religion.

(2) Royalism in politics.

(3) Classicism in literature.

Eliot was consistent and logical. Although American-born, he became a subject of the King of England; he joined the Anglo-Catholic Church; and he brought out a book of essays facetiously referred to as *For Launcelot Gobbo* the actual title of which was *For Lancelot Andrewes,* the title essay being in praise of the prose style of the sermons of the Bishop of Winchester who died in 1626.

It was very comical the way the New Humanism of the twenties developed out of the espousal of it by Eliot. Babbitt's whole doctrine was compounded of snobbery and was anti-democratic and anti-Christian; it recognized property rights as the one sacred fact; it denied the Christian virtue of humility; and proclaimed the rights of privilege for the aristocracy while outlining the obligations of the aristocracy to the masses also.

The Babbitt-Eliot doctrine had a snob appeal for the wistful literary yearners of the academies who had been under the hatches for many years in fear of the whirlwind that had swept over academic dry rot, feeble dialectics masking as erudition, complacency in American life, shams and pretensions of all sorts. There had been a lull of four years during which there was no voice of the reaction to be challenged. During this lull, dreary little aesthetes and academicians swarmed out of the hatches like so many cockroaches, all proclaiming themselves the New Humanists and hailing Babbitt as the Allah and Eliot as the prophet, and proving that they were true disciples by never writing two hundred words without appending footnotes. Seward Collins, who had begun to leap around like a flea from one intellectual fad to another and who had inherited a fortune, undertook to become the patron of the movement; he financed a rally in Carnegie Hall at which Babbitt was the principal speaker and turned the *Bookman* (after I severed my connection with it) into a medium for New Humanist propaganda.

This began to alarm young writers such as C. Hartley Grattan, John Chamberlain, Henry Hazlitt, Malcolm Cowley, Edmund Wilson, and Lewis Mumford, and after the New Humanists published a book which was a sort of manifesto, Grattan got together a symposium by way of a counterblast, called *Critique of Humanism,* to which I contributed reluctantly because, as I said to Grattan at the time, the New Humanism died the night the senescent Babbitt spoke so emptily and feebly at Carnegie Hall.

Nothing I could cite at the moment better illustrates the mutability of human affairs than the story I have just told; for when I first knew him, Collins was not a doctrinaire but a very liberal-minded young man, with whom I was closely associated for several years, two of them as editor of a magazine which his father had purchased for me to edit. He figured much in the "Daybook" as a host on week ends to writers of the liberal movement at his father's estate near New Canaan, Connecticut, where Seward had a house of his own with a magnificent library, and where there was a swimming pool, a lake, gardens, and always congenial company.

I had met Collins in 1921 while I was still on *McCall's.* I was browsing in Terence Holliday's bookshop when Holliday told me there was a young man in the shop who recognized me and wanted to meet me. I was introduced to Seward, who had followed my work, he said, on the Chicago *Tribune* and in the New York magazines. Later I learned he was a sub-editor on *Vanity Fair* and had a book-lined apartment in the Rodin Studios on Fifty-seventh Street and Sixth Avenue, where, in his leisure, he said he was working on a biography of Havelock Ellis, his particular idol at the moment. Among his close friends were Edmund Wilson, John Peale Bishop, and F. Scott Fitzgerald, who were Princetonians like himself.

But toward the close of 1928 Collins's views changed and he came to oppose all that he had previously espoused. It was an abrupt and drastic switch in his whole set of values but he had been too prominent a factor in my career and too long a friend for me to feel anything toward him except a sort of troubled pity.

When I read the work of some of the popular historians of the twenties I wonder where they were when the events they relate occurred. It would seem as though they wrote their books from the headlines of the more sensational stories in the press. I was in the thick of things, as a working newspaperman throughout the period, and yet I did not sit on a flagpole, participate in a marathon dance or a bunion derby, try to get 1,000 per cent on an investment with the swindler Ponzi, nor did I know of anybody, personally, who did. Every age, every period, every decade, every day, every hour brings forth some evidence of the fantastic misuse of human energy.

Late one afternoon in June 1927, from a window on the ninth floor of the Manufacturers Trust Building in Columbus Circle I watched with some other employees of Johnson Features the surge of what seemed like a sea of human beings climax a full day's hysterical worship of a young aviator named Charles A. Lindbergh who had done nothing more remarkable than fly the Atlantic in a non-stop hop to Paris solo, after the Atlantic had already been flown by others. Dow Walling, a cartoonist employed by Johnson Features, had reminded me that night that I had met Lindbergh. I didn't remember it. Walling said, "He was that tall, skinny young fellow I introduced you to when he came in here with Max Miller."

But I had no more wish to join that hysterical crowd than later on I had wished to join the mob in attendance at the court trial of Hauptmann for the kidnaping of Lindbergh's child, or join the equally hysterical crowd of publicists who still later were to denounce Lindbergh for warning the United States that Hitler had the most powerful air force in the world, after he had been sent by our government to learn just how powerful Hitler's air force was.

One did not have to be as old as I was then, and I was only thirty-five, to know that the adulation of the mob is never more than of a day's duration and that it can easily be changed to execration or to quick forgetfulness; for Admiral Dewey had received almost as much adulation on his return from Manila as Lindbergh had, and I have never yet found a person who knew that the triumphal arch in Washington Square was a permanent one erected in Dewey's honor after a temporary one had been erected in Fifth Avenue, off Madison Square, for his triumphal march through the city, or, indeed, what became of Dewey after that day of homage.

Most of the people I knew in the twenties worked very hard, as I did, and if we seemed to play a great deal also, it was because we had the energy to do so. We weren't moping long in a state of "postwar disillusion," even if we found *The Waste Land,* like the wailing pathos of Gershwin's *Rhapsody in Blue,* a thing of haunting and disturbing beauty, indicative of a mood. Nor were many, except as a mood seized us—as it seizes everyone from time to time in all eras—among those whom Fitzgerald called "all the sad young men," which is a sentimental and rhetorical descriptive, properly applicable to adolescents of every age. It was peculiar to some of those of the twenties only because it was a fashionable pose, rather run into the ground by them. It was like the fashionable pose of being a Communist during the thirties and early forties, like that of Vincent Sheean, who nevertheless took care to hobnob with the British nobility and with Winston Churchill on the playgrounds of the Riviera, not with the workers; or like that of many another who found the pose rewarding without suffering any of the obligations of his avowed convictions.

When I was literary editor of the *Tribune* and *Herald Tribune,* we lived first in an eight-room "railroad" apartment in a converted slum building in East Eighty-first Street, between Park and

Lexington, and later in a flat very much like it on East Ninety-second Street, between Madison and Fifth avenues. Both apartments were on the fifth floor and we had to walk up; there were no elevators. I had about 10,000 books, for which I had open shelves built, extending from floor to ceiling of the large living room and the walls of my tiny study. The back room I used for a study was designed to be used, I suppose, by a maid who "slept in." I know that its counterpart in the apartment below was used for such a purpose, because, sometimes when I would be working late at night in my study, my thoughts would be disturbed by the ardent love that her sweetheart made to her, words that came up through the apertures from the radiator pipes. I took pains to discover that this maid was a very pretty young Italian girl and that her sweetheart was handsome, young, and also Italian, who obviously had read the most romantic books of Italian gallantry. He addressed her as if he were the hero in the passionate scene in the second act of all the Italian dramas at the Teatro Italiano. It was an indignity, I thought, that his visits to her had to be made by stealth; he made his way up to her by the fire escape and through the kitchen window. There was always the danger that he might be shot by some mistaken householder or some policeman as a burglar and that, perhaps, added to the romantic excitement of his visits. He was forced to climb higher than Romeo.

Our furniture in those days was serviceable without being in the mode; it was the same miscellany of mission and bird's-eye maple that had served us in Chicago. In the first year of our marriage I had spent many happy nights and holidays sandpapering it down to the plain wood, repainting and revarnishing it. In those New York apartments I had to work much at nights, often until three or four o'clock in the morning, because it is necessary for a book reviewer to read all or parts of many new books daily, not only to find one that is worth writing about but also to keep in touch with what is being said in books. One never knows when some unheralded book may turn out to be, through this process of winnowing, a rare treasure. And, besides, I was not only writing between 5,000 and 8,000 words weekly for the book-review section I was editing but also writing an article every month for *Arts and Decoration* and the *Detroit Athletic Club News,* and, for a time, *Vanity Fair* and *Shadowland,* besides contributing occasionally to the *Bookman,* the *Nation,* the *New Republic,* and the *Reviewer.*

Our maid, who was also the cook (although my wife preferred to participate in this function), was a very religious young Jamaican Negro girl, who was very fond of our children. And they were very fond of her. She went to the Baptist Sunday school and attended prayer meetings. Because she was so pious a Baptist I was astonished to discover that she had many voodoo superstitions. I didn't learn this from her; I learned it at secondhand, from my children. She had taught them that there were certain things you must do and must not do, in certain circumstances, and there were certain simple means of warding off evil. Hers weren't the superstitions of Southern whites and Southern Negroes which I had been familiar with as a child; they were practices and beliefs which, I had learned from books, were peculiar to the Negroes of the West Indies.

I did not take umbrage with Edith for teaching my children these primitive beliefs as I knew that they would have little effect on them. It would have offended her and intruded upon the privacy of her conscience for me to take a reasoning and superior attitude toward her beliefs or to have forbidden her to talk of such things with my children. Also, it would have deepened the impression which these voodoo superstitions had made upon my children's minds if I had made anything of them. I was right about this, for years later they were amused to learn that they ever had believed in these voodoo superstitions, and had forgotten all about them.

Edith was race-conscious, and she had a caste system of her

own which I found difficult to fathom. Once we had Countee Cullen, the young Negro poet, and Eric Waldron, a young Negro novelist, to dinner. Edith was greatly disturbed by this, so greatly disturbed that, after she had served the soup, she called my wife into the kitchen and protested so vigorously that my wife served the rest of the meal. The next day I tried to get at the root of her objections to our having Negroes to dinner. The objection, it seems, was not to our fraternizing with Negroes but to the humiliation she suffered, as she said, "in their eyes," less, it seems, in Cullen's eyes than in Waldron's, because Cullen's father was the pastor of Edith's church, whereas Waldron was a stranger. It was very complicated, but vaguely I understood. She had not been, like them, a guest at our table. I mentioned this and reminded her that she often ate with the children and that I should like to have her as guest the next time we had a Negro to dine with us. But she said she could not do that. I could understand that also, because it would be a false situation; I wouldn't otherwise be inviting her to dine, because she was not a poet as Cullen was or a novelist as Waldron was. I gave up trying to rationalize Edith's conditioning after I had told her that, if she worked in a restaurant in Harlem, she would have to wait on Negroes, and she had replied she would not work in a restaurant in Harlem.

In the early twenties the liquor one bought from bootleggers for home use was unreliable, although there were many speakeasies where liquor was expensive but non-poisonous. It was not until about 1926 that the bootlegging industry became well enough organized for the quality of bottled goods or liquor over the bars to be depended upon. Many had been temporarily blinded by bad liquor in the early days of Prohibition. That was why so-called "bathtub" gin became so popular and why it is today identified with the twenties. The most reliable liquor was synthetic gin which one made oneself. A great many drugstore proprietors were in the bootlegging business. They dispensed bonded whisky on prescription and grain alcohol without it. It was easy to find a doctor who would write such a prescription (the druggist, if he knew you, would give you the name of such a doctor if you did not know of one yourself) ; but this was very expensive, because you not only had to pay the prescription writer but also pay a whopping price for bonded whisky, which the druggist sold only in pints. Most druggists, however, seemed to have an unlimited supply of grain alcohol in gallon cans, tested and guaranteed to be pure.

Grain alcohol sold for from four to eight dollars a gallon and it made two gallons or more of synthetic gin. One mixed the grain alcohol with equal parts of distilled water, dropped in sixteen drops of oil of juniper, added a half ounce of glycerine to emulsify the solution, and shook the mixture well. Omitting the juniper oil, one could buy extracts which produced a synthetic liqueur, such as benedictine, anisette, chartreuse, and so on, but this was not very satisfactory either in taste or in aftereffects, because the extracts tended to produce headaches and to impair digestion. Nearly everybody who drank used synthetic gin for cocktails until bootlegging became a well-organized business, which had to maintain high standards of quality, even in synthetic scotch, in order to meet competition.

Some, like Robert Chanler the artist, who gave big parties, served applejack, usually as an ingredient of punch. Chanler made his own applejack on his farm near Woodstock in the summertime for the fabulous parties in his vast four-story studio in East Nineteenth Street. But applejack is a drink to be used with caution unless one's stomach is abnormally robust; and at Chanler's and elsewhere where applejack was served I either abstained or found access to weaker and more palatable stuff.

Before Prohibition went into effect many people, who could afford it, laid in large stocks of liqueur. T. R. Smith, the editor of *Century,* a gourmet, who liked to entertain in style, had a grotesque apartment on the upper West Side. The largest room in his flat had rows of shelves like those in a public library. The shelves were filled from top to bottom with fine liquors of all sorts from scotch and champagne to distilled gin and rare brandies. His cloakroom and kitchen were stacked with cases of liquor.

As fine a liquor as I tasted anywhere during Prohibition was that served in the homes of residents of Richmond, Virginia. It was pure bourbon, "moonshine," but carefully distilled, aged six months in charred kegs, and delivered in the keg to one's home at eight dollars a gallon. The merchant retained ownership of the kegs. One ordered several kegs at a time, and as one keg was being slowly drained of its contents, the other kegs were aging. This pure-grain bourbon made excellent mint juleps; and the butler in every Richmond home prided himself on the perfection of his mint juleps.

When we lived on East Eighty-first Street and on East Eighty-ninth Street my evening's work was frequently interrupted by revelers who would troop in unannounced; but I was not disturbed in this way to the extent the Scott Fitzgeralds were when they lived near the Lardners in Great Neck. In an article Fitzgerald wrote for the *Saturday Evening Post* entitled "How to Live on $30,000 a Year," he explained how his friends used his home as a private roadhouse. Ring Lardner told me he did not see how Fitzgerald got any work done, so inconsiderate were the friends who piled in on him. But this lasted, I think, only one summer; the Fitzgeralds moved elsewhere.

We lived within short walking distance of the Metropolitan Museum of Art and it was my custom for more than two years to take my children there almost every Sunday until we had become familiar with the museum's entire contents; we even attended the free concerts in the main hallway on Sunday evenings, where we sat on the stone steps of the grand staircase when we could find room. Riding through the park in a victoria on summer nights was a treat my wife and I indulged in when we felt flush or exuberant after a dinner at the Brevoort or the Lafayette, or after an evening at the theater.

The "Daybook" gave the impression, and seems to give me the impression now as I read old scrapbooks containing it, that we were always on the go—or, as Kazin put it, as if I were animated by "a gusto so great that he began to live on it." In a way this was true; I was young and my zest was so intense, my curiosity so strong, that, holding with Terence that "I am a human being; nothing that is human is alien to me," I was eager to savor as much of life as I possibly could while my responses were keen.

But luncheons at the Algonquin, parties, even week ends in the country occupied only a fraction of my life, and much of this which seemed play was in the nature of work; because everything is grist for the writer's mill, and especially was this true of me while I was writing the "Daybook." But life was not all beer and skittles, or gin and jazz music, for any of us in the twenties. We were responsible citizens with jobs to do; we had troubles and anxieties; we were daily confronted with news of corruption in high places, outbreaks of crime, and of sadistic mob actions. We were daily given evidence that human beings are very fallible and prone to act less like gods than like human beings. We were bedded by common colds, exasperated by the ill-nature and unreasonable tempers of others (ourselves always being reasonable and just, of course). We had income-tax payments to meet, bills to pay, moving to contend with—and, occasionally, we were struck a crushing blow.

I got a succession of these blows in the spring of 1924. My son contracted pneumonia and hovered for nine weeks on the brink of death. We had to employ day-and-night nurses and my wife and I were racked with anxiety; the crisis came and passed but empyema developed. An operation was necessary; there was the trip to the hospital in the ambulance, the wait for word, the long convalescence—costing me more than $3,000. And, while it was going on, I was given notice that my successor as literary editor of the *Herald Tribune* had been chosen and that, although my year ended on April 1, I could remain until October 1, because my successor could not take over the job until then.

I was in the humilating position of having to hold on to a job where I was not wanted, because I could not afford to chuck it. The one hundred and forty dollars a week for nurses for nine weeks, hospital and ambulance fees, including fee for the operating room, all had been paid on the dot. I had paid the surgeon five hundred dollars but I still owed the physician some money. There was no "severance pay" in those days. My bank balance was very low.

As soon as our disrupted household resumed some sort of normality and our boy was up and well again, I set to work night after night, until late in the morning, turning out extra work for magazines to pay my bills and lay by some reserve against the time when I might have a long wait before I could find a regular job again. I wrote and sold extra magazine stuff which brought me in $2,000 in five weeks and, of course, I had my regular income from *Arts and Decoration* and the *Detroit Athletic Club News,* so the outlook wasn't so bleak.

Then, just after my connection with the *Herald Tribune* ended, that curious thing again occurred. I was offered a job by a man I had never heard of and the job was the sort I had *known* very definitely (and without anything on which to base my knowledge) for three years would be offered me—the job of writing a daily column, not about books, but about life in New York, which would be syndicated all over the country.

A man called me up and said he was William H. Johnson, former syndicate manager for the New York *Herald Tribune.* He asked me to have lunch with him. We had met. Don Marquis had introduced us one day when I had gone up to see Don at his little office in the dome of the old *Tribune* building. The syndicate office was on the same floor. Johnson had lost his job on the *Herald Tribune* about the same time I had. Meanwhile, he had planned a blanket newspaper syndicate service of cartoons, photographs, text features, and a complete colored Sunday supplement similar to Hearst's *American Weekly* and had sold it to a great number of papers on a when-as-and-if basis. Then he had got Mrs. Mary Rumsey, daughter of E. H. Harriman, the great financier and railroad builder, to finance it. She was the widow of C. C. Rumsey, the sculptor. He offered me a contract guaranteeing me twice as much as I had been making on the *Herald Tribune*. I was to write a daily New York column and act as an associate editor, starting to work January 1, 1925, three months hence, by which time Johnson expected to have his mat service perfected, his printing arranged for, his office established, and his staff organized.

I signed the contract, met Mrs. Rumsey, and spent several evenings with Johnson and Mrs. Rumsey at her country home near Port Washington, discussing plans for the magazine. Then one day in early October I dropped down to my bank to inquire how much money I had. (I never kept stubs and always knew from my monthly statements only approximately what my balance was. I still banked at the Clark Brothers' venerable institution in the old *Tribune* building on Nassau Street, a bank I had used when the *Tribune* was downtown and from which I had never transferred my account. Later it somehow got dragged under at the time of the failure of the Bank of the United States, before the crash of 1929.) The teller told me I had a balance of $2,137.43.

On impulse and without a previous thought of going abroad, I drew out $2,000 and went to the office of the French Line in Whitehall Street and inquired about sailings and prices for cabin liners. The *De Grasse,* which I had known as "the artists' and writers' ship," was sailing at noon on Saturday. It was Thursday noon. I bought passage for two then and there. I phoned my wife to tell her we were sailing for France on Saturday. Naturally she, not having heard me say anything before about going on a trip, said it was impossible—that she had nothing to wear. I said we were going anyhow, because I had the tickets in my pocket and she would have to meet me downtown that afternoon to get passport pictures made. Following my son's illness my father had come from Oklahoma to take the children to the farm for my son to recuperate so we were free to go abroad.

After we had our passport pictures I thought all I would have to do was apply for a passport at the Custom House and would get it right away. So I did not bother about it until the next day. That evening my wife and I had dinner with Bill Johnson at Mrs. Rumsey's town studio residence on East Fortieth Street. The place had been the former Harriman stables but had been converted into a studio for Mrs. Rumsey's late husband. The other guest of the evening was Col. E. M. House. Casually I remarked that my wife and I were sailing for France on Saturday to remain until I had to return to work for the syndicate.

Mrs. Rumsey exclaimed, "Then of course you must have my apartment in Paris! I'll cable Angeline, the bonne, to kick Augustus John out if he is still there—he has been there long enough—and to have the place all ready for you when you arrive. You will love it. Nothing pretentious, a small place, and you will love Angeline; she's a veritable little angel of a cook. Also I'll write you a letter of introduction to Herrick (United States Ambassador to France) and he will see that you meet all the right people."

That amazing and charming woman thereupon sat down to her writing table, wrote the letter to Ambassador Herrick, handed it to me, took up the phone, and sent a cable, just as she said —including the direction to "kick Augustus John out if he is still there"—and, standing up, said, "There! It's all fixed! I am sure you will have a wonderful time, and if there is anything I can do for you while you are there, just cable me; or see Herrick; he's a good friend of mine."

I was overwhelmed. So we already had an apartment in Paris,

rent free; we wouldn't have to stay in a pension or in a hotel! Then Mrs. Rumsey said, "Oh, but the address!" and she wrote it out—62 rue Boissière.

(Throughout the evening I had studied Colonel House. He had been Wilson's chief adviser, especially during the peace conference, and was allegedly the man "behind the throne" throughout Wilson's presidency. He was small, thin, gray-eyed, gray-haired, gray-faced; his head was long and narrow and his forehead high. He had a reputation for being as impenetrably silent as the Sphinx and as wise, and on the two occasions I saw him at Mrs. Rumsey's he seemed to be making an effort to preserve that reputation when there was no need for it. Throughout the dinner Mrs. Rumsey tried to get an answer to a question: "Tell me, Colonel, was Lloyd George in cahoots with Clemenceau?" He replied, "Cahoots? Cahoots? . . . That reminds me of a story," and launched into a long and completely pointless narrative which he apparently made up as he went along. Nothing daunted, Mrs. Rumsey asked the question again, whereupon he told another story. After a third try, with the same result, Mrs. Rumsey gave up.

House's performance, I thought, was silly, because it was obvious enough that Lloyd George had been in cahoots with Clemenceau; the two of them, with Orlando, had ganged up on Wilson to nullify the Fourteen points and there was no sense in House's being so secretive at that late date. But being noncommittal had, I suppose, become second nature with him; it had been one of the reasons for his behind-the-scenes political power. The other reason, I decided, was that the man had a peculiar formation of the muscles and tissues around the mouth which gave him a perpetual cat-that-swallowed-the-canary expression. It was unchanging. It could readily inspire a belief that he knew all the answers if he chose to tell them. Wilson, on the contrary, had the habitual expression of a man who is seriously in doubt even about his deepest convictions but anxious for the correct answers. House's expression could make a man like Wilson consider him a compendium of uncanny wisdom, even if he knew nothing whatever about the subject under consideration. House's memoirs, published long after I met him, substantiated my first impression : it was a voluminous rigmarole of very little historical value, as if he had been reminded of a story when he had been asked about cahoots.)

That night I packed and my wife got started on getting her things ready. I paid Edith a month's salary in advance and said I hoped she would return to work for us when we came back; I paid all bills and the rent up to January 1, notified the superintendent of the building of our intentions, stopped the papers and the milk, but did not have the telephone service temporarily suspended because resumption of service might be delayed on my return.

Armed with our hideous passport pictures, I blithely walked into the Custom House next morning and asked for our passports. I had no birth certificate or other proof of citizenship. By lucky chance the clerk who waited on me recognized my name and said he was a reader of mine. He took a copy of Who's Who, thumbed through it until he came to my name, and said, "This information will suffice." He prepared my passport and said it would be ready in about a week.

"A week !" I gasped. "But I am sailing at noon tomorrow." He said the passport had to go to Washington to be signed by the Secretary of State. He said he could put it into the diplomatic pouch for speed and immediate attention but he didn't see how I could get it before Monday. I phoned Julian Mason at the *Tribune*. He said he would see what he could do. At midnight Mason phoned me he had routed Secretary of State Charles Evans Hughes out of bed at ten o'clock, having been unable to reach him before then, and that the Secretary had signed the document and seen to it that it was mailed under special seal. He said I could pick up the passport at the Custom House the next morning. I was there by nine, dropping my wife and the luggage off at the French Line pier on my way. The passport had not arrived. I waited an hour; the clerk and I talked about books and plays. I waited another hour, phoning my wife at the pier meanwhile. Ten minutes after eleven the clerk returned from the receiving room and handed me the passport, reminding me that I still had to get my visas, for I had included all western Europe in my itinerary. The French visa, he said, would be necessary; the others could wait.

A French consulate officer had an office at the pier. He took an unconscionable amount of time to earn his ten-dollar fee, I thought, so we got aboard only five minutes before the gangplank was withdrawn. The French Line photographers snapped some pictures of us which I was later to see in the window of the company's office in Paris, along with pictures of other "notables," including Owen Johnson, the novelist; and Tamara, the dancer.

We had a surprise awaiting us. After we had been assigned to a cabin, the chief steward notified me that, as a special courtesy, the company was changing our inside cabin to an outside suite; there would be no extra charge. We also received an invitation from the captain to sit at his table, which I was not blasé enough to decline, though I was informed by Owen Johnson, an experienced voyager, that it was infra dig or something to accept the captain's invitation; that the proper thing to do, as he did, was to decline, and thereby raise one's social status with the captain. Johnson reminded me that I couldn't very well order special wines without buying for the whole bunch and would have to drink the *vin ordinaire*. This did not prove a handicap, because there was a Brazilian coffeeman at the captain's table who ordered champagne for the whole table every night, until the captain himself on the last night out spread himself royally in the way of vintage wines and liqueurs. On my left was an old gentlewoman from Boston who had made thirty-six voyages to Europe, the first more than fifty years before, and remembered details about her first trip. On my right was a vivacious Cuban beauty.

The voyage to Le Havre took eight days, most of it on a calm, smooth sea, restful and invigorating. We danced every night except Sunday; the food was excellent; and all the passengers were friendly—somewhat Bohemian and not in the least bit stuffy. The most delightful person we met aboard ship was Mrs. Frank Morgan, wife of the actor and herself an actress, who had suffered a broken leg in an automobile accident and was going to the Riviera to recuperate. Her leg was in a cast and she got about on crutches, but she was high-spirited and jolly. She also sat at the captain's table, at the captain's right, in fact. She was followed about by three handsome young French Air Corps officers whose devotion to her was so complete that they paid little attention to young, pretty and unattached females who were unabashedly envious of Mrs. Morgan's power to charm. My wife and I became especially attached to a young Pittsburgh steel man and his wife and to a young University of California professor and his wife.

CHAPTER 7

Parisian Impressions

PARIS IN THE MIDDLE TWENTIES. YOUNG PA-
RISIANS "FLOG THE CORPSE" OF ANATOLE
FRANCE. DIDOES OF THE ROYALISTS AND DADA-
ISTS. HEMINGWAY, FORD, STEIN, AND THE EX-
PATRIATES AT THE DÔME. HOMEWARD BOUND.

Cigarettes and chocolate were contraband at the French port of entry and inasmuch as nearly everyone still had cartons of cigarettes left over from the voyage, there was much discussion among the passengers on the *De Grasse* about what to do with them. The consensus of the experienced travelers was that cartons should be opened and single packs of cigarettes distributed among various pockets of one's wardrobe, but all chocolate (of which my wife and I had none) should be given to the crew. I put a few packs of cigarettes in the pockets of my extra clothes, as directed. Inspection at the pier at Le Havre was courteous and perfunctory, only a few quick pats on the tops of clothes displayed when luggage was opened, no rummaging about underneath. But when our trunks were delivered to our apartment in Paris the next day, the cigarettes—nothing else—had disappeared.

Rolling along the Norman countryside on the train to Paris, I kept my nose pressed against the windowpane like a child on his first railroad trip; the rolling terrain, the thatched roofs, the oxcarts, the immaculate fields were a continuous series of luminous Corots seen through the gray-blue mist of the late-autumn dusk. There were no signs of the devastation of the war; all was serene and beautiful.

Lewis Galantière met us at the station and rode with us in a taxicab to our new home. Our apartment was on the second floor, just off the Avenue Kléber. At the other end of the street was the Place Victor-Hugo; we were within a short walk of the Place de l'Etoile and the Avenue du Bois-de-Boulogne. One reached our apartment through a court entrance which was guarded by the concierge and his wife by day and night; one had to ring for the iron gate to be unlocked.

Angeline, a dumpy little woman in a black satin dress, greeted us as though she had known us all our lives. A living room and a bedroom faced on the street. Between them and a largish dining room was a vestibule. The dining room had a fireplace. Beyond it was that great rarity in a Paris apartment—a modern bathroom with a real porcelain tub as well as the inevitable bidet and a toilet. (Most Parisians either went once a week to public baths or had tin tubs into which they, or their maids, poured hot water from kettles. The Galantières had a collapsible tub of waterproof canvas.) It was a large tiled bathroom, with a dressing table and full-length mirrors; the hot water came from an instantaneous heater, in which the gas under the boiler was ignited by turning on the hot-water faucet. Beyond the bathroom was Angeline's room. We had dined on the train, which was over an hour late getting into Paris. We were fatigued from the journey, and Lewis, after seeing us settled, had a nightcap with me and left.

Next morning my wife and I were treated to service such as we had never known before. Angeline awakened us by drawing the curtains and letting in the morning sunlight. Then she placed before us trays containing hot chocolate, fruit, and sweet buns. For me there were copies of *Figaro* and the *Temps*. Angeline told us that after we had made our toilet and had dressed there would be a more substantial breakfast, and there was—oatmeal with cream, sausages and eggs, toast, marmalade, and coffee. After getting out of bed I discovered that during the night Angeline had pressed my trousers, shined my shoes, and laid out fresh linen

178

for me. She had also washed and dried my wife's stockings and pressed her dress. This extraordinary performance was to be repeated every night during our stay. During breakfast Angeline asked if we were dining in; I said we were. She then asked me what entree Madame would prefer. She built her dinners around the entree; it was not necessary to specify beyond that. Dinner consisted of soup or hors d'oeuvres, relish, fish, entree, salad, dessert (usually some delicious example of Angeline's superb art) cheese, and coffee.

It was made clear to me that Angeline's services went with Mrs. Rumsey's free loan of the flat and that I would be required to pay only for gas, electricity, kindling and briquettes for the fireplace, laundry, soap, flowers, wines, and liquors. Angeline produced a new black account book in which she said she would list all purchases and submit them to me at the end of the week. She suggested two good table wines to be delivered daily and I arranged for her to purchase whisky, gin, vermouth, brandy, and liqueurs, giving her a 500-franc note on account. She did the purchasing (and the haggling with the vendors, which all French cooks enjoy) early every morning, not forgetting a posy for the dining table and flowers for the other rooms. I have her account book before me now. Ordinarily Angeline's day's purchases ran to about 90 francs or $5.50, but I shall take November 29, 1924, a day when we had four guests for dinner: *pain,* 2.60; *lait,* 1.80; *journeaux,* .70; *oeuf coque,* 1.00; *fleurs,* 3.50; *poisson,* 21.00; *faisan,* 30.00; *boucherie,* 11.00; *pommes terre,* 2.00; *salade cresson,* 3.00; *beurre table,* 5.40; *beurre cuisine,* 5.00; *fromage,* 3.75; *camembert,* 4.50; *citron,* 1.00; *glacé,* 15.00; 3 *vin,* 11.25; *cognac,* 29.00; *eau,* 1.75; *macaroni,* 1.50; *tomate,* 1.25; *café,* 1.00; *champignons,* 2.50; *oeufs,* 2.50; *gaufrettes,* 1.50; *pourboire,* .50.

Upon whom Angeline bestowed three cents by way of a tip I cannot imagine, but I'll bet he paid through the nose for it. If the French concierge is a petty tyrant, the French *bonne,* or general housekeeper-maid-and-cook, is a matriarch who is absolute ruler in her domain, the home. She occupies an entirely different position from that of a British or American servant; she is on a plane of equality not only with her mistress and master but with their guests; she does not hesitate to upbraid a guest for being late, if by doing so he (or she or a couple) has marred the absolute perfection of the meal she has prepared. Galantière was forty-five minutes late one night for a dinner which Angeline had gone to great trouble to prepare in his honor. Angeline met him at the door with an enraged torrent of French Billingsgate, called him an "infamous barbarian," and said that "with such a deficient sense of obligation to cuisine" he should be permitted to eat only at the stalls for teamsters in the market of Les Halles. Angeline's cooking was so superb that even our meals at Foyot's, the Marguery, and other famous places seemed flat and uninspired in comparison.

On our first morning in Paris my wife and I were out early for a stroll in the Avenue du Bois-de-Boulogne and my steps led me directly to the little dead-end street, called the Villa Saïd, that I might look at the granite château-like residence which had for so long been the home of Anatole France, who had died at his country home near Tours just two weeks before I reached Paris. There was a *conciergerie,* or porter's sentinel post, of brick at the entrance of the street. I went into the post to chat with the woman on duty. She talked exactly like the benevolent old harridan of a housekeeper in France's books. I asked what France was like, because she said she had known him for many years. She said, "He was just a feeble old man like any other. He didn't believe in God and was forever chasing after women and forgetting his overshoes. He led Madame a dog's life and when she died, he married his housekeeper." She referred to Madame Arman de Caillavet, who had long been France's mistress and taskmistress, and to Emma Laprévotte, whom France had married in 1920, when he was seventy-six. This was not news; it might have been read in any newspaper.

I knew the streets of Paris, from study, better than I knew the streets of New York, and I immediately familiarized myself with the bus and subway lines. Taxi fares in Paris were ridiculously cheap until midnight, when the fares doubled in price, so that one could ride from one end of Paris to the other for the equivalent of fifty cents, including the tip. An ordinary trip cost only about a dime. For that reason, Galantière and many other Americans I knew who had lived for several years in Paris had never been inside the subway. But I liked the subway and always rode second-class, at the cost of about half a cent American money. Galantière worked at the International Chamber of Commerce in the rue Jean-Goujon, near the Grand Palais, and lived on the Ile St.-Louis in the shadow of Notre Dame Cathedral. I kept in touch with him by telephone (we had one in the apartment) and *pneumatique,* but I had told him, on my arrival, that I wanted to wander about the city alone for several days before meeting any of the Americans whose rendezvous was the Dôme or the Rotonde.

Thus I was able to enjoy all the things that were considered the hick things to do—such as going up in the Eiffel Tower; visiting Napoleon's tomb; climbing up to the bell towers of Notre Dame to see the gargoyles at close range; visiting the Victor Hugo Museum, the Louvre, the Luxembourg, the Trocadero, the Palais de Justice, Saint Sulpice, the Sacré Coeur.

It amused me to run into Harold Loeb, one of the founders of *Broom,* in the rue de l'Odéon and find, on our way to the Dôme for a drink, that he had passed by the Luxembourg every day for six years and had never been inside it. I took him in and showed him the Manet room, with its famous "On the Balcony" group and the portrait of George Moore and, for good measure, the original of Paul Chabas's "September Morn" which a press agent had once managed to get banned in Chicago, thus promoting the sale of reproductions of it from the nationwide publicity that ensued.

I sought out the places made familiar to me by Balzac, Zola, Hugo, Anatole France, and Maupassant; visited the haunts of Verlaine and Baudelaire; walked the narrow streets in the district of the Sorbonne and spent hours in the Cluny Museum, not neglecting to view the *ceintures de chastité*. I bought a complete set of Montaigne from a *bouquiniste* on the Quai Voltaire within a few feet of the building in which Anatole France was born; walked the streets of the Faubourg St. Germain with Marcel Proust in mind; and visited the rummage counters of the department store, Aux Trois Quartiers, across from the Madeleine in which the fabulous Comte Montesquieu de Fezensac, the original of the Baron Charlus in Proust's narrative, selected his costume and always set the fashion in men's wear of his day.

I took in *L'OEuvre,* the Leftist daily, for the pleasure of reading the pungently satiric column of Guy de la Fouchardière, who could begin an article deriding the American immigration authorities for not allowing Luis Firpo's mistress to enter the country with him by saying, "The United States is a country where it is forbidden to drink, to make love, and to be a Negro." I also took in the Royalist sheet, *L'Action française,* to follow the coruscating fulminations of Léon Daudet, son of the great Alphonse Daudet, and a man whose excitable pen got him with equal celerity into duels and into jail.

Paris was a great place for public funerals and they were often the occasions for political "demonstrations" which ended up in street fights. While I was there the Socialists had persuaded the government to exhume the body of the great Socialist leader, Jean Juarès, who had been assassinated just before the outbreak of the war in 1914 and, with ceremonial pomp, to entomb the body along with the bodies of other national heroes in the Panthéon. The Royalists, under Daudet, protested, and, failing in their protest, organized a rival procession on the same day that Juarès was being honored. Neither event would have been a success if quite a few heads had not been cracked in the street and café brawls that followed.

Copies of *Un Cadavre* were still to be had on the newsstands of Paris when I arrived. This was an astounding pamphlet, inconceivable in America, published by a group of young Surrealist writers among whom were Drieu de la Rochelle, Philippe Soupault, Jules Bréton, and Louis Aragon, on the occasion of Anatole France's death. The ghoulish aspect of the sheet was emphasized by the fact that it had been prepared while France was still alive and was actually on the newsstands two days before he died, because a false report had reached the group from Tours that France was dead. Copies that had been hastily delivered to the kiosks were withdrawn until news of France's death was official.

The leading article of *Un Cadavre* asked in a streamer headline across the tabloid-size sheet, "Have You Ever Flogged a Corpse?" Beneath it De la Rochelle proceeded to flog the corpse of Anatole France in orgiastic frenzy and the others joined in to mutilate France's reputation. On the face of it, it was a revolting display of bad taste, but it was no more than the bid of a new literary group for attention. Some of the young Surrealists had talent and they were in revolt against the literary tradition which France had brought to perfection—a tradition of clarity, simplicity, and urbanity. The syntax of the Surrealists was as bizarre as the non-representational work of the Surrealist painters, their vocabulary was raw and startling and their epithets barbaric.

The Surrealists, in fact, were out to supplant the Dadaists, who had sprung up immediately after the war and had added to the gaiety of the literary life. Galantière introduced me to the already somewhat outmoded Dada leader, Tristan Tzara, at the Dôme. He was an intense little Roumanian, black-haired and very dark-skinned, whom I considered no more than a clown; I had read some of his "poetry" and considered the hoax called *Spectra* which Arthur Davison Ficke and Wytter Bynner had published back in 1916 under the names of Emanuel Morgan and Anne Knish, infinitely superior to it as amusing nonsense. But Tzara represented something I considered very precious in the intellectual life of Paris, where even the most serious and responsible persons never took themselves too seriously to engage in buffoonery. Tzara had arranged a mock trial of Georges Clemenceau in which the old "Tiger of France" was accused of living too long. Tzara was his prosecutor, Rachilde was his counsel, and Clemenceau took the stand in his own defense. He was asked to show cause why he should not be permanently anesthetized. The verdict of the jury was "guilty, with extenuations. Leniency recommended."

One can only try to imagine an American bigwig participating in such an event to realize that it could not happen in the United States. Nor can one imagine an American "immortal" of the Academy of Arts and Letters being guilty of the joke Anatole France played at a session of the French Academy whereat the uses of the word "aneau" were under discussion for the dictionary. All the uses of the word had apparently been exhausted and the discussion was about to close, when France noticed that one of the most learned and venerable of the "immortals" was fast asleep. He nudged him awake and whispered, "They have forgotten Hans Carvel's ring! Tell them they must not forget the ring of Hans Carvel!" The old gentleman, a model of piety and rectitude, not knowing what he was saying but concerned for the probity of French scholarship, cried, "You forgot Hans Carvel's ring!" The reference was to the bawdiest story in Rabelais.

Ford Madox Ford, about whose work I had written off and on for seven years and whom I had met and entertained in New York, learned I was in town and sent me a *pneumatique* inviting my wife and me to dinner at a small family restaurant on the Boulevard du Montparnasse. At the restaurant he introduced us to a handsome, ruddy-complexioned young Australian woman as his wife.

After dinner we went to a *bal musette* near the Panthéon where Ford introduced us to Nancy Cunard, E. E. Cummings, Robert McAlmon, and a number of other people whose names I did not catch—and to Mrs. Ernest Hemingway. Hemingway was there, but he and Ford were not speaking. Hemingway came up to me and introduced himself. After Ford had asked my wife and me and Mrs. Hemingway to sit at a table with him, Hemingway said to Mrs. Hemingway, "Pay for your own drinks, do you hear! Don't let him [nodding toward Ford] buy you anything."

What had happened was that Hemingway had attacked T. S. Eliot very savagely in the *Transatlantic Review*. Ford had permitted the attack to appear, but when Eliot angrily protested, Ford apologized in the editorial columns of the magazine, saying, in part: "We wish we could reconcile it with our conscience to excise the paragraphs in which our chroniclers make attacks upon individuals. Thus two months ago one of these gentlemen made an attack on Mr. T. S. Eliot; he stated, that is to say, that he desired to grind Mr. T. S. Eliot into fine powder to be sprinkled on the shrine of another writer. We hesitated for a long time over the ethics of the matter, deciding in the end that our standards must prevail. We had invited that writer to write, we had indicated no limits to his bloodthirstiness; our hands fell powerless to our sides. . . . We take the opportunity of expressing for the tenth time our admiration for Mr. Eliot's poetry."

Hemingway had thereupon severed his connection with the *Transatlantic* and ceased to speak to Ford, although night after night they met in the same gathering places; and Hadley Hemingway and the Fords remained on good terms. The *bal musette* favored by the group around Ford was a small place, with a tiny dance floor and music furnished by an accordion player in Spanish costume who played American jazz music very acceptably. (Incidentally, American jazz rhythms had taken Paris by storm in the early twenties and the Parisian intellectuals were vying with each other in writing serious treatises on it; but French musicians who played for the *dancing*—which we in America called *these dansantes*—on and off the boulevards could not get the hang of it; therefore American bands were in great demand.)

Hemingway and I got along famously from our first meeting. He asked me to come to lunch the next day, saying he would offer me the best bouillabaisse in all Paris. Hadley Hemingway went home early, because, she said, she had to take care of the baby. Hemingway left with us, walking as far as the Boulevard du Montparnasse, where my wife and I picked up a cab. Hemingway was stocky and boyish; he walked with an odd gait as though he were walking on skis or snow shoes. (I learned the next day that skiing was his favorite sport and that he was leaving presently for the Austrian Tyrol.)

I went next day to the *Negre de Toulouse* in the Boulevard Raspail, to which Hemingway had directed me. The restaurant got its name from a figure of a Negro mascot carved in wood which stood outside the door. The bouillabaisse was of a very superior quality. Hemingway outlined the fine points of bullfighting for me and told me what one has to learn to be a good bullfighter. He said he had palled around a lot with a famous bullfighter in Seville and had even gone in for bullfighting himself for the experience and fun of it. He asked me not to miss the boxing matches at the Cirque d'Hiver, and Hadley described the match they had seen the night before, using boxing terms as technical as her husband's. They lived, at the time, in an incredibly bare hovel, without a toilet or running water, and with a mattress spread on the floor for a bed; it was in the court of a lumberyard, on the second floor, to which one climbed by a flight of rickety steps. Hemingway's only income was from occasional newspaper dispatches for the North American Newspaper Alliance. The place in which they lived seemed utterly comfortless, but the Hemingways were well dressed and the baby's carriage was new and luxurious.

A few days later I ran into Hemingway in the Luxembourg Gardens and he and I went to a café in the rue Guynemer for a brandy and soda. While we were sitting on the terrace an artist friend of Hemingway's came and sat with us; he told us the story of a man whose wife had left him on his wedding night. After he had left, Hemingway said, "That's curious. That's what happened to him. He is putting the story into the third person and torturing himself with it."

Gertrude Stein lived around the corner from where we were sitting, in the rue de Fleurus. Hemingway took me to meet her and left me there; he had some work to do. Miss Stein looked, just as Sherwood Anderson told me she looked, like the wife of an Iowa corn doctor. Her secretary-companion, Alice B. Toklas, got tea while Miss Stein sat like a jolly Buddha on a divan, surrounded by her Picassos and Braques and talked to me of Carl Van Vechten and Sherwood Anderson, both of whom she liked personally but whose work, so different in character, she dismissed. She said she had written a history of literature that morning. I blinked. She pulled it out from under a pillow. It consisted of one typewritten page, about three hundred words in all, each sentence a paragraph. It *was,* in a way, a history of literature. Because I said I liked it, she presented it to me. The dress she had on was like a Mother Hubbard and there was a homey earthiness about her. Before I left she showed me a stack of letter file boxes that reached the ceiling. She said they contained her unpublished manuscripts. It was not difficult for me to conceive that she had been William James's favorite pupil in psychology or that she had been a promising student of brain surgery at Johns Hopkins, but her connection with either painting or literature seemed remote to me. I didn't see how anyone who had a feeling for painting would juxtapose a Picasso of the painter's "blue period" and a raw and blatant Braque exercise in planes; and her interest in literature seemed like that of a casual dilettante, as if she rarely bothered to read anything. I suspected she had read no Hemingway or Anderson and had merely accepted their homage.

Victor Llona interviewed me for *Le Journal Littéraire* and later invited me to his house one evening to meet André Gide. Gide wore a turtle-neck sweater and kept on his overcoat throughout the evening, and still he shivered frequently, though the room was not cold. His French had that clear, precise, syllabic enunciation of the cultivated French Protestants, the easiest of French for an English ear, unpracticed in French, to follow, and when he chose to speak English it was clear, natural, and without accent. He had known Oscar Wilde in Wilde's last days in Paris and he had also known Conrad. I noticed that Gide's face and Conrad's were very much alike, except that Gide's head was massive and Conrad's small, and Gide was clean shaven and bald, whereas Conrad's hair was thick and he wore a mustache and short beard. The lines of their countenance were the same, however, and they had the same somber, remote expression. Llona said Gide had a phobia about drafts and, before coming, had requested that all windows be tightly closed.

One Sunday Galantière took us to the home of Archibald Mac-Leish in St. Cloud. MacLeish had a large beautiful white frame house, which had formerly belonged to the mistress of a Russian grand duke. He showed us the hidden vault for her jewels in the principal bedroom of the house. E. E. Cummings was there, and for eight solid hours he talked incessantly; but he was not boring; on the contrary, he was enormously entertaining. His head was a storehouse of remembered verses from Sappho in Greek, Laforgue in French, Horace in Latin, and Amy Lowell, Shakespeare, and Longfellow in English and he could weave the most incongruous quotations together spontaneously, with effects sometimes very funny and sometimes of a startling beauty. No one else had a chance to talk throughout the afternoon, during dinner, or after dinner; but no one minded this, because Cummings's flow of words was so entertaining. He even talked all the way into town on the train and was still talking when he asked to be dropped at a certain corner, on our way home in a taxicab.

We had parties at the house and made the rounds of the dance halls and bars from the Moulin Rouge to Zelli's, from the Ritz to Harry's New York Bar, and from dives off the Place Pigalle to even more unpleasant places. We went several nights to enjoy the Fratinelli Brothers, the pantomimic clowns, at the Cirque Médrano; I got one of the great thrills of my life seeing Lucien Guitry enact the title role of Tartufe; we chuckled at the *conférences* of Vincent Hyspa and attended the première of Diaghileff's *Ballet Suedois* where top hats were smashed and a great racket was raised among the fans and contemners of a very inferior performance. (Green wigs were the fashion among the women of the *beau monde* that season and there were many in the audience.)

Paris is a state of mind of foreigners, to which Parisians contribute by a philosophy implicit in their behavior, which comes down to "Live and let live." The French are as bourgeois and puritanical as the residents of small American towns; their interests are largely centered upon their families and their immediate material interests; they are thrifty and even catchpenny; and they are self-centered in the exercise of their rights. But so long as your behavior does not threaten their private interests, they do not care what you do or what you say or how you dress or how much money you make or how poor you are. They consider that the way you live your life is your own affair, provided it does not affect the general welfare. That is why Britons and Americans, who are often so afraid of what people will say, feel as if they were in a freer world when they are in France. And that is why so many who are circumspect and strait-laced at home shed their inhibitions in Paris and indulge in conduct that would be shocking at home. But anyone who is free of the fear of taboos at home does not conduct himself in Paris otherwise than on his native soil. But he does feel as if he were at a Mardi Gras, if he is on holiday.

I did not stay long enough in Paris to know as much about the French as I have been able to learn from Edith Wharton's *French Ways and Their Meaning* or from Galantière's *France Is Full of Frenchmen,* and I was merely charmed by the aspects of it, some of which I later recorded in brief impressions, such as these:

Mental Snapshots of Paris

The huge white-bordered and white-initialed black drape which covers the front of a house as a sign of mourning.

The fascinating illusion of a rapidly changing expression produced by the Mona Lisa in the Louvre.

The actors and actresses from the Théâtre Français at midnight supper at the Café de la Régence, the café famous as a haunt of Voltaire, Benjamin Franklin, Rousseau, and Napoleon Bonaparte.

Students from the Ecole des Beaux-Arts, with adolescent faces and pointed beards.

The flower market alongside the Madeleine and the bird market in the Rue St.-Honoré.

The rows of stores in the Rue Bonaparte which sell religious effigies, ecclesiastical costumes, and utensils for sacred rites.

The façade of Notre Dame viewed from the Petit Pont on a winter night, giving the impression that this vast mass of medieval stone has no more weight than a castle of playing cards.

The white turrets of the Church of the Sacred Heart on Martyrs' Hill, standing out above the mists that hung low over Paris and seeming to me, as I stood on the second landing of the Eiffel Tower, to be a fairy domain resting upon creamy clouds.

The guides and map sellers in front of the Café de la Paix who can spot an Englishman or an American half a block away.

Latin Quarter students with floppy Windsor ties and broad-brimmed black hats sipping vermouth and water at the sidewalk tables of the Deux Magots.

The first glimpse of the Venus de Milo down a long corridor of the Louvre, her exquisite outlines set off by a great square of dark velvet hanging on the wall behind her.

A close-up view of her, showing her badly in need of a bath, because covered with dust and soot.

The Citroën, or the tin lizzie of Paris, and all the old Ford jokes that are made over to apply to it by the entertainers in the cabarets of the Boulevard St.-Michel.

The perpetual gas flame at the head of the grave of the Unknown Soldier under the Arc de Triomphe, flickering and wavering behind a whistling gale and sheets of rain as I rounded the Place de l'Etoile in a cab at five in the morning.

Rich and paunchy Argentinians, blazing diamonds in their full-dress shirts, breakfasting on beefsteak and champagne at seven in the morning at the café of the Tranquil Fathers. . . .

When Hemingway, whom I had encountered on the Boulevard St.-Michel, learned I was returning home, he insisted that he must give me a present to remember him by on the voyage. He said there were only a few bottles of twenty-year-old "Napoleon" brandy left in the whole Montparnasse section and he knew where they were. He took me to the far end of the Boulevard St.-Michel to a wine and liquor store that was also a delicatessen. He told the proprietor what he wanted. The proprietor regretted that he had none left. Hemingway told him he was a liar and pointed to a top shelf, near the ceiling, in a remote corner. The proprietor still denied that the brandy was there. Hemingway seized the ladder which ran along the shelves on coasters, pushed it to the corner, mounted to the top, pulled out a bottle, and brought it down. The proprietor tore his hair, protested, begged; said he had promised to save the three bottles for an important

191

customer; that he would be ruined if he parted with even one of the bottles. Hemingway paid him the standard price for the bottle and handed it to me, saying, "Don't drink it until you get aboard ship. Bon voyage!" We parted at the Dôme, to which we had walked for a farewell drink, and I did not see him again for fourteen years, and then only for a few minutes in a hotel room in San Francisco when he was seeking funds to provide ambulances for the Spanish Loyalists.

The night before we left, Cummings, Galantière, Morris Gilbert, Morris Bishop, my wife, and I had dinner at the Café de Paris and, having consumed much champagne, we made a night of it, going from one bar to another and landing up finally at a restaurant in the market amusingly named *Aux Pères Tranquilles* where, as Cummings has for years never ceased to remind me, I consumed the entire contents of a large tureen of soup. It had been a bad night to get around—the worst fog in Paris for many years, and we had to bribe taxi drivers to haul us (many refused to do so, even when we brandished fifty-franc notes in their faces).

Angeline had packed and dispatched our luggage when we got to the apartment at six in the morning. She prepared a fine breakfast. We did not have time to change clothes, because our train left for Cherbourg at eight o'clock. At Cherbourg we had to spend the night in a hotel, at the Red Star Line's expense, with all the other passengers, because the *Zeeland* (which was the only ship on which we could book passage at the last moment) was twelve hours late from Southampton. We had to board the ship from a tender in a drizzling cold rain. The ship was crowded with immigrants in sweaters and carpet slippers from Poland, Galicia, and Germany, whom an agency had undertaken to get into America under the quota for the year. Our ship had a stormy passage. It was entirely encrusted with ice for three days and all the doors to the decks were locked and barred. The floors of the lounges were strewn with very sick peasants; the liquor ran out

(Hemingway's present, which I carefully guarded in my cabin, was a lifesaver), and the only thing we could do was play penny-ante poker in the clubroom. I lost thirty-six dollars but my wife, who played in only one session, won seventy-five dollars because she didn't know any better: she thought she had a straight and it turned out that she had a straight flush. All of us dropped out when she gave her hand away by asking a question which indicated that all she had was a straight, but an elderly gentleman and his "nephew" who we all suspected were sharpers, because the old gent was a consistent winner, was out for blood and refused to allow a no-stakes decision. He had an ace high full. It was a large pot, according to our picayune standards. The old gentleman was very angry and acted so badly about it that all the rest of the players cut him the remainder of the trip.

We arrived in New York with just eight dollars and seventy-five cents, after tipping all the members of the staff who had served us. It was lucky that my wife won at poker. The money was mostly exhausted by taxi fare, express charges for our luggage, and dinner. But I had $137.43 in the bank and my salary started the next morning.

CHAPTER 8

New York in Jazz Time

I WRITE A DAILY NEW YORK COLUMN. "GENTLE-
MEN PREFER BLONDES" AND THE "AMERICAN
MERCURY." BLIND PIGS AND BATHTUB GIN. PAR-
TIES OF THE TWENTIES. GIRL-IN-THE-CHAM-
PAGNE BATH AND OTHER SINGULAR EVENTS.

Editors Features Service, W. H. Johnson, president, was a scattered organization. The editorial offices were on the ninth floor
of the Manufacturers Trust Company building in Columbus
Circle; the mechanical plant for printing and distributing our
daily features was in Cleveland; our Sunday-magazine supplement was printed in, and distributed from, Pittsburgh; and all
matters relating to money, income and outgo, were handled by a
staff of financial experts connected with Mrs. Rumsey's estate,
whose offices were somewhere in the Wall Street district.

The Sunday supplement was edited by Mark Wiley, who had
been trained for that sort of work under Morrell Goddard, the
genius who had founded Hearst's *American Weekly,* a magazine
of instruction in the wonders of science and of moral lessons in
the vices and follies of this world, piquantly illustrated by reproductions of some of the finest works by the classical painters of
the nude and therefore enjoying the largest weekly circulation of
any periodical in the world.

Mark had two staff writers, Caroline Gordon (who was later
to become a novelist whose very considerable merit, I think, has
never been fully appreciated) and Vivian Brown, a beautiful and
brilliant newspaper product of Chattanooga. Mark also had as
an occasional contributor Charley MacArthur, who would ask

194

for an assignment to do a Sunday-supplement story whenever he needed money to pay his rent or to maintain his reputation (fostered by Alexander Woollcott) as the irrepressible faun of the Algonquin set.

Clark Kinnaird, our managing editor in Cleveland, and his staff assembled and edited material from the New York office, wrote news features and stories, bought and captioned pictures, and supplied page and galley proofs, stereotyping mats, and photographs to newspaper clients. Dow Walling, a former crack oarsman from the University of Washington, was our first comic-strip artist. Our second was one whom we had a great deal of trouble convincing that his real forte was not that of making third-rate "modernistic" wood and linoleum cuts, which were a dime a dozen in Greenwich Village, but that of making millions laugh with his whimsical and sympathetic portrayal of boyhood life.

"Little Bill" Johnson and I had the same idea for a new comic strip concurrently. Each of us had been following the work of Percy L. Crosby in *Life* (then the country's foremost magazine of humor) and had come to the same conclusion; namely, that the adventures of "Skippy," a boy character created by Crosby, and Skippy's picturesque and individualized ragamuffin friends, would make a highly successful comic-continuity strip. Skippy was a willful but endearing boy, wise beyond his years, and equipped with super-normal grace, whose heroic escapades were probably a romantic compensation for the sort of boyhood Crosby thought every man was entitled to but which neither he nor anyone else had experienced; therefore, it had a universal appeal for adults rather than for children. Skippy was reminiscent of a character created around 1910 by Quin Hall, a Newspaper Enterprise Association cartoonist, though developed beyond Hall's original conception; and it was possibly a sense of being indebted to Hall that caused Crosby to try to avoid being too indissolubly identified with "Skippy" and to seek creative satisfaction as a "gallery"

195

artist and as writer. Moreover, he had originated a Sunday-page comic-continuity idea which had been tried out by the New York *World* with no success, and he was somewhat soured on the idea of doing a comic strip. Counting his occasional covers for *Life,* he was averaging about one hundred and fifty dollars a week, which enabled him to maintain a studio apart from the small flat in which he lived with his wife and child. I visited this studio during the weeks of our negotiations. It contained a drawing board, pens, brushes, gum arabic, India ink, a set of etcher's and woodcut artist's tools, reams of Bristol board, a chair, a typewriter, a cot, and little else except, surprisingly, cheap reprint copies of Kant's *Critique of Pure Reason* and Schopenhauer's *Essays.* As I picked the books up with what must have been an inquiring lift of the eyebrow, he said rather sheepishly that he was "going in" for philosophy. I said, "A very worthy pursuit," secretly hoping that he would not get bogged down in it.

When Johnson finally persuaded Crosby to sign a three-year contract with us, the agreement called for a daily cartoon by Crosby but not specifically for a Skippy strip. For weeks Crosby turned in a daily cartoon which could be accommodated to two, three, or more columns, with comical gag lines pointing the joke. They were mostly satirical buffooneries about the prize-fight racket. I thought they were funny, but the editors upon whom our salesmen called did not share this opinion. Crosby was then persuaded by Johnson to try a Skippy strip; out of sheer pride he compiled because he did not want to face failure again in the syndicate field.

The Skippy strip caught on immediately, and in less than six months Crosby's income from it was more than $60,000 a year. Thereupon W. R. Hearst, who liked the strip, directed Moses Koenigsberg, of the Hearst King Features organization, to try to wrest Crosby away from our E.F.S. The contract for the daily strip was found to be ironclad, but Hearst contract lawyers discovered a loophole: the contract did not preclude Crosby from drawing a Sunday page of Skippy stuff. Crosby therefore signed with Hearst, further agreeing to the distribution of the daily strip by King Features on the expiration of his contract with Johnson Features. Thus within a year after Johnson had persuaded Crosby to make Skippy a comic-strip character, Crosby's income shot up from about $5,500 a year to around $125,-000.

In my capacity as a feature editor as well as a writer of a daily New York column for the syndicate, I was responsible for our securing the syndication rights to Donald Ogden Stuart's fantastically satirical lampoon on go-getterism, *The Crazy Fool,* which was about a chap who inherited an insane asylum and a fortune, provided he put the asylum on a paying basis. I thought the buffoonery was hilariously funny, but our potential clients were of a different opinion and declined in great numbers to buy it. Clark Kinnaird was much more successful with a coup whereby Johnson Features got the exclusive rights to newspaper serialization of the novels of Beatrice Burton. This writer proved to be a worthy rival of the author of enormously successful newspaper fiction serials entitled *Chickie,* the heroine of which was a brash and slangy product of the new freedom who went through dangerous fires of temptation as a breadwinner in a highly competitive business world and remained a salamander of purity. The Beatrice Burton and the "Chickie" stories received a prodigious amount of free advertising by being denounced from many pulpits and by officials of purity leagues as shocking displays of the bad bringing up and the loose living of the younger generation.

My copy of *Gentlemen Prefer Blondes* bears the date November 7, 1925, and this inscription signed by Anita Loos, "To Burton Rascoe, who really knows a real piece of literature when he really sees it." (Those who recall the diction of Lorelei Lee will recognize the parody.) The date marks a rather humiliating defeat for me, wherein the author talked my boss out of what I was sure would be a fine syndicate property for us, something

197

that would make the syndicate a great deal of money. It turned out that I was right in my enthusiastic prophecy about the book, but that was cold comfort to me that day.

Miss Loos wrote the first chapter of *Gentlemen Prefer Blondes* to while away the tedium of a four-day trip by train from New York to Los Angeles. She completed it at odd moments while working for a motion-picture studio as a scenario writer, in which profession she had been adept ever since she was in her teens, and had sold a script entitled *The New York Hat* to David Wark Griffith, who had paid her fifteen dollars for it and used it as a comedy vehicle starring Mary Pickford and Lionel Barrymore.

The *American Mercury,* edited by H. L. Mencken and George Jean Nathan, was in its second year and the most talked-about magazine of the time. (It was the legend that every newspaper reporter carried a copy of the green-covered magazine in one pocket of his topcoat and a bottle of gin in the other, and that coeds who considered themselves sophisticated carried copies on the campus with the cover prominently displayed in order that their advanced ideas might not go unnoticed.) Miss Loos submitted the manuscript of *Gentlemen Prefer Blondes* to Nathan, who was a personal friend of hers. Nathan thought the story very amusing but too frivolous for the *Mercury;* another account, from Nathan, many months after the novel was a great success, was that he reluctantly turned it down because of the magazine's policy of using no serials, the story being too long for publication in one issue.

But Nathan did turn the story over to Ray Long, editor of the *Cosmopolitan* and executive head of all the Hearst magazine publications, including *Harper's Bazaar,* of which Henry Blackman Sell was the editor. Long could not see the story as a feature for *Cosmopolitan* but asked Sell to take a look at it. Sell was enthusiastic and bought it for serialization, turning the job of illustrating it over to Ralph Barton. Curiously enough the story caused no stir as a magazine serial, possibly for the reason that

198

the magazine was largely bought on the strength of its fashion pictures and advertisements.

I read it as a serial in *Harper's Bazaar* only because my wife subscribed to the magazine and I happened to be turning the pages one day when my eye was attracted to the Barton drawings and thence to the text. Some time later on I read a note in *Publishers' Weekly* announcing that Boni & Liveright were scheduled to publish *Gentlemen Prefer Blondes* in book form. The next day I dropped into Horace Liveright's office to congratulate him on this, saying, "The sale of that book will be over 150,000 copies and will pay your overhead for the year."

Liveright said, "You are crazy. We will be lucky if we sell a thousand copies. We are printing a very small edition. We are bringing it out only as a favor to Anita, whom I like. She is a swell girl."

I then told Liveright's editor, T. R. Smith, what I had told Liveright. He said, "No; we will lose money on it. It is amusing, but the public won't buy small books. There is not enough to it. We had to use a thick coated paper and fill it up with a lot of Ralph Barton drawings to make it look like a book at all."

Nevertheless, I went out on a limb in the *Detroit Athletic Club News* (a handsome monthly magazine limited to club members) and in *Arts and Decoration,* predicting a sale of over 100,000 for it and saying, in the latter publication, not only that it was "the literary treat of the season," but:

"It is something more than an ingenious satire; it is a tour de force of comic realism that is quite as deep (Bring the camphor bottle for the swooning Jacobeans!) yes, quite as deep as *Daisy Miller*. Many learned arguments have been waged over James's Daisy. She has been held to be the symbol of America, and her story been said to illustrate the contrast between the naïve and intrepid ignorance of America and the corrupt wisdom and experience of Europe. With nothing but beauty and innocence to commend her, lacking in wit, culture, and urbanity, Daisy could do anything that came into her silly head, without being aware of the danger of her actions, and come through unscathed. The implications of *Gentlemen Prefer Blondes* are more considerable than that."

I analyzed the book in relation to Henry James's treatment of the same subject, showing that actually Miss Loos had deeper insight into the discrepancy between the real and the articulated motivation of human action than had James. I concluded by saying, "The story of the Madonna-appearing casual murderess, who is the central character, is less a satire upon her type than it is a satire upon male susceptibility and gullibility. . . . Miss Loos's knowledge of the psychology of the sentimental male is outrageous."

After I had reread my advance copy of the book, I told Johnson that the book was certain to be the most popular literary sensation of the year; that everybody (a false assumption, incidentally) would recognize this as soon as the book came out; and that we ought to get the jump on others not only by sewing up the second-serial rights but by signing Anita to supply the text for a comic-strip feature relating the further adventures of her blond little gold digger. Johnson was infected by my enthusiasm and agreed to clinch a contract if I would arrange a meeting between him and Miss Loos.

I phoned Miss Loos's house and got her husband, John Emerson, an old friend of mine, on the phone. It was ten-thirty in the morning and I asked him if Johnson and I could come right over to talk about the serialization of Anita's book. He said, "Come on." Johnson and I were at his door before eleven. I introduced Johnson to Emerson and said, "Anita has not only written a sure-fire best seller but a novel as deep, fundamentally, as Henry James's *Daisy Miller*." John called up the stairs: "Sweetheart, come down! Your favorite literary critic is here and is talking wildly. Puts you in a class with Hank James."

Anita came downstairs and I reiterated my points about the

popularity, sales possibilities, and distinction of the novel. Both Anita and John were very gloomy at the time. John had had a series of very costly failures as a play producer on Broadway and he was not hesitant about confiding to Johnson and me that he was broke. Anita was not only incredulous over my enthusiasm but had been thoroughly convinced by Liveright and Smith that the book would not sell.

"Both Horace and Tommy [T. R. Smith]," she said, "have told me the book has had no advance sale and that they will lose money on it. Frankly, I wrote the book for fun and didn't expect to make anything out of it. I have already received something from the serial, but I shouldn't like to see the book cost Horace money, as he says it will. Besides, I should like to see Ralph [Ralph Barton] make money; he needs it. He worked so hard making so many drawings for it, and he was to be paid a royalty."

All this time I could see that Johnson was being thoroughly unsold, by the author herself, on the business proposition he was supposed to make to her. He hadn't read the book or even heard about it except from me. I told Anita I was as sure of the great popularity of the book as I had ever been about any book in my life and that I had predicted sales on many of them in advance of publication. I said, "This book will make you rich." John said, "Well, we could use some money right now." And Anita said, "I wish you could convince Tommy and Horace, but I very much doubt if you can. They have thoroughly convinced me that the book is a flop, even before publication."

The upshot was that Johnson never said a word, even about second-serial rights. If the book were a flop, we would not only be unable to sell it to newspapers for serialization but we would be out the guarantee and the cost of promotion. Anita autographed the copy which I had brought along for the purpose and, after some pleasantries, Johnson and I left. I felt defeated but not deflated; I told Bill, "We have just lost a big bet; somebody is certain to have that comic-strip idea after the book begins selling."

Bill said, "If it does. We can't have too many 'if's' in this business."

For three months it looked as though I had guessed wrong. Reviews of the book were perfunctory and confined to the back pages of the book-review sections, where it was dismissed as pleasant froth. Sales did not justify any expenditure for advertising. It looked as though a third of the first edition of 3,000 would be remaindered. Then, in the middle of February, nearly three months after publication, orders began to pour in, exhausting the edition and catching the publisher short of stock. A new edition was ordered, and by the first of March there was an avalanche of demands. Within a year, the book had sold over 400,000 copies and soon it had been translated into nearly every language on the continent of Europe and into Japanese. It was, in translation, the year's literary sensation of Paris, Berlin, Vienna, Stockholm, and other capitals of Europe. It was made into a play starring June Walker. And, just as I predicted to Johnson, a syndicate very successfully exploited a comic strip relating the adventures of Lorelei Lee, the blonde of *Gentlemen Prefer Blondes,* and her sister, Dorothy, the cynical brunette. Miss Loos's total income from the book was close to a million dollars. Its sequel, *But Gentlemen Marry Brunettes,* was as wise and deep as the first book but was not so amusing; its sale was comparatively slight, because the vogue of the first book had run its course.

Another feature I counted upon never got into our hands because the author, James Stephens, was so charmingly irresponsible. For many years two books among those I dip into most frequently and always with an afterglow of satisfaction and sense of well-being are Stephens's *The Crock of Gold* and *Demi-gods;* and I delight to read to people who are ignorant of them several favorite poems of mine from *Songs from the Clay.* Stephens had just concluded a successful lecture tour and I wanted him to write for us a series of his impressions of the towns and people he had seen.

Before I got in touch with him I had queried, by wire, a number of clients about the proposed series and had got enough commitments on a when, as, and if basis to justify our paying a considerable sum for the work, with equal profit to the syndicate. He and Mrs. Stephens came to the office. He was a veritable leprechaun of a man, small, under five feet, with a forehead so high and wide and a chin so narrow that his head looked like a crescent-topped cone with curly hair sticking out in wild disorder above his ears, which were large and pointed at the tips. He was the most unearthly creature I have ever seen, with the long face of a comic Irishman, timid brown eyes, dark skin, tiny feet and hands, and the rudiments of a goiter that, when I first knew him, had been large but had been shrunken considerably as the result of an operation.

Never have I seen a man who impressed me as being so easy, free, and natural, so untamed by society, so untouched by conventions, so spontaneous, pagan, and joyous as Stephens. The first time I met him was at Ernest Boyd's flat in East Nineteenth Street, shortly after his arrival in New York in 1925 for the lecture tour that had brought him to my office at Editors Features. (Stephens had received enough publicity during this tour to make his name familiar to newspaper readers throughout the country, or, more importantly, to editors of those newspapers to justify our commissioning him to write the articles I was to suggest to him.)

Ernest and Madeleine Boyd had invited John Farrar, Thomas Beer, Marc Connelly, and myself to lunch to meet Stephens. Madeleine was an excellent cook and had been at great pains to prepare a meal that Stephens (and the rest of us) would remember. We had all had a round of cocktails waiting for Stephens. A half hour passed; lunch was ready to be served. No Stephens. Like all good cooks, Madeleine began to fret lest the food she had prepared would remain too long in the oven. Three quarters of an hour passed; then an hour. Madeleine was frantic. She called the private home where Stephens was a guest and was informed that he had left an hour and a half before, with a slip of paper in his hands giving him explicit directions. Madeleine kept her head out of the window, looking down into the street. At last she screamed, "Stephens, *ici! Ici,* Stephens!" and waved her arms.

Farrar, Beer, Connelly, and I were standing rather stiffly in the living room when Ernest ushered Stephens in; Madeleine had hastened to her kitchen, probably muttering a prayer that her food had not been spoiled. Stephens did not wait to be introduced; he began talking to us as though we had all grown up with him. He explained that the reason he was late was that he was so fascinated by a Negro man who sat opposite him in the bus that he rode all the way to the end of the line watching him and had to be directed back to East Nineteenth Street. There were no Negroes in Dublin, Boyd explained, when the expression on our faces seemed to show puzzlement as to why the sight of a Negro should prove so interesting to Stephens.

"Yesterday," said Stephens, "I had a most glorious experience. I rode on top of an omnibus the length of Fifth Avenue to a Roman triumphal arch at the end of the street where the bus turned around and brought me back again. The conductor shoved a metal box in my face and asked for my fare. I took some coins from my pocket and held them out in my palm for him to choose the proper amount. He selected a ten-cent piece but did not pocket it. He handed it to me and instructed me to drop it into a slot in his metal box. I did so, and the box played a little tune."

Boyd asked him how he had left "Æ" (George Russell), and Stephens replied, "He is in fine health. Two nights before I was to leave Dublin by the boat train Æ came to my house. We talked through dinner and until five in the morning. He was back at

204

nine, and we talked all day and all night and we were still talking when I climbed aboard the train—and we hadn't begun to scratch the surface of the things we wanted to talk about."

We had had pen pictures from George Moore and others of those inseparable companions, Stephens and Æ, the one so small and the other so huge, as they walked down the streets of Dublin, but Connelly asked what Æ looked like. Said Stephens, "He is an e—NOR—mous man, inconCEIVably covered with whiskers."

At that moment Madeleine announced lunch, which consisted of a purée, pheasants in casserole served with a good sauterne, a pie of Madeleine's own baking, cheese, coffee, and cognac. We talked little during the meal, so delicious was it; but Stephens told us some tales of Oliver St. John Gogarty (the prototype of Buck Mulligan in Joyce's *Ulysses*), including the tale Gogarty relates himself in *As I Was Walking Down Sackville Street,* about how George Moore had come to Gogarty (who is a physician) with a face rash, which Gogarty knew was the result of a slight disorder and would disappear within a few days; but Moore had recently behaved badly at a house to which he and Gogarty had been invited, and Gogarty decided to punish him. He told Moore, gravely but ambiguously, that the rash was a "memoir of his dead life." Moore protested that it had been all of twenty-five years since he had bedded with a woman (though he was forever boasting of his amorous adventures), whereupon Gogarty replied, "Nevertheless!" and gave him some sugar pills, with directions for taking them, and forbade him to see anyone or to leave his room for two weeks, after which time, Gogarty told him, the rash would disappear and no further symptoms would develop. Then Gogarty persuaded Lord Invercastle, who abominated Moore, to invite Moore to a formal dinner party, guaranteeing to Lord Invercastle that Moore would not show up. It was one of the great desires of Moore's life to be invited to Invercastle's home and, receiving an invitation to do so when he was helpless to accept, Gogarty knew, would cause Moore almost intolerable anguish. Thus a Gogarty revenge.

After lunch Stephens entertained us with the sort of monologue of which only a Dublin poet is capable. He quoted Irish poetry with a divine eloquence running, with no sense of incongruity, straight from Yeats's *The Cold Heaven* to Gogarty's bawdy parody of Keats's *On First Looking into Chapman's Homer,* and from the Celtic twilight poems of "Æ" into tavern ballads, giving to each its proper mood and measure. Later I, who ordinarily avoid lectures and poetry recitals with a particular horror, went five times to hear Stephens talk before large gatherings, and on each occasion I was utterly enchanted, so so natural, so spontaneous, so passionate, and yet so earthy about poetry was he.

When Stephens and his wife came to see me at the office that day he was all for talking of poetry and of Dubliners rather than of business. His wife, a handsome patrician woman, a foot taller than he, eyed him like a fond but anxious mother, fearful of what her undisciplined but brilliant child would do next. Stephens said he had a world of things he wanted to write about concerning his tour of America and was all for telling me of them at once. But I knew that a Dubliner had much rather talk than write, even if writing is his profession, and that once having related something in speech he is likely to consider it a part of his conversational repertory and never put it down on paper. I asked him to save it all for the articles he was to write for us; told him how much we would pay for each article—an amount he considered very liberal—and that I would cable him payment on receipt of each or all of the articles, which we tentatively fixed as six in number, each about one thousand five hundred words.

He promised to get to work on the articles aboard ship and to mail the first one shortly after his arrival in Dublin. Weeks passed and there was no word from him. I wrote him but received no reply. I told Boyd about this. He said he could guess exactly what had happened: that Stephens had conscientiously written the articles as promised; but that just as he had finished the first one, the young editor of one of the numerous little starveling literary publications in Dubin, which pay nothing for contributions, had called upon him and asked him for something, so Stephens's name might appear in the table of contents, giving the magazine prestige, and that Stephens, in the generosity of his nature, had given the article away, even though the payment he would have received from the syndicate would have substantially improved the state of Stephens's finances. Boyd was correct in his surmise: Stephens's impressions of his trip to America (which would have delighted millions of newspaper readers and brought him enough to live on for six months or longer) appeared gratis in a coterie publication which probably reached no more than three hundred persons in all Ireland.

Percy Pyne, Jr., grandson of the New Jersey industrial and financial baron Moses Taylor Pyne, was a member of our staff at Johnson Features, more as an apprentice in newspaper syndicate work than as a contributor. Johnson had made a place for him at the request of Mrs. Rumsey, because Percy, whose nickname was "Toughy," had been a poet at Princeton before he joined the British Royal Air Force (later converted into the Lafayette Escadrille) in World War I and had not cared for the sort of work—that of banking or selling bonds—to which, by family tradition, he was destined. Toughy, as he preferred to be called, was so lacking in a sense of what a newspaper requires that he submitted several sonnets, including one to the pigeons of St. Mark's in Rome, as syndicate possibilities, which I had the unhappy duty of rejecting.

He was a tall, very handsome, black-haired young man in his late twenties, whose experiences as a combat flyer—in the days when our frail and faultily constructed fighting planes killed three times as many aviators by crashes than were shot down by the

Germans—had left him with more psychic scars than anyone I
know. He was an idealist and dreamer who had served with the
British Air Force long before the United States cast its lot on the
side of the Allies. He had gone to war, not from choice, but
because joining the "gentlemen's club" of the R.A.F. was considered an obligation of young men of wealth and social position
when he was in Princeton. Shy, diffident, sheltered, with the
predilections of a poet and a scholar, he had been drawn into a
frenetic life of dueling in the air, alternating with a frenetic social
life in London, where the spirit was "drink and kiss tonight
because tomorrow you may go down in flames." He had survived
the war without contracting cynicism or falling into embittered
disillusion. Yet he was a spiritually "displaced person," a young
man unfitted by background or upbringing for anything except
following in the footsteps of his father and grandfather in the
complexities of finance, and temperamentally averse to that. He
had no trade, no profession, no training except for poetry and for
dueling in the air.

Nor did any of the usual activities of the young men of wealth
and leisure of his class appeal to him. He did not care for polo
except as a spectacle to be watched, with mild enthusiasm, when
his friend, Tommy Hitchcock, who had been in the air force with
him, was playing. Riding to hounds in Virginia, with an excessive amount of drinking to follow, appeared to him a stupid use
of conspicuous leisure. (He had read Veblen's *Theory of the
Leisure Class* and had considered it a just indictment, attaching
much more importance to the work than I thought it deserved.)
Nor was he temperamentally inclined to exploration like his
friend, Suydam Cutting.

He preferred the society of writers and artists to that of the
class into which he was born and yet, even among those of his
class, such as Robert Chandler and Mrs. Harry Payne Whitney—
who had made careers of painting and sculpture—he seemed like
a wistful outsider. The bond of friendship between him and

Mrs. Rumsey, whose husband had been a noted sculptor as well as a noted polo player, was that she, by preference also, cultivated people who were engaged in the creative arts and was ceaselessly furthering the interests of painters, sculptors, composers, musicians, playwrights, novelists, and poets.

But Mrs. Rumsey's interests in the arts included a nervous, even fluttery, enthusiasm for ultra-modernistic expressions in form and color, to which Percy did not respond either with pretended or actual comprehension or sympathy. This was an experience common enough; there were many artists as well as laymen who could regard these paintings or the music of Varèse or Satie only with the emotion of puzzlement. But Percy's failure to find in such art what others seemed to find deepened his sense of being very faultily equipped for the experience of life.

He and I lunched together two or three times a week for many months, at a restaurant in Columbus Circle, and he seemed to be a serious, lonely man, eager for a compelling direction in life but finding none. His favorite poets among the moderns were Robinson Jeffers and Edna St. Vincent Millay; but these poets also seemed to disturb his sense of moral values and to present conflicting concepts of conduct to him—Jeffers with his wrestling with the deep, dark forces of primitive passion and Millay with her airy acceptance of the "biological imperative."

Toward the caste conventions of his class—which were those of a self-conscious group whose pride in lineage was a pride also in the social and civic obligations of the aristocracy, coupled with that disdain for mere wealth which those who for generations have been financially secure make a convention of disdaining—was that of amused tolerance. He once told me how his father (who must have been a delightful man with a humorous turn of mind) had displayed his amusement over the seriousness with which elderly members of New York's most class-conscious society took their sense of exclusiveness.

Percy Pyne, Sr., it seems, was leaving the Knickerbocker Club with a judge who was also a member of one of New York's old families when they encountered John D. Rockefeller, Jr., with whom Pyne was acquainted. He introduced Rockefeller to the judge. They chatted a moment and parted, Rockefeller going in one direction and Pyne and the judge in another. The judge said, "Young Rockefeller seems a nice enough chap. I hear he is spoken well of." Pyne answered, "He is, indeed," and then added, with sly malice, to draw out the judge's prejudices, "We might propose him for the club." The judge exclaimed in horror, "The Knickerbocker? Oh no! The Union, perhaps, but not the Knickerbocker!" (As I compare the biographies of John D. Rockefeller, Jr., in Who's Who for 1925 and for 1947 I see that he has "made" the Union Club since then, but *not* the Knicker-bocker.)

My path did not cross Toughy Pyne's after he left Editors Features Service; the next I learned of him was from Elliott White Springs, some years afterward, who told me Toughy had been attacked by a strange illness that had partially paralyzed him. I talked to Toughy on the phone the next day and asked if I might go to see him; but after we had set a date, his valet had to phone me on the afternoon I was to go there that Toughy was too weak to see me. When he died, I was deeply depressed for several days, rather inexplicably, for he and I were never close friends and could hardly ever have been, because our social orbits and our interests were so far apart. But it had seemed to me that he had been struggling within himself for something to give meaning to life, and that, in his diffident way, he had plied me with questions in that search and I had, without realizing the importance of these questions to him, replied to them casually as mere attempts to make conversation.

Once Toughy had taken me to lunch at the Brook, the very exclusive club of which his cousin, Percy Pyne, II, was governor, and had introduced me to a number of his friends. Afterward he had told Springs, rather sorrowfully, that I had "high-hatted" his friends. He did not realize that it was not snobbery on my part which kept me aloof from the conversation at table that day; but simply that I was unable to participate in their conversation, for they were talking about the dogs that were to be used in a coming hunt near Leesburg, the condition of Tommy Hitchcock's ponies, the handicaps of the Argentine players, incidents relating to a recent society dance at which they had all been present, and the affairs of persons to whom they referred by their first names and whose last names I probably should not have recognized even if I had heard them. Scott Fitzgerald was right when he said, "People who are used to wealth are different from us," and their difference sometimes is most apparent when they try very hard not to show it.

Mrs. Rumsey I could understand, admire, and be fond of, and be completely natural with, precisely because she had not been conditioned by the sort of early environment to which Toughy, for instance, had been subjected. No breadwinner of a poor family, indeed, had had a less carefree life than she had almost up until the time she was married. Her father, the great financial genius and railroad magnate, E. H. Harriman, who had begun his career in Wall Street at fourteen, was so mistrustful of others that his daughter Mary was taught stenography and type-writing and put to work as his secretary while still in her early teens. Her hours were long and arduous; she was kept severely dressed and severely disciplined; she was not permitted to enjoy even the ordinary social life of a young woman brought up in a strict middle-class family; until her father's death in 1909 she was a slave (she told me) to an exacting taskmaster, who de-manded almost as much concentration from her as he demanded of himself in his multifarious schemes whereby he gained almost absolute power in the railway world. Released by her father's death from the bleak discipline he had imposed upon her, she naturally rejected everything that reminded her of it. Her asso-ciations were almost from the first with the (to her) glamorous and exciting world of artists rather than with the world of high finance, fashion, and society. She married the gallant poloist C. C. Rumsey, who was also a sculptor who insisted upon living gaily, freely, and creatively rather than in a world of money-making and stuffy convention.

An exquisite little woman with a flaming store of nervous energy, when I knew her, Mrs. Rumsey was natural, free, and capable of infinite and continuous enthusiasms. Her husband had been killed in an automobile accident in 1922, two years before I met her, and her life was dedicated to the activities she thought would please him. Heiress to a huge fortune, money was to her an instrument for doing exactly what she pleased—on impulse. Deprived of the normal life of girlhood and young womanhood and widowed early, she sought fulfillment in restless activity; it didn't matter much to her what the activity was, provided it amused her. Secluded for so long, she liked to have people around her, all sorts of people, and, because she was truly democratic, with none of the inverse snobbery of those who affect disdain for snobs, she would bring the most incongruous people together at house parties on her estate near Port Washington and yet somehow, through sheer force of her bubbling happiness at having them as guests, make them unself-conscious also. Thus it was not uncommon of her to have as house guests a Wall Street buccaneer of finance, a seedy White Russian refugee painter, a prim spinster from a very hidebound and exclusive old Long Island family, a journalist, an old polo player somewhat daffy from being hit over the head too many times with a polo mallet, a Greenwich Village poet, and an Italian princess. She was, of course, an easy touch for anyone who came to her with a sufficiently bizarre scheme for promoting modern art.

One of the most fantastic of these schemes came to fruition in January 1925, with the inauguration of the "Artel of the Arts" on the site of the Harriman stables, which Mrs. Rumsey had converted into a sculptor's studio and apartment for her late husband. The first floor of the studio was given over to an exhibition of paintings. On the second floor there was an auditorium and a stage with a single set designed by Nicholai Cikowsky, which combined a suggestion of stairs, a semicircular platform, an Alhambran archway, a Borgian dungeon entrance, a ceremonial altar, a radio aerial, and a touch of the girders of Brooklyn Bridge, all in blue, yellow, and white.

On the night of the inauguration of the Artel of the Arts I recognized among guests of Mrs. Rumsey, Brancusi and Archipenko, the sculptors; Gatti-Casazza, the spade-hearted impresario of the Metropolitan Opera; Yvonne George, the French *chanteuse;* a marchesa and two princesses whose pictures I had seen in the society pages; Ivan Narodny, a lovable but eccentric Russian mystic philosopher whom the fabulous "Sheriff Bob" Chandler, the society-born painter, had retained as his secretary, wrote the manifesto of the organization, which was weird enough to be quoted in part:

"The Artel of the Arts is an intellectual legion in today's life which, ridiculing philistine sophistry and time-eaten platitudes, pursues those spiritual essentials upon which the great cultures of the past were built. The Artel of the Arts aspires to new ideas in art and literature, not for newness's sake, but for the sake of an evolutionary principle. It advocates a more noble and sincere civilization than the one we have today. It emphasizes the idea of the essential, not the form. Our modern effeminate society reflects the emptiness of its boasted education in the banal stage, empty literature, and stilted art which have resulted from art's separating itself from the stage and altar and each raging after the obvious —success.

"The Artel of the Arts becomes in its metaphysical aspects, as it were, a religious community of the future. The Old World's life is practically in the grip of a reckless mobocracy, while the New is a bureaucratic machine with money interests on one side and organized labor on the other. The social revolution lies not in new social systems and better legislative laws but in more spiritually inspired individuals."

This deriding of "money interests" was quaint when one read on to discover that the subscription price for five performances, of which a sample was to be offered that night, was fifty dollars per person and that the project had been financed by Mrs. Rumsey, who was also contributing to the support of most of the artists connected with the enterprise. The program consisted of an indifferent cello performance of familiar standbys from the works of Bach and Musorgski, a few old English ballads by a male singer, an "aesthetic" dance by three awkward girls—and Edwin Markham. The venerable poet, then nearly eighty, of course read the only poem by which he was known, *The Man with the Hoe,* which was inappropriate enough against such a non-representational background but downright appalling when he explained what the poem meant and how he had come to write it. That, I believe, was the end of the Artel of the Arts.

In writing a daily syndicated column about New York I was in competition with O. O. McIntyre, who had, over a period of fifteen years, built up his "New York Day by Day" column from a give-away press release in which he managed to mention the hotel for which he was press agent into the most widely syndicated text feature of the time. His column appeared in eighty papers and was so popular that the McNaught Syndicate was able to charge very high prices for it. Within a year's time my column was appearing in more than four hundred newspapers, or in five times as many media as McIntyre's; but his income was reputed to be more than seventy-five thousand dollars from the syndication, whereas my income, to say the least, was very considerably less than that.

McIntyre had a very simple formula for his column. It had a wide appeal and also did not necessitate his ever leaving his rooms (which for a long time were in the Ritz Hotel and later in a spacious and luxurious apartment in a fashionable district). The formula was this: to give his readers in the cities and small towns away from New York (his column did not appear in a New York newspaper until the last years of his life, after the Hearst organization had acquired the syndication rights to it) the illusion of participating, vicariously, in the glamorous life of New York, and at the same time assuring them that life in New York was perfectly dreadful and that they were much better off in whatever town they lived in. His native town bore the homely name of Gallipolis, Ohio, and he was forever pretending that life in Gallipolis (and, inferentially, in other towns of its size or smaller) was ideal, whereas life in New York was a rat race in which the participants were nearly all phonies, sharpers, crooks, or shady characters; that the average New Yorker was a yokel, compared with whom the average villager was a shrewd and worldly-wise man.

McIntyre created an entirely unreal New York conforming to the small-town reader's conception of it—a city of sinister sin, Chinese opium joints, decadent thrills, ostentation, and, of course, the visiting place of celebrities of the stage, of the popular magazines, and of the screen, whose names were sprinkled through McIntyre's column with an air of easy familiarity. His sentences were short and colloquial, though he was given to fancy words like "purlieus" for "region," or "neighborhood" and "jezebel," "denizen," and "outré." He occasionally lifted whole paragraphs from other New York journalists without credit and, when Christopher Morley protested, he innocently, and probably quite honestly, said he thought that anything printed in yesterday's newspaper was in public domain. His column gave pleasure to millions; it brightened their lives and enheartened them, which I am constrained to believe was a more beneficent mission in life than that of some of the "deep-thinking" columnists who came after him, whose thundering, contrary, and specious winds of doctrine can only confuse and trouble them.

I was tempermentally incapable of creating an imaginary New York for the readers of my column. I could only report what I saw, heard, felt, and thought, convey impressions, relate that which seemed new and interesting to me. Nor could I repeat myself or keep hammering home the same idea, which is the secret of a certain kind of success.

My method of working was, to me, just as rewarding, in that it brought me an immense readership in cities and towns all over the country (which means success in syndication), and it also added an immense amount of experience and information about human behavior which is the stock in trade of a writer and upon which he may draw as long as his creative life endures. When I decided I had exhausted the vein of ore I had been mining and that I would find fresh adventure in prospecting elsewhere, I gave up the job of writing a daily column about New York and its people (and also a weekly book review which was syndicated to sixty-three newspapers). V. V. McNitt, the syndicate manager who had succeeded Johnson, tried to dissuade me with a guarantee of $1,000 a week and promises of extensive promotion which he said would build my income up to $75,000 or $100,000 a year. He showed telegrams to me from editors from Portland, Oregon, to Portland, Maine, and from Oakland, California, to Montgomery, Alabama, pleading with me to continue the column. These offers and these pleasing telegrams were persuasive, but I knew that the more successful I became, commercially, the more restricted would my life become and the less likely would it come about that I would publish my first considerable book at forty.

I had long held that, just as the novelist or playwright is great in proportion to the number of characters, from hero to villain, from philosopher to clown, within him that make up his creative being, so also should any writer, as long as he is receptive to impressions, live as though writing were not his profession in order that the experience which accrues to him may not be prejudged by him and thereby become, when articulated, a mere attitudinizing.

216

(Upon such principles of approach I have tried to base my professional work as a critic of literature and drama; that is, I have opened a book, as a lover of literature, hoping to find pleasure and instruction in it, not as a critic conscious of an audience awaiting my reasoned judgment on it; on going to a play or listening to music I have figuratively divested myself of my robes of office and have even kept them in the closet while recording my impressions.)

Writing about life in New York, then, for nearly three years was interesting and fascinating work, just as I imagine Dickens found the work of gathering material for *Pickwick Papers,* Addison and Steele gathering material for the *Tatler,* Lafcadio Hearn gathering material to write about in a newspaper in New Orleans. After nearly three years it became something of a chore, and an exhausting one.

When I was fresh at the work, I roamed the streets, kept my eyes peeled; investigated; I went to the theater, to the opera, to concerts, to burlesque shows, to art exhibits, museums, and night clubs; I trudged through snow to St. Mark's-in-the-Bouwerie for services in which the rector had managed to combine Episcopal ritual with pagan aesthetics without offense to the solemnity of worship and with exhilarating effect; I sat through services in Salvation Army missions during which former derelicts testified they had attained the grace of God; I went to burlesque shows in East Houston Street and to basement dives in Harlem; I attended the First Regiment Armory horse shows, marveled at Huber's flea circus, and dropped pennies in the kinetoscopes of arcades off Times Square.

I ate in the ancient restaurant of the East India Company and drank in water-front speakeasies; I discovered that (at that time) one could find a forest on Manhattan Island as primeval as that of the Maine woods—at the northern tip of the island, which is now Inwood Hill Park—and found on the south shore of Spuyten Duyvil mounds of clamshells piled there by the Indians centuries ago; I familiarized myself with the many foreign quarters of New York, to which immigrants from Europe and Latin America gravitate, each according to his origin, there to create a community retaining the habits and customs of the Old World among the conglomerate races of the New.

I became a commuter to the suburbs, which is an act whereby one attaches oneself to a small town or village as a daily escape from the megapolism of the city. I sat on the glacial boulder called Mount Tom off Riverside Drive, near Eighty-third Street, where Edgar Allan Poe had sat; read Chaucer in the little park where Masefield had thus beguiled his leisure from his labors as a porter in a nearby saloon; I attended the riotous Greenwich Village balls in Webster Hall and danced to the music of Paul Whiteman's band at the Palais Royal and to the music of Vincent Lopez's band on the Pennsylvania Roof. I was my own Harun Al Rashid in O. Henry's Bagdad-on-the-Subway and sat and drank where O. Henry had sat and drank at a tavern in Irving Place.

But I had no more intimacy with some of the more sensational occurrences in New York during the twenties than had any resident of Shawnee, Oklahoma, or Fulton, Kentucky, who read the daily newspapers. The Snyder-Gray and Hall-Mills murder cases, the Hauptmann trial, the Kip Rhinelander scandal, the "Peaches" and "Daddy" Browning escapades, and the hysteria occasioned by Valentino's funeral, were spot news events, handled by the wire services; I was as remote from them as I was from Mammoth Cave, in Kentucky, where Floyd Collins was caught in a narrow fissure and penned there until his death, while the world waited his fate, or from Nome, Alaska, to which the half-breed Malamute, Balto, won immortal fame in the annals of dog lore when he led the team which carried Gunnar Kasson and his sledload of diphtheria anti-toxins to the beleaguered plague victims of the frozen North.

Nor was I temperamentally capable of active participation in the crazes of the period. Emile Coué, the faith healer from France, came, conquered, and departed, and not once did I tell my beads with the magic words, "Day by day, in every way, I am getting better and better." Ely Culbertson, with probably the best-conceived, best-conducted, and most successful publicity stunt in American history, made contract bridge practically compulsory for millions of Americans and yet I never even watched a game, much less learned to play it. Nor did I take up mah-jongg, although it was almost socially obligatory. Margaret Petherbridge, Prosper Buranelli, and Gregory Hartswick, puzzle editors of the New York *World*, at the instance of a new publishing firm, Simon & Schuster, in 1924 got together the first of a series of crossword puzzle books which started a craze that swept the country; and yet I never indulged in the pastime until I was hospitalized eight years later. I attended a six-day bicycle race one evening at Madison Square Garden, only because Paul Morand had written a good short story about such a racer in *Open All Night;* but it was such a bore that I left after an hour. After looking at newspaper pictures of the tortured faces of the participants in the marathon dances, I would no more have gone to watch such a spectacle than I would have gone to a garbage dump to make love. I read about the publicity-mad creatures who sat for days on end atop of flagpoles but I could not conceive of myself even craning my neck to observe any such display of human imbecility.

I did see death come quick and awfully though one afternoon. Carol Frink, a newspaper feature writer, had got the life story of a "human fly" and called me up one morning asking me to sit with her and the "fly's" wife in a restaurant opposite the McAlpin Hotel where we could watch the "fly" crawl down the wall of the hotel from a window near the top. His was a hazardous and very specialized profession, possible only through prolonged exercises whereby his fingertips had become abnormally prehensile and his toes extraordinarily sensitive and sure; he had had to develop a sense of balance to an acute degree, for the shift of an ounce of weight beyond his calculations might mean a plunge to death. It is also a skill for which there is very little demand, so his workdays were infrequent and he had to keep in daily practice; and one is overage in the work earlier than is a prize fighter. The "human fly" and his wife were very poor but he had the pride of a great artist in his work, the same concern with perfection; he disdained concealed mechanical aids, which he said some "human flies" were unprofessional enough to use.

The three of us sat there at a table beside a window from which we watched the crowd fill the street and the sidewalk, except for a small area roped off and guarded by policemen where the "human fly" would land, if he fell. The young, pretty, plainly dressed, and haggard-looking wife sat there pale and tense as her husband waved to the crowd, crawled out of the window, and began his slow, cautious descent, hanging by half-inch ledges and supporting himself by toes in canvas shoes, the tips of which touched slight projections or fitted into crevices in the masonry. Then, three stories down, he slipped. His body seemed to float earthward, turned slightly sideways. But that was an optical illusion; the descent was swift and horrifying. I never saw the body, but the news pictures showed it crushed like an egg that had dropped and spread on the sidewalk.

Every adult male in New York, except teetotalers, had cards to a dozen or more restaurants which served liquor at bars or tables during Prohibition. The process of getting a membership card to such a "club" was easy; one had only to be vouched for by a customer who had already obtained a card. As soon as the bootlegging business got organized and the shakedown for federal and municipal "protection" had got stabilized into smooth-working plans, the speakeasies became not only safe places for public drinking but the best places to eat. Good food was the attraction, not for the profit on the service of a meal (often, indeed, the kitchens in the most popular speakeasies were run at a loss), but for the enormous profit on the tax-free and license-free liquor served.

Thus the blind pigs, which were constantly subject to raids before "protection" was organized, were dangerous places to patronize; their profit had to be made quickly, so their liquor was raw and adulterated, "cooked" alcohol in counterfeit bottles, and often contained fusel oil and actual poisons, resulting in blindness and paralysis. One wise and humane newspaper proprietor, alarmed by the disastrous effects upon his staff from the consumption of hard liquor, financed a restaurant and bar, admission by membership card only, near his newspaper in order that his reporters and other staff men might have a place to eat and drink where both the food and the liquor were of the best quality and reasonably priced. Thus clubs called "Artists and Writers," "Manufacturers and Engineers," "Brokers and Bankers," "Pen and Pencil," "Bowling and Boxing," et cetera, et cetera, sprang up in strategic locations all over the city, usually in old mansions. The furnishings were clublike, the atmosphere comradely, the food and service excellent.

There was a certain piquancy of adventure, for a while, in finding new places where good liquor was to be had, in basements off the main thoroughfares and in respectable residential districts, where a rap at the door resulted in the opening of a slot through which a lookout peered and demanded identification. Much of this sort of thing was showmanship and was exploited in the more garish dens of Greenwich Village for the benefit of tourists. Inside, the liquor was served in teacups instead of in glasses, further to add to the devilishness of the sense of lawbreaking. In the better-established and less garish places, where the customers were regular, a doorman sufficed, and if there was any doubt about one's identity, the doorman called the manager while the prospective patron waited in a reception room or vestibule until his registration was produced or the manager politely explained that the club was open to registered members only.

The syndicate which ran the Piccadilly, the Piccadilly Rendezvous (a night club on the top floor of the same building), the Palais Royal, Montmarte, the Café de Paris, and other places in the Times Square district were not in fear of federal agents or the local police but they were in fear of their waiters, cooks, bus boys, and scullions. These employees could be inefficient, discourteous, insubordinate, demanding in their hours and wages, and yet they could not be fired, because they could file complaints that would result in raids, whether the raiders wanted to make the raids or not.

I was at Texas Guinan's El Fay Club on Third Street one morning about three o'clock, talking to Texas, who had come to my table, when a patron staggered up to her and loudly protested a bill. (The El Fay Club was what was known as a clip joint and one of the first night clubs with a floor show established during prohibition. It was financed by Larry Fay, a racketeer, who was later shot to death while he was making a call in a telephone booth in a speakeasy uptown.) The aroused patron had been buying champagne for his party all evening, passing out twenty-dollar bills to the scantily clad young girls of Miss Guinan's chorus, and giving the orchestra leader large bills to play the popular tunes he asked for.

The "champagne" served at El Fay, like the "champagne" served at nearly all other night clubs which featured a floor show, was carbonated cider with grain alcohol added. It cost about fifteen cents a quart, including the cork and phony labels, and sold at from twelve to fifteen dollars and up to thirty dollars. The food was scanty and correspondingly overpriced, chicken chow mein (the principal dish, which came in a container from a wholesale caterer) cost three dollars a person. The patron (a steel man from Pittsburgh, so Texas told me) had added up the items on his bill, and the correct tally of the figures printed by the cash register was $399. The penciled tally was $499. The patron had thrown almost that much around in cash, in a silly display of free spending, but in his drunken state he had had a moment's shrewdness and added up his bill.

Texas added the figures and called the waiter. She bawled out the menial, using very blistering language, and told him to get his coat and his pay and to leave immediately; that he was fired. He looked very abject. Then she apologized to the patron and corrected the tally. When the satisfied patron had gone, she said to me, "Naturally you think we made that overcharge. We didn't. God knows we gyp the suckers enough on what we serve here, but that hundred bucks would have been split between the cashier and the waiter and we would never have known about it. In the checkup the penciled tally would be rubbed out and the correct amount, $399, would have gone into the till. It happens all the time. But we can't fire the cashier or the waiter; they'd get the joint closed in no time. That waiter isn't being fired. He will put on his coat and leave the same time the patron does, so the patron will enjoy the satisfaction of believing he has caused the crook to lose his job. But the waiter will walk around the block and come back. He will stay out of sight if the customer ever shows up again."

The press agent for the El Fay Club was Milton Raison, a young poet who had made quite a stir in the early twenties with a volume of poems called *Spendrift*. Raison and I were friends. He told me about Fay. Fay had laid the foundations of his racketeering fortune during the war. Drafted, he was put to work driving trucks which took supplies to Camp Mills on Long Island because he had been a taxi driver. He would drop off government goods at a warehouse on the road, where he had confederates, and later sell the stuff through a "fence" or dealer in stolen goods. With cash thus accumulated, he went to Chauncey M. Depew, president of the New York Central, and offered the company $250,000 for the exclusive concession of taxi service at the Grand Central Station. Depew considered the cash only so much velvet for the company and accepted it. Fay got the concession at the Pennsylvania Station in the same way. He sold both concessions to large taxi corporations at a profit of about a million dollars.

Fay had a sweetheart in a show in Chicago. He used to charter a special train, consisting of an engine, a combination club and dining car, and a Pullman sleeper, to visit the girl nearly every week end. Once he decided to go to the Saratoga races while he and Raison were in a taxicab on their separate ways home after the club was closed for the night. He wanted Raison to go along to keep him company. He peeled three one-hundred-dollar bills, handed them to the hackie, and told him to drive to Saratoga, remain with him and Raison while there, and drive them back. He put the taxi driver up in the same elaborate suite occupied by Raison and himself. He went to the races once, won a lot of money, and decided to return to New York. On their return, Fay instructed the taxi driver to go to the company that owned the cab. There he bought the cab and presented it to the driver.

It must sound curious that a night club, operating in violation of the law by selling liquor, should find any need for a press agent. One would think their operations would be clandestine and the less printed about the clubs the better. But the clubs thrived on publicity, because the patrons and the press were in tacit conspiracy to nullify the Prohibition Law by ignoring it. Because Texas Guinan was a colorful and amusing character, whose greeting to a customer was "Hello, sucker!" she was good copy for the press; she was interviewed, her shows were reviewed, the club was described in newspapers and magazines. But no mention was ever made of the fact that liquor was sold there, much less of the fact that the club's only reason for existence was from the enormous profits derived from fake champagne, cut liquor, outrageously priced food, and a heavy cover charge for a dreary and skimpy floor show. The night clubs were all ill-ventilated, stuffy, noisy, garish, vulgar, overcrowded, cheap, shoddy, and expensive; but they were places to go and places to be seen by actors and others who thrive on publicity and, inasmuch as conspicuous spending is not only an indication of prosperity in New York but is a fetish in the process of advancement, advertising men, automobile and radio executives, wholesalers, promoters, play producers, magazine editors, and go-getters of all sorts patronized night clubs as much for business reasons as relaxation.

The syndicates, of course, had nearly a monopoly on the night-club business, and when they began fighting among themselves over disputed areas of monopoly, such assassinations took place as those which put an end to the careers of Larry Fay and "Dutch" Schultz. Those who tried to invade the night-club business as independents were never interfered with by the syndicates—directly; they were nearly always put out of business, legally, by the enforcement officers at the direction and connivance of the syndicate managers. The profits from night clubs were so enormous, however, that it was estimated that if a place with a floor show, costing $100,000, including rent, furnishings, tableware, and linen, could keep open for nine weeks without being raided and padlocked the profit would be nearly $250,000. From that one can get an idea of the free spending of the times, and of the fabulous profits.

One of the popular resorts was the Piccadilly Rendezvous where Gilda Gray introduced the Hawaiian hula-hula. It was a small place, where both real and fake champagne were served at enormous prices; but it became a favorite of college boys from Princeton, Yale, and Harvard, because of the publicity accorded Miss Gray's dance, and this soon caused the place to operate at a loss. The reason was that the collegians and their girls would arrive early and in force, bringing their own liquor, and remain for hours, paying only the cover charge and for setups of ginger ale at one dollar and fifty cents a pint, which they would often make last throughout an evening. The origin of the slang word, "heel," was among the waiters of the Piccadilly Rendezvous, who used it to describe a college boy or any other night-club patron who was close with his money; it had reference to the fact that economical men wear rubber heels, which can be replaced cheaply when they get worn down, whereas free spenders have many pairs of shoes, all with full leather heels. From an expression of contempt for a man who is careful of his money it came to mean what it means now—a person without honor or any principles of decent behavior. Waiters had a trick of standing between the floor show and the customers who were slow spenders, cutting off the view, but this didn't work with the collegians and their girls: they got up and stood with the waiters, shutting off the view of liberal spenders. They couldn't be ejected without serious reprisals; and the management did not dare raise the cover charge out of the reach of the collegians. The management gave up and closed the place; Miss Gray went into the *Follies*.

The Piccadilly Restaurant on the ground floor was a charming place, decorated in the style of an English inn, with red-and-white checked linen and featuring chops, kidney-veal pies, and steaks. The liquor was also excellent but sold so openly (liquor was served in cups, but there was no difficulty about getting into the place and anyone got what he asked for) that I asked Gil Boag how they managed it. Boag knew I would not betray him in my columns but that I would describe the arrangement, without mentioning the Piccadilly, and thereby increase the interest of out-of-towners in New York—and would be likely to mention the restaurant in connection with its excellent food. So he took me downstairs where there was a wall of bottles and glassware on racks, before which were tables where bartenders mixed drinks as they were ordered through a speaking-tube system and sent them upstairs by dumb-waiter. He asked the bartenders to stand aside while he pushed a button. The wall turned around. The other side of it was utterly blank. The syndicate owned the building next door and kept it empty. When federal agents arrived with a search warrant, a signal was given. All cups and bottles of liquor upstairs were seized by waiters and thrown into the several hatchways contrived for that purpose and conveyed to the basement of the building next door; the revolving wall was turned, while the mixing tables and bartenders were shunted into the adjoining basement. Within less than a minute, Boag said, there would be no liquor on the premises indicated in the warrant; and the searchers bore no warrant to search the adjoining building. Here, again, the help had to be treated with great tact, for the only two raids they had had were the results of revengeful waiters.

I was a "charter member" of a restaurant in West Forty-ninth Street, just off Fifth Avenue, which was greatly favored by writers, editors, stage folk, and others connected with the various arts; and because I lunched there nearly every day, I would get a letter from one of the proprietors if I remained absent for as long as a week, asking if I had found anything to complain of in the service. This restaurant occupied three floors of an old brownstone residence and was known as Jack & Charlie's. (When they moved to more elaborate quarters in West Fifty-second Street, the restaurant became nationally known as "21.") The proprietors were sons of a famous restaurateur on the lower East Side and they had been brought up in the tradition of serving excellent food. They preserved this tradition at their speakeasy; they were as jealous for the reputation of their food as they were for the reputation of their liquor. So, by word of mouth, it rapidly became known as one of the best restaurants in the midtown section. In their beginnings the magazines *Time* and the *New Yorker* were practically edited either at the basement bar or at the tables upstairs; and publishers were often there with their authors discussing future books.

At a table at Jack & Charlie's I once created a mystery in my own mind which I have not solved to this day. After I became

editor of the *Bookman* I received from a literary agent the manuscript of *The Sisters,* one of the two unfinished stories found
among Joseph Conrad's papers after his death, the other being
Suspense, which was published in 1925. Conrad had begun *The
Sisters* in 1896 but had put it aside for *The Nigger of the "Narcissus"* and had never completed it.

I bought the story but, as it stood, it was only the beginning
of a novel, in which the background was established and the two
principal characters introduced.

There was no indication of how the story was to develop. Ford
Madox Ford was in town and I got an idea. Ford had collabo-
rated with Conrad on *The Inheritors, Romance,* parts of *No-
stromo,* and *The Nature of a Crime,* during the time Conrad
was dubious about his ability to write English. Ford was closely
associated with Conrad, therefore, during the period when *The
Sisters* was begun and laid aside. Why wouldn't it be a literary
coup if I could engage Ford to complete the story in the Conrad
manner?

I knew that Ford had a memory in which fact was often
mixed with fancy and that, although he had written some novels
of his own which probably will survive as long as any of Conrad's,
he had somehow missed the fame which Conrad finally achieved
and, because of this, he was rather pathetically subservient to
Conrad's reputation, as though, if he could gain popular recognition in no other way, he could arrive there by hanging on to Conrad's coattails as Conrad's collaborator and expositor. There was,
at the time, a sort of tug of war between Ford and Richard
Curle over the question of Conrad, as to which one had the better right to be identified with Conrad. I was definitely rooting for
Ford, though I did not see why he should contend with such a
minor literary hack as Curle and why he did not dissociate himself entirely from Conrad's memory and stand on his own com-
mendable feet.

But Ford had made some rather extravagant claims in print

about Conrad's indebtedness to him, in substantiation of which he quoted conversations of thirty-odd years before, which were somewhat implausible. I was of the belief that Ford knew nothing of the existence of the manuscript of *The Sisters,* but that if I could implant in his mind the idea that *I believed* he did, and that I thought he knew how Conrad intended to develop the story, he would say that of course he knew all about the story and would consent to finish it, or at least tell the *Bookman* readers how Conrad intended to develop it. If I let Ford disclose that he had never heard of the story before I spoke of it, my plan would fall through; Ford could not pretend to know how a Conrad story was to develop if he had never heard of it.

I phoned Ford at the Brevoort and invited him to lunch, asking him to come to the office of the *Bookman.* Meanwhile E. E. Cummings had dropped in and I not only invited him to lunch with Ford and me but told him my plan and asked his help in carrying it through. The idea was to prevent Ford's disclosing that he knew nothing about the story, if that were the case. Ford came. We went to Jack & Charlie's where I ordered for the three of us (since neither of them had been to Jack & Charlie's before), specifying cocktails, filet of sole Marguery with a good dry sauterne, and brandy with coffee. It was not until we were on the second brandy that I, speaking as rapidly as possible, told what was in the Conrad manuscript and said, "Of course you are familiar with it and know how Conrad meant to develop it. I should like you to finish the story for us or at least tell us what Conrad intended to do with it."

Not to my astonishment, Ford said he was familiar with the story and that Conrad had discussed it thoroughly with him. He engaged to write a history of the story and relate the plot which Conrad had discussed with him. Afterward Cummings said in an aside to me while Ford was getting on his topcoat, "Good work! He swallowed it hook, line, and sinker." But Ford turned in such an interesting and plausible article about Conrad's intentions that I have never been able to decide to this day whether what he wrote is true or imagined.

His explanation for the reason that Conrad never completed the story was that Conrad wanted to write a story of incest (in the canonical sense) and that he was afraid of it. The Stephen of the story, he said, was to marry one of the sisters but to fall in love with, and have a child by, the younger one, and that the story was to end with the slaying of the child and its mother by her uncle, a fanatical priest, who had destined her for the religious vocation of a nun. Ford had a daughter who became a nun and he liked to remind people that he himself was "a Papist." The plot seems hardly Conradian, but Ford's account seems highly plausible.

As we were walking down Fifth Avenue to my office, where Ford was to pick up the Conrad manuscript, he excused himself and asked us to wait while he went into the Guaranty Trust Company bank, at Forty-fourth Street. Cummings expressed astonishment to me that Ford should have business with the bank. He asked Ford, when he came out, if he had an account there. Ford said, no, he didn't, but that he had once gone there with John Quinn and had discovered that the bank had an *urinoir;* since then he had often used it, because, he said, "American cities are not so solicitous of a man's comfort as Paris is." Cummings said, "It *would* take Ford to find an *urinoir* in a bank on Fifth Avenue and have the courage to use it without having an account there."

For some years prior to 1920 mechanical-minded boys had amused themselves by constructing homemade wireless receiving and transmission sets from various parts that were commercially available and by "talking" to one another by using the Morse code. Newspapers had wireless editors who instructed these young mechanics, by diagrams and text, in the developments of wireless telegraphy. It was not until 1920 that the first public broadcast was tentatively tried out and even then it was considered a passing fad. Radio parts were sold by different companies which controlled certain patents, but receiving sets, factory-assembled, were not generally available until 1924 and even then they were so expensive that most of the radios you saw in the homes of friends had been assembled by some bright lad in the neighborhood or by some adult who liked to tinker with such things in his tool shop in basement, attic, or shed on his days off or after dinner in the evenings.

The first radio I ever owned was a homemade one I purchased from a young broker's clerk who wished to sell the one he had in order to buy parts with which to make a more elaborate one, accommodating eight tubes instead of four. That was in the spring of 1924, when I seemed suddenly to go in for ownership of mechanical contrivances, for in that year I presented my wife with our first automobile—a two-door Buick sedan—bought an allegedly noiseless typewriter (which made a heavy, rumbling sound instead of a light clatter) to supplement my still-serviceable Underwood which I had bought secondhand ten years before, a 16-millimeter motion-picture camera and projector, a boy's chest of carpenter's tools, and a camera with a developing outfit.

Of these the automobile gave us the most pleasure, after my wife and I had taken our driving tests (we knew how to drive Model-A Fords because there were two of them on my father's farm, but not how to handle the self-starting modern machines). My wife drove me to the Mamaroneck station every morning and met me every night, though our home was within easy walking distance; we went for long drives every evening and explored the Westchester and Putnam County countrysides on Saturdays and Sundays until the novelty wore off. The radio was of very little use except when we gave parties, because you could get nothing but dance music on it. This was a sort of blessing, because it saved the trouble of changing records on the phonograph, and in those days there were no commercials. By the fall of 1924, however, the radio clamored for recognition with the broadcasting of the rival oratory of the Republican and Democratic politicians. Even those who would never think of attending a political rally listened to the campaign speeches. (It was true, of course,, that one could turn off one's own radio on a summer evening and still hear every speech, because most radios had loudspeakers without volume control and the blare could be heard a block away; one often turned on one's own radio, in fact, in sheer self-defense.) Within a year radio had come entirely into its own, with all the horrors of the Cliquot Club Eskimos, the A. & P. Gypsies, the Happiness Boys, and other singing commercials, but also with all the satisfaction of being able to dance in one's own home to the latest Kern, Tierney, Gershwin, Berlin, and Porter tunes by Ben Bernie's, Paul Whiteman's, and Vincent Lopez's orchestras.

In my rounds of the dance-and-supper clubs for material for my syndicated column, I had first heard a young man with a narrow face, close-set eyes, and auburn hair sing caressingly behind the measure of the music as played by the orchestra, into the microphone of an elegant and intimate night club. He was Rudy Vallee, who was to become the darling of millions of women throughout the country, by the magic of radio.

George Gershwin, the composer whose fame and millions were made by a happy combination of genius, the orchestral ingenuity of Ferde Grofé, and well-managed publicity, is as definitely identified with the twenties as the speakeasy, the flapper, the stock market boom and crash, and "the new freedom." Indeed, although as late as 1935 he wrote the closest approach to an American opera in *Porgy and Bess* that we had had up until his death in 1938 of a brain tumor, his most individual composition, "The Rhapsody in Blue," is definitely allied to the mood of the year he wrote it, 1923.

By 1922 the country had recovered somewhat from the postwar depression and the mood of despondency had been dissipated by an upsurge of carefree gaiety; cynicism was still in the air but it was a tolerant cynicism. Then, in 1924, there was a business recession; things were looking dark again; the aftereffects of the economic and spiritual calamity in Europe had not worn off. The mood of 1924 was that of romantic melancholy. "The Rhapsody in Blue" expressed that mood as definitely in native American idiom as did T. S. Eliot's *Waste Land* in poetry. Like that poem, it mixed classico-heroic themes with barrel-house wails of sorrow with a brooding overtone of lost loveliness.

I was in the last row of the top balcony of Carnegie Hall on the epochal night when Gershwin played the piano score of his masterpiece with full orchestra under Paul Whiteman's baton, and it was the ideal location from which to see and hear that tremendously thrilling event. It was the occasion on which the peculiar American musical idiom known as "jazz" was accorded its rightful place in the history of the development of music. The program gave the history of the development of jazz, with examples from the earliest low dance-hall form using piano, banjo, and snare drums, through the introduction of the saxophone, clarinet, and trumpet, to "The Rhapsody in Blue."

Parties are the normal part of social life of any community at any time; but during the Prohibition era they seemed to be more elaborate and more frequent than I have known them before or since. They were not a phenomenon of New York; I heard about fantastic ones in London, Chicago, and Hollywood and about some that were very bizarre and alcoholic in towns such as Tulsa, Detroit, Reno, and elsewhere. Like the ancient illusion that the grass grows greener in other fields than in one's own, it seemed, during the twenties that all the better parties were elsewhere. I was always hearing about parties given by Carl Van Vechten in the Savoy in London (in which, it was said, Van Vechten took several floors of the hotel, stocked them with liquors and vintage wines, and held open house for days and nights), by Vincent Bendix in Chicago (at which hordes of people were invited and entertained for days), and about orgies in Hollywood. All of these, on report, appeared to be more interesting than the parties I attended in New York, but they were probably pretty tame too.

The most notorious party of the twenties took place after midnight of February 23, 1926, in the Earl Carroll Theatre. It landed the host in the federal penitentiary in Atlanta. And it was a newspaper sensation for months. No party since the "Girl-in-the-Pie" supper given by the millionaire Henry W. Poor in the mid-nineties created so much scandal; and yet, if James Huneker's description of the Poor party in *Painted Veils* is to be relied upon, the party at the Earl Carroll Theatre was like a small-town church social in comparison, and so I have always suspected that the Poor shenanigans were exaggerated. I attended the Earl Carroll party and found it inordinately dull, decorous, and tawdry. I have seen much wickeder stags held for the benefit of the volunteer firemen's associations in small towns.

In a letter I have from Huneker, dated January 4, 1921, he says that "the bacchanalian episode" he describes in *Painted Veils* "is an exact transcription of the famous dinner given by the late Henry W. Poor for the sculptor Augustus Saint-Gaudens at the studio of an amateur photographer, James Laurence Breise, on Sixteenth Street, near Fifth Avenue. The affair made an enormous scandal, and the yellow journals had their usual carnival of mud-slinging. Names were duly printed and the little girl of the pie became a marked character."

The Poor episode, as Huneker describes it, involved not merely a tableau of nearly nude women who served the formally attired male guests with champagne and canapés after their posings were concluded, nor the *pièce de résistance* at the supper table in which a very young and beautiful girl, entirely nude, arose from an enormous pie and danced on the table, but a dance in which the guests and the nude entertainers participated in a manner that seemed to shock the professedly blasé Huneker, as he narrates it.

The "girl-in-the-champagne-bath" party was given by Earl Carroll for a Texas oil millionaire, W. R. Edrington, who had backed a number of Earl Carroll *Vanities* (imitations of the Ziegfeld *Follies*) and had built the theater for Carroll. The audience was mixed; about a third of the guests were women, among whom was Countess Vera Cathcart. The countess was very much in the newspapers at the moment, because she had been detained on Ellis Island by the immigration officials on the quaint and ambiguous charge of "moral turpitude" (it seems she had made a trip with the Earl of Craven without a chaperon). Carroll had taken advantage of the publicity, on her release, and had announced that he was starring her in a musical. I recognized none of the other women except Dorothy Knapp, whose pictures were often in the papers at the time.

The reception was on the stage, where there were two bars, one for beer on tap and served in seidels, the other for hard liquor, cocktails, and wines. A table in between was attended by carvers who sliced hams, chickens, bologna, and cheeses for sandwiches. Members of the cast of the current *Vanities,* including the stately showgirls, mingled with the guests and made themselves available for the dances, for which a full orchestra supplied the music.

After the reception on the stage, the guests, about five hundred of them, were asked to take seats in the orchestra for the show. I sat with Philip Payne, then the managing editor of the *Mirror.* I recognized a great many newspapermen, including drama critics, columnists, editors, and desk men as well as reporters, but I recognized only two of the other male guests, Irvin S. Cobb and Harry K. Thaw. The show began with some vaudeville skits, brief and ordinary. The most audacious of the acts of the evening was not the bath incident; it was a Charleston contest in which various members of the chorus participated for cash prizes and consolation prizes of lingerie. The award was made on the strength and duration of the applause from the audience. The first prize of $100 was won by a very pretty young girl, very fresh and innocent-looking, dressed in the ordinary street clothes of flappers of the period, in contrast with the other contestants, who wore abbreviated chorus costumes. The winner, however, wore black silk stockings and girdle with garter straps. But she had omitted to put on panties. Carroll put a damper on the spirits of the clappers and made them look very much disturbed by saying he was glad "that little girl got the prize, because she is going on the operating table at ten o'clock in the morning for the removal of a cancer in her breast. She needs the money."

Carroll then announced that a beautiful girl would take a bath in champagne on the stage and that those who wished to drink from the bathtub should line up to the right of the theater; cups would be given them and the champagne would be drawn from a faucet in the tub's outlet until it was gone. Two attendants then erected a screen in the center of the stage while a bathtub on a mobile trestle was rolled from the wings behind it. A tall, dark girl, wrapped in a huge bathrobe, came out, acknowledged the applause, stepped behind the curtain and, from the neck up, could be seen getting into the tub. Then the screen was removed. A line began to form at the right as one chap walked up from the first position, dipped his cup into the tub, and walked off-stage very awkwardly and in obvious embarrassment, not having glanced in the direction of the bather.

Then the girl's head slumped as though she had collapsed. There was immediate confusion on the stage as Carroll and others rushed to the tub and lifted the girl out, meanwhile covering her with towels and robes. The line withdrew and the audience sat mystified, not knowing whether this was all part of the act or not. Then Carroll came forth and announced that the girl had fainted but had revived. He said her act was to conclude the show and that he was sorry but the party was over. He thanked all for coming.

Entrance to the theater had been through the stage door in an alley; the front entrance was barred and darkened. Phil Payne on our way out stopped to inquire about the girl. Carroll said she was a little hysterical but would be all right; she had suffered from the chill of immersion. (Incidentally, I was told the liquid was ginger ale in champagne bottles.) Then, whether Payne's next words were spoken on impulse, in which he forgot that all newspapermen had pledged themselves not to print a word about the party, or whether he shrewdly took advantage of Carroll's confusion of mind, I don't know, but this dialogue ensued:

"This would make a whale of a story for you, Earl. Can I break it?"

"Sure, sure, sure," said Carroll, his head bobbing around to return salutes of his departing guests.

"What's the girl's name?" asked Payne, taking a used envelope and a pencil from his pocket.

"Joyce, Joyce, Joyce—Joyce Kilmer."

Payne was about to write that name down when I said, "For God's sake, Phil, that can't be the girl's name. Joyce Kilmer is the name of the poet who wrote 'Trees' and was killed in the war."

Payne repeated almost my exact words to Carroll, who asked at random, "Anybody know the girl's name?" A chorus girl stepped forward and said, "Her name is Joyce Hawley." She watched Payne write it down. We left.

The next morning the *Mirror* played the story on pages one, two, and in runover columns, with pictures. No other morning paper referred to the party. The afternoon newspapers carried follow-ups and the story was splurged sensationally for weeks. But Payne became something of a pariah among newspapermen, who did not know that Carroll had specifically, in my hearing, granted Payne permission to print the story. Payne was deemed to have violated one of the sacred unwritten rules of the profession, of never breaking a story when under pledge not to do so. Payne, a simple, sensitive, sentimental, and very ingenuous soul, in spite of his job as managing editor of a sensational tabloid newspaper (it was said of him that the reason he was so successful as a tabloid editor was that he believed everything he printed), was depressed by the outcome, and it was possibly for this reason that he decided, at the last moment, to board as a passenger the *Mirror's* airplane which was going to try to break the time record for a transatlantic flight. The plane was lost somewhere in the ocean without trace.

As a result of the scandalous publicity about the party, Prohibition enforcement agents were obliged to act. Carroll was arrested on a charge of possessing and dispensing alcoholic beverages at the party. He denied the charges, against the advice of his counsel, so I was informed. Witnesses were called and the fact was overwhelmingly established that liquor was dispensed that night at the theater. Forgotten was Joyce Hawley, forgotten too was the original charge of violating the Volstead Act. Carroll was indicted and found guilty of perjury. He was sentenced to the federal penitentiary in Atlanta for a year, of which he served less than three months, in very comfortable quarters, where he was allowed to entertain visitors.

The most celebrated party giver of the twenties was Robert Winthrop ("Bob") Chandler, a descendant of Peter Stuyvesant and a member of the Astor clan, who was an eccentric but very talented painter. He became nationally known in 1910 as a result of a famous telegram sent him by his brother, John Armstrong Chaloner (the brothers spelled their last names differently), who inquired, "Who's loony now?" on hearing of Bob's marriage to Lina Cavalieri, a then-famous Metropolitan Opera star, upon whom Bob had made a prenuptial settlement of $150,000. The point was that John had been committed to an insane asylum by his family and had escaped; he was then in hiding somewhere in Virginia. Bob's was a loony act, as it turned out, because La Cavalieri left him on the day after their marriage, $150,000 richer, never to return. Sheltered as a lad, as the sons of the rich often are, Bob was allowed to make the "grand tour" of Europe when he reached his majority and in Italy he decided to become a painter. This was an act of apostasy from the traditions of an Astor and a social cleavage between Bob and his family developed. But he did become a painter whose panels representing peacocks and cranes in gorgeous greens and reds were highly praised by European and American art critics. Rich, jovial, fun-loving, bohemian, he was known to everyone in the art world of two continents. He was a Viking of a man, with a wrestler's body and a head like that of a bull, the crown covered with crinkly hair the texture of steel shavings. He had an impediment in his speech, which limited his vocal communications to a few words which he bellowed.

His studio was a converted four-story house at 147-49 East Nineteenth Street. On entering the place one found oneself in a bare room, the walls of which were covered with paintings of weird animals. On party nights this was the dance floor, at which a Negro jazz orchestra supplied the music and Japanese servants served punch, usually strongly spiked with applejack. The second floor was reached by a narrow staircase, at the head of which was a large room, with window seats, cushioned divans, and nooks with tables as in a restaurant. Bob received his guests from a high Renaissance chair placed upon a dais, crying "Papa! Papa!" in greeting to each, whether the guest was a prince of the royal blood, a famous painter, or a penniless poet. At a large dining table bottles of whisky, brandy, gin, and wine were arranged helter-skelter, with ice-cube containers, soda, plain water, ginger ale, and glasses, presided over by his chief butler and major-domo, a wiry little Jap. Off this second-floor main room one was inevitably taken by some friend of Bob's, on one's first visit, to gape at Bob's huge bed, over which was a mirrored ceiling. The walls of this room were covered with futuristic paintings by Bob and his artist friends, many of whom were czarist exiles from Russia who lived largely upon Bob's bounty and slept in the rooms upstairs when they had no homes. On the top floor was Bob's workshop, a vast room with skylights, unfurnished except for easels, huge canvases in their frames, palettes, paintbrushes, and tubes of paint—and a high stool on which Bob sat when he painted. (At any time during a party, even when the party was in honor of the Prince of Wales or the King of Belgium, Bob might leave unobtrusively and go up to his studio and paint until dawn, while the revelry continued below. I found him there, alone, on several occasions.)

Bob's parties were as noisy, colorful, and crowded as Canal Street in New Orleans on the night of Mardi Gras; but they were parties without ringers: everyone who came had to pass muster at the door as one who had received an invitation from Bob or from one of his party organizers—Clemence Randolph, Louise Hellstrom, or Ivan Narody. The parties were conglomerates, with guests in all sorts of costumes, from full evening dress to sweaters and corduroy trousers, from Russian smocks and baggy panta-loons to gypsy garb; one overheard conversations in French, Russian, Italian, Danish, Spanish, and German. Men and women who hated each other often met there, but once inside Bob's door they had to hold their tongues and treat each other with respect. Critical or sarcastic remarks about any one of his guests was something Bob did not allow, and anyone who was guilty of such an offense might find himself suddenly seized by the collar and the seat of the pants, in the jujitsu grip of Bob's Japanese major-domo and propelled down the stairs and into the street. Or Bob himself might bellow to a woman offender, commanding her to leave. Such an occurrence happened rarely, but it had happened a sufficient number of times for any of Bob's regular invitees to warn a new guest against that one breach of decorum which Bob would not permit. Bob himself was a hard worker, devoting days and nights to panels, murals, and stained-glass windows, which decorated public buildings, private homes, and the walls of famous art galleries. His parties were his recreations where he wanted to see others of talent and distinction in the arts drop their problems, relax, lose their inhibitions, and enjoy themselves.

One always saw at Bob's parties certain special cronies—Benjamin de Casseres, Konrad Bercovici, T. R. Smith, Barliuk (the Russian painter, who wore one earring), Helena Rubinstein, Clemence Randolph, Vladimir Dukelski, Miguel and Rose Covarrubias, John Sloan, and (when he was in America) Jo Davidson. Besides, there were always a great number of beautiful women—Russian, French, and American—whose names one never learned, because no one was introduced by Bob or announced on entrance, but who, one understood, were singers, actresses, ballerinas, or wives or mistresses of painters, sculptors, composers, or writers. I was there one night when he gave a party for the Prince of Wales (now the Duke of Windsor), who was greeted with the usual "Papa! Papa!" but was otherwise thrown, with his party, upon his own in the hubbub of music and dancing, so much so that he was still there dancing or drinking at five in the morning when I left. Augustus John, Carl Van Vechten, Gatti-Casazza, John Barrymore, architects, sculptors, painters, newspapermen, novelists, critics, columnists, playwrights, diplomats, noblemen, society folk, anarchists, revolutionists, royalists, Cubists, Expressionists, Dadaists, and academicians (if Bob thought they were interesting enough to be invited or had any appreciation of the arts) comprised the motley. Bob would allow no stuffiness or reserve at his parties. By midnight the scene might be like that of a kermis; and Bob might sneak off to paint for an hour or crawl into his huge bed for a nap. Once, at three o'clock in the morning, while the party was in full swing, he suddenly took a notion that he wanted my wife and me, T. R. Smith, and some young woman whose name I never learned, to go up to a Negro dance hall in Harlem with him. We sneaked out, all piled into one taxi, went there, had one drink, and came back. Bob knew precisely at what time a certain Negro girl sang a song; he wanted to hear it; he heard it; we came back; nearly everybody was gone. Bob ordered breakfast for the eight of us who remained and my wife and I got home at eight in the morning.

Horace Liveright's parties were nearly always impromptu; they would start in the afternoon, usually on Friday, and last until one or two in the morning—at his publishing house in an old residence in the West Forties. People would hear about the party and drop in—Theodore Dreiser, Otto Kahn, Sherwood Anderson, Elinor Wylie, Sinclair Lewis, Paul Morand, Edna Ferber, Herbert Bayard Swope, Beatrice Kaufman, Edgar Lee Masters, Paul Robeson, Ernest Boyd, Maxwell Bodenheim, and actors and actresses, because Liveright dabbled at play producing as well as publishing, made a fortune out of *Dracula*, lost money on *Hamlet* in modern dress, made another fortune out of *The Firebrand*, and lost on some other ventures.

Lee Meader, the architect, had a penthouse on the roof of a skyscraper he had designed in West Thirty-eighth Street in which he gave two or three parties a year which were unusual in that the entertainment of the evening was planned and executed by professionals. His parties were not large; everyone was required to appear in full evening dress, only champagne was served, and the entertainment might be a boxing match between professional fighters, a ballet, or a one-act play, followed by music and dancing.

Condé Nast, the publisher, was famous for his parties, of which he had two kinds—a small one for three hundred guests and a less exclusive one for a thousand or fifteen hundred. I rated among the *hoi polloi* so I was invited only to the large parties. These were dress affairs, and celebrities of the screen and stage, the arts and letters were invited. There was a huge ballroom, at each end of which was an orchestra; while one orchestra rested, the other played, so the music was continuous. Champagne only was served. These parties were decorative, decorous, and charming.

But all these parties pale into insignificance beside the wildest of them all—the stock market orgy of the twenties, in which I, as so many others, became involved.

CHAPTER 9

Boom and Bust

UNWILLINGLY I BECOME A STOCK MARKET GAM-
BLER. EVERYBODY'S DOING IT. THE BOOM, MR.
COCHRANE, AND MR. NICHOLES. BLACK WEDNES-
DAY. THE END OF AN ERA.

One Sunday afternoon, late in the summer of 1925, when my
wife and I were week-end guests at Collinswood, the country
estate of Herbert Collins near New Canaan, Connecticut, Mr.
Collins drew me aside after dinner and asked me if I would drive
over to the country club with him. He said that, as an officer of
the club, he was responsible for some construction work going on
there. His invitation was unusual for him, because he was somewhat in awe of his son Seward (inexplicably so, it seemed to me),
and he looked upon us as Seward's guests rather than his own
and was shy and deferential toward the swarm of writers and
their wives and unattached actors and actresses who overflowed
Seward's own house on the estate and cluttered up the big house
on summer week ends.

I considered Mr. Collins by far the most interesting person
present at those house parties and I seized every opportunity to
hear what he had to say. I never heard Mr. Collins express an
opinion or make an observation that was not cogent, free from
the usual clichés, and somewhat heterodox, and always illuminating. Whatever he had to say had more depth to it, in my opinion,
than all the stage and literary chitchat and shoptalk that were
the conversational stock in trade of us who gathered at Collinswood on week ends.

Mr. Collins was about five feet eight inches in height (both of his sons were considerably taller than he was), weight about one hundred and sixty pounds; he had a full head of fair hair only slightly streaked with gray at fifty; he reminded me of a blond John Drew without a mustache and might easily have been mistaken for a distinguished star of the stage; his voice was gentle and resonant and his countenance was always (when I saw him) alert and friendly. He was quiet-spoken, never assertive or dogmatic; he kept in the background of his business partners and associates. He was courteously deferential to his bankers, his brokers, his lawyers, his employees, his wife and sons, his acquaintances and servants. His gentility was innate: his reserve was not from any lack of self-confidence, for, when called upon to express an opinion, he was extraordinarily frank and straightforward, saying exactly what he thought even if it were in thorough disagreement with what had just been said. It was a pleasure to watch him in action, because he was perfectly relaxed at all times and his co-ordination was perhaps the most remarkable I have ever seen. He reminded me of Hoppe when he was playing billiards; he reminded me of Bobby Jones when he played golf; he was so relaxed and yet so surely expert in everything he did.

I learned from Mr. Collins the history of the United Cigar Stores, which were conceived by him; and I did this only by pumping him, for Mr. Collins was loath to talk about his affairs. Once I went with him to his office in the United Cigar Stores building in West Eighteenth Street, and his complete lack of ostentation was evident here also.

Mr. Collins was a multimillionaire; he was vice-president and cofounder of the United Cigar Stores chain; an officer and stockholder in Tobacco Products, a holding corporation for the United Cigar Stores, General Cigars, Loft Candy Stores, Whelan Drug Stores, the Happiness Candy Co., Barking Dog Cigarettes, a restaurant chain, and vast amounts of real estate; he carried an investment and speculative account with brokers amounting to about $20,000,000; he had homes in Connecticut, on Park Avenue, in Pasadena, and permanent apartments in various capitals of Europe; he was a director member of numerous clubs; he selected the sites and negotiated the leases for the thousands of United Cigar Stores throughout the country; he regularly inspected individual stores to check on their stock, management, and earnings.

And yet his office consisted of only a plain flat-top desk, five feet wide by three feet long, with an ordinary office chair, placed in a large room which was entirely filled with other desks just like it and occupied by bill clerks, file clerks, and accountants! There wasn't a pencil or a piece of paper on top of his desk, let alone a desk set. He had no secretary; if he wished to dictate a letter, which was seldom, he could call upon one of George Whelan's secretaries. He had only one phone on his desk.

This amazing man carried the minute details of the tremendous ramifications of his estate and enterprise in his head! When he died suddenly, as a result of a stroke suffered while playing nineteen holes of golf on a hot day, it took a corps of Federal Treasury accountants three years to figure out his taxes, because in that desk there were only a few scraps of paper in the way of memoranda and he kept no files. He had checkbooks but the stubs were blank; he had bankbooks and safety-deposit vaults filled with leases, bonds, deeds, insurance policies, annuity agreements, and a will. But of receipts, canceled checks, and other records they could find few: he apparently registered in his mind the amount and date of every payment large and small and never bothered with a receipt, a check stub, or a canceled check. He might buy and sell one million dollars' worth of securities by phone in the course of a day, register it in his memory in detail, and when he got a monthly report of his transactions from a broker, he would apparently glance through it and throw it away. His trust in his bankers, brokers and business associates was unbounded; and I should have imagined that he might have paid many a bill twice if I had not known that he not only promptly paid every bill presented him but, if it were a monthly account, knew exactly what he had paid each month previously for many months back.

How I learned this was when he asked me, when we were having lunch alone one day in a newly opened restaurant owned by one of his companies, what he should do about Seward's book-purchasing mania. He had just paid a bill of $754 to one bookseller, representing one month's purchase by Seward. This had represented, he said, a jump of $400 above the usual bill; and, said Mr. Collins, "He already has more than 20,000 books and subscribes to hundreds of newspapers and magazines from all over the world. He can't possibly read a fraction of what he already has." I said, "Seward has an income of $35,000 a year from an annuity you established for him. He is unmarried. Let him pay his own book bills."

Mr. Collins's career was simply amazing. He was married and the father of one son and working as a shipping clerk in George A. Whelan's wholesale cigar factory in Syracuse. Cigar makers worked in the front of the store and young Collins worked in the back. The store was on a corner past which hundreds of workmen employed in shirt and collar factories had to go twice every day. When the cigarmakers were out to lunch or when Whelan was away, young Collins frequently had to respond to the ring of a bell which sounded when the door was opened. Almost invariably it was some workman who had seen the word "cigars" on the sign out front and had not known what "wholesale" meant, and so had come in to buy some cigars or tobacco.

Young Herbert persuaded Whelan to allow him to set up a counter in the front of the store and lay in a stock of cigars, pipe and cigarette tobacco, chewing tobacco, and snuff to accommodate these workmen. He said it would not interfere with his packing and shipping duties any more than did the necessity of answering the bell and turning prospective customers away. The retail counter was a success, and young Herbert decided that the reason for this was that the store was on a favorable corner for such trade.

He began to make a private survey of locations in town where the greatest number of men passed by during a day. Then he figured that if he could rent holes in the wall, under short-term leases, at or near these locations, he could successfully operate a number of such tobacco stores on a small amount of capital. Whelan advanced the money for an experiment, and when it proved successful, he allocated the profits to a fund for establishing more such stores.

When a half dozen of them were showing a net profit each month, young Collins approached Whelan with the idea of letting him try the experiment in New York. Whelan was receptive but kept putting it off. Moreover, he had never raised Collins's salary or given him a share in the profits in the retail stores. The owner of the tobacco concessions in several hotels in Buffalo who bought cigars from Whelan offered Herbert twenty-five dollars a week to move to Buffalo and manage his stores. Herbert, despairing of Whelan's dilatoriness, was about to accept the offer when Whelan visited Mrs. Collins one afternoon and told her not to let Herbert take the Buffalo job, stating that he would go to New York and try to raise the money to finance Herbert's scheme. Herbert stayed on at eighteen dollars a week.

Whelan at length went to New York and tried to interest Bernard Baruch, Thomas F. Ryan, and James B. Duke in Herbert's scheme, but none of these financiers could see any money in it. Finally, Henry Weill, a broker who had backed Thomas W. Lawson in some of Lawson's financial plunges, agreed to put up $5,000 if Whelan would put up an equal amount. With $10,000 capital, Herbert surveyed the New York scene for several weeks and finally negotiated for a short-term lease on a tiny store in Nassau Street near the Brooklyn Bridge. He had the front painted red to attract attention. This later became the identifying color of the United Cigar Stores. The gross receipts were under ten dollars a day, but Herbert leased eight other holes in the wall on Third Avenue and thus was born the retail tobacco chain which expanded and made millions.

"All success is a matter of luck," Mr. Collins told me one day. "If that Buffalo retail cigar dealer hadn't offered me a job at a raise over what Whelan was paying me, Whelan probably would never have taken any active interest in my chain-store plan for New York. If I had taken the Buffalo job, I might still be running those hotel stands at fifty or seventy-five a week. George couldn't have founded United Cigars alone and neither could I. In a business like that it takes the partnership of two different kinds of men, an idea man and a man who can raise money. The latter has to sell the former to the financiers. If George had gone to New York investors and told them *he* had a great idea he wanted them to invest in, he wouldn't have been able to raise a cent: the money-raiser doesn't sell himself or his idea; he says, "I've got a man who has a great idea." We needed each other, because, although I know something about retailing merchandise, I have no talent for promotion. George has no talent for organization and raising money. He is always promoting something, and once he gets his organization financed and operating successfully, he is no longer interested in it, except for stock-juggling purposes. He has wrecked several concerns, which he organized, through stock-market manipulations; he had made and lost fortunes and made them again, because gambling in stocks is a game he gets a great kick out of."

Mr. Collins also told me, with wry amusement, about the peculiar ethics of managers of gambling syndicates in Wall Street. He said that frequently a market operator would get a number of rich men to come in with him in a combine to push a stock up. He would be in charge of the operations. He would use the money the others put up to push a stock up ten or fifteen points and then "pull the stopper," that is, go heavily short of the stock, forcing a twenty- or thirty-point drop, wiping out the investment of his partners, and cleaning up a huge profit for himself.

I asked Mr. Collins what happened when men found out that a syndicate partner had double-crossed them like that. He said, "They just shrug their shoulders or laugh. They consider it all in the game. They don't even stop speaking to such a fellow, as you and I would. In fact, he could come along right after he had rooked them and they would go in with him on another bull or bear operation he proposed and let him manage it, knowing full well that he might rook them again but figuring that he would give them a break the second time and win back for them what they had lost or more. They consider him a smart operator. And, moreover, they would do the same if they had the chance. For myself I never join in a pool. I work alone."

Much of what Mr. Collins told me about behind-the-scenes market operators, back in that summer of 1925, I have forgotten simply because I had no basis of reference whereby I could understand the procedures. I knew no more about stocks and bonds and the securities exchanges than a Presbyterian minister would know the operations of a bootleg syndicate. I thought of Wall Street as a sort of malign Monte Carlo, the more sinister in that stock manipulations there sometimes affected the economy of the whole country, bringing poverty, ruin, and unemployment to millions who did not know a stock from a bond, whereas the only losers at Monte Carlo were the players themselves. In this I shared the general misconceptions of my fellow writers who were to write about the stock market debacle years later; most of them had a Sunday-supplement writer's superficial grasp of the subject; they knew nothing about the fundamental importance of a free securities market, where one's assets may be daily, even hourly, determined, in the functioning of a capitalist society. There were even economists in the New Deal and among popular writers on the subject who wanted to put a ban on short selling on the ground that it is immoral and detrimental to the public welfare.

They did achieve measures of restriction on short selling. It was as if they argued that, if you had a dozen pencils and were offering them for a dime apiece and I knew where I could get a dozen of the same pencils on credit for three cents apiece, it was immoral for me to undercut you five cents a pencil and make a profit of two cents each, instead of a profit of seven cents each. Or, in gambling terms, it was as if the rule was that you could not play the red, you had to play the black. Short selling is a check on runaway inflation.

That Sunday afternoon when Mr. Collins asked me to accompany him to the country club I was pretty sure he was going to say something to me about my investing in the stock market. Seward had told me that his father had made some tidy sums for his poor relations and for servants in his employ. They had turned over certain sums to him out of their savings and he had put them into his general brokerage account. Then he would buy stock and sell stock in their names in the limit of their pro-rata share of their investment in the total account and in the limit of their individual capacity to purchase stock on margin to the extent of the amount of money they had subscribed.

Seward had said that his father had expressed a desire to make some money for me in the same way but did not know how to approach me on the subject. I had told Seward, in turn, that I did not know how to approach his father in the matter either, for it seemed to me that it was very like holding out a tin cup and asking Mr. Collins to drop some coins into it. I would be asking Mr. Collins to take a risk in my behalf which I would not myself assume and in which I knew he would not permit me to lose, even if he guessed wrong.

We drove for some time before Mr. Collins said anything and I was getting a little nervous about what I should say if he broached me in the matter of gambling in stocks. Then, to my surprise, he sounded me out on quite a different matter. He said that he was eager to see Seward established in some sort of work he liked and that the idea which seemed to please him most was that of owning a newspaper with me as the editor of it. This was startling, for Seward had never mentioned such a thing to me. He said that both he and Seward had great faith in my editorial judgment and journalistic abilities. He asked me what I thought of the idea.

Up to that moment the notion of editing a newspaper had never entered my head—except the vague one that nearly every young newspaperman entertains of someday editing and owning a small-town daily or country weekly, like William Allen White or Ed Howe, and thereby gaining country-wide influence by writing what he pleases. On the first impact of the idea, however, I did not doubt my ability to edit even the New York *Times* successfully. Yet I knew how much newspapers cost. The New York *Tribune* had recently paid Frank Munsey $5,000,000 for the *Herald,* which had been losing money steadily (as had the *Tribune,* until after its merger with the *Herald*), and I was staggered at the enormity of the financial aspect of the suggestion.

I said I thought the idea was attractive, naturally, but what kind of newspaper did Seward want—a New York newspaper or one in a smaller town; and did he want to start from scratch or buy an old property? He said Seward had heard that the *Morning Telegraph* was for sale and could be bought for about $1,000,000. That newspaper was (and is) devoted almost exclusively to horse racing and other sports. It was Seward's idea, Mr. Collins said, for me to turn it into a newspaper of general appeal, but on a high level of editing and writing competence, while retaining and expanding its sports and entertainment features, and to reduce its price from a quarter to a nickel.

I remindid him that the New York *Post* was costing Thomas W. Lamont $200,000 a year, that the *Tribune* was facing a large annual deficit, and the morning *World* was not prospering even under the dynamic guidance of Herbert Bayard Swope and his brilliant assemblage of trained seals. I told him that, in addition to the $1,000,000 he would have to be prepared to lose perhaps as much as $300,000 a year for three years, by changing the character of the paper, before it turned the corner and began to make money. I said I was confident I could turn the trick within three years and that, after that, it might make money hand over fist. I told him that, on the whole, experience had shown that it was less expensive to start a new newspaper or a new magazine than to revive one that was financially on the skids; that the New York *Times,* after Adolph S. Ochs took it over, and *Collier's* were notable exceptions; but that the advantage of buying up an old property lay in having a press, plant, paper supply, and basic staff already at hand.

He said that was all he wanted to know and that he would have his business agents start negotiations for the property at once and have his lawyers draw up articles of incorporation with Seward and myself as partners and with me as editor. (Later it developed that, although the widow of the founder of the *Telegraph* wanted to sell the paper, she could not do so, under the will of her husband, except under conditions of stringency which did not prevail. The deal collapsed. Mr. Collins asked me to look around for some other property, newspaper or magazine. I was offered the *Century* by ex-Attorney General George W. Wickersham, as agent for the owner, for $60,000; but when I asked for an inventory of assets, I found it consisted of subscription stencils most of which had long ago expired. I had asked Mr. Wickersham what the $60,000 was for and he had answered, "The good will of the *Century* name," to which I replied that while the name had once been a great asset, it was now a definite liability.)

By this time we had arrived at the club and Mr. Collins took me around the grounds and told me how it had been running at such a heavy deficit that the members had been kicking about assessments until he took over the management, improved the cuisine, and made it generally more attractive to members as well as less wasteful of upkeep and so had made it pay its own way and build up a reserve besides. He explained how he had done this, in a simple, matter-of-fact way, without boasting and with amused citations of the way in which big businessmen and financiers—directors of the club—had run the club in such a wasteful and unbusinesslike manner as to make one wonder how they had ever succeeded in anything else.

After we had got back into the car and had driven in silence for several miles, Mr. Collins said in a soft-voiced, casual tone, "I should like to make some money for you, if you will let me." I said nothing, because I had been expecting this, and he continued, "I do a little trading in the stock market and I have made some money for some of the old people among Mrs. Collins's relatives, our servants, and some friends of mine, enough for them to put by tidy sums at interest against retirement or a rainy day. If you can spare $2,000 I'll purchase some good stocks for you and hold them for the rise. You take a risk, of course, but I don't think you need to worry. I never invest in a security without first having a thorough investigation made of the company's assets, management, and future possibilities in the way of earnings."

I thanked him and said I thought I could raise the money but I would have to consult my wife before deciding. I could have spared the cash. I had put away $2,000 in gold in a safety-deposit vault against any emergency that might arise, through a bank's failure or any other calamity. (Ironically enough, I had to turn over this gold to the government at fifty-two and six tenths cents on the dollar by presidential fiat in the spring of 1933, right when I needed it most; for the bank in which my wife and I both had considerable savings accounts as well as comfortable checking-account balances had previously failed and the president of the bank had shot himself. In the liquidation, which took three years, we had received only ten cents on the dollar the first year and fifteen cents on the dollar two years later.) And I had a fair

253

balance in my checking account as well as a savings account to which I added when my checking balance exceeded $1,000. But I had been in too many worrisome states over money in my life to risk, in any sort of gamble, any part of what I had been able to accumulate.

In fact, I had a thoroughly bourgeois attitude toward financial risks of any kind. I had not realized, as I do now, that all life is a gamble; that one gambles on a successful marriage when he takes unto himself a wife; that young men gamble years of their lives on making a go of it as a lawyer, doctor, or member of any other profession when they devote those years to preparation for a career; that a young novelist, who takes two years (or ten years, as Margaret Mitchell did in the case of *Gone with the Wind*) in writing a novel, gambles his time and potential earning power in other endeavors against the chances of winning stakes which justify his gamble; and that America's vast industrial expansion and the rising standards of our living are the result of speculative risk.

But, as I have said above, I thought of investment or speculation in corporate securities as something akin to playing roulette with more than roulette's odds against you. So I made a curious compromise with my principles. I wouldn't risk any part of my savings from my income as a writer of a daily syndicated column or as a regular monthly contributor to two magazines. But I would write extra magazine articles, as a free lance, and if I sold them I would consider the money so much velvet and apply it to the amount I would turn over to Mr. Collins. If I lost it, that would be that.

As a result of this strange process of reasoning, I went furiously to work on this extra writing and within four weeks I had accumulated $2,000 in checks from magazine editors. I sent a check for this amount to Mr. Collins. Mr. Collins, as I have mentioned before, almost never wrote letters or kept memoranda of any kind. I didn't hear a word from him by letter or phone.

254

Then, on the third of the month, three weeks later, I received through the mails a document from a brokerage house that threw me into almost a paralyzing tizzy of anxiety. It was an oblong piece of foolscap, seventeen inches wide by five inches deep, with double-entry rulings in red, at the top of which was printed the name of the firm and this announcement: "This is a statement of your account as it appears on our ledger. Please examine and advise us of any errors or omissions." There was some writing in various columns, with figures of amount, days, and interest. It appeared that I had bought and sold some Tobacco Products and some General Cigars and had bought some Montgomery Ward. But at the bottom of the sheet were these ominous and terrifying words, "Balance on Mont. Ward...$5,712.05." And it was on the debit side of the sheet!

All I could figure out from this document was that I owed the brokerage house $5,712.05 and that this was a dun for the amount. I couldn't spare that out of my checking and savings accounts put together. I tried vainly to reach Mr. Collins at his office and at his home. I considered this a matter between Mr. Collins and myself, so I refrained from phoning Seward. I was too frightened to call the brokers for fear they might say something I didn't wish to hear. I was in a blue funk for hours and scared to mention the catastrophe to my wife. Desperately I phoned Mr. Collins's office, saying that I had a very urgent business matter to discuss with him. I was told he was on his way to Florida and would be at the Royal Poinciana Hotel in Palm Beach at eight o'clock that evening. At precisely eight o'clock I put in a long-distance call and got Mr. Collins on the phone. In as calm a voice as I could muster I told him I had received a bill from a broker for $5,712.05 and that there must be some mistake, because I had meant to invest only the $2,000 I had turned over to him. Mr. Collins laughed and told me to forget about it. He said I didn't owe anybody anything; that I had bought 200 shares of Montgomery Ward stock at thirty-seven dollars a share, making $7,400 in all, and that the stock had gone up five points since I bought it, and it was now worth, according to the closing quotation for the day, a little over $8,000. He said not to pay any attention to the broker's statement; that he would attend to everything.

I was comforted but confused. My stock was worth $8,000 and I had paid only $7,400 for it; that left me with a $600 gain, but it was still apparent that I owed nearly $6,000. . . . From that day on, for nearly two years, those statements came every month and I never opened one of them. I hid them from my sight. Nor thereafter did I ever mention the stock market to Mr. Collins, even though during that time I lunched and dined with him many times. Once, while we were walking up Fifth Avenue, he said: "I can't for the life of me understand what is going on behind the scenes in Tobacco Products unless George Whelan or somebody is up to some monkey business. By all logic the stock should be going up instead of down, and it has been dropping steadily. I pulled out of it sometime ago because I didn't like the looks of its action on the tape; but if figures mean anything, it is 'way underpriced."

I didn't know what he was talking about, so I said nothing. I didn't know then that Tobacco Products was a holding company for United Cigars and other companies, and that insiders had rigged the stock until they finally got it into such a mess that Kuhn, Loeb & Co. took it over, reorganized it, and found, too late, that they had been badly stung. Otto Kahn, head of Kuhn, Loeb & Co., being personally so badly stung by the stock that, after the crash, he threw his $6,000,000 castle and estate on Long Island on the market; offering price, $800,000.

In September 1927 Mr. Collins suffered a stroke while playing golf and died shortly thereafter. I received a letter from his broker, enclosing a card. The letter said, "We are herewith enclosing a card which is signed by all our customers carrying margin accounts. When you return this card will you kindly state that you waive any guarantee of your account by the Estate of Mr. H. S. Collins."

Inasmuch as I had been afraid to look at the monthly statements from the broker, I hadn't the slightest idea how the account in my name stood. I was now obliged to assume the responsibility of it. I resolved to visit the brokerage house and learn what was what. I had never been in a broker's office before, so I took my last statement (unopened) out of its hiding place and the letter from the broker, as means of identification, and went to the address on the letter.

There was no receptionist to stop me, so I walked right into what looked like a prayer meeting, with the faithful sitting in chairs and waiting for the services to begin. There was little activity, except on the part of what seemed to be ushers. Along a window-lighted wall some men at desks were answering telephones.

I approached one of the men who looked like an usher and said I would like to see Mr. Blank. I used the name of the firm. It turned out that, although this gentleman had founded the firm, he had been dead for forty years. The man said there was nobody by that name connected with the company. He looked at me as though I were a particularly benighted salesman trying to sell him a left-handed butter churn. I produced the envelope containing my statement and the letter from the firm. He looked them over and his whole manner changed.

He led me to the desk of what turned out to be the senior partner and introduced me. That gentleman, in turn, introduced me to my guide. He looked over my credentials and we began to reminisce about Mr. Collins. Then I said, "I understand I have a little account here which you wish me to take over. I know nothing about these things, so instead of continuing the account I should like to close it. Will you please let me know just how I stand?"

He glanced again at the statement, smiled, and said, "I should say you have got quite a little account with us! Your Montgomery Ward opened at ninety-three today. On that and your other stocks you have a profit of over $14,000 on a $2,000 investment. Not bad!"

"You mean, sir," I asked, "that if I closed my account now I could get $14,000 in cash?" That seemed an awful lot of money to me and I was ready to grab it.

"Yes," he said. "You can write out an order for the sale of all your holdings right now, and we'd have a report for you within a few minutes on how much you got for them. Within half an hour or less we could give you a check for the full amount due you. But I wouldn't advise you to sell now. All stocks are acting very strong. See there! Your Montgomery Ward has gone up two points while you have been sitting here."

He pointed to the Translux. The price changes and the volume on each sale—with the stock exchange code number of each stock—were flitting across a narrow strip of frosted-glass screen. It was the same as the tape strips on the several stock tickers in the office but projected, by an electrical device, so that the customers of the brokerage house, who were sitting in rows watching this thing as solemnly as though they were in church, could tell whether they were losing or winning without moving out of their seats. I didn't know the meaning of the symbols of the stocks, much less the rows of figures after an active stock, which ran something like this: "X 97⅝, 99, 98¼, ½, 99, ⅛, ¼, ½, ¾, ⅝." It conveyed nothing whatever to me.

"Just what does 'up two points' mean, sir?" I asked.

"You have 200 shares of Montgomery Ward. It has gone up two dollars a share while you have been sitting here. It means that you are $400 richer than when you came in."

I was getting dizzy. To me this made no sense. I, who had worked hard all my life for a living, had, according to this pleasant old party with a benign face who was instructing me, made $400, without doing a stroke of work, in about five minutes. It was more cash money than a small farmer in Oklahoma saw in a year; I had known times when $400 would have seemed like a fabulous sum if I were the possessor of it.

"No, I wouldn't get out of the market now if I were you," he continued. "With Mr. Collins, we went very thoroughly into the affairs of Montgomery Ward before Mr. Collins invested a cent in it. Our analysis showed that the potential earning power of the company, under its present management and with its program of expansion, justifies a much higher price than it is selling at now."

Incidentally, the conclusion proved to be right: the original shares that Mr. Collins bought were selling at more than $1,000 a share even at the lowest point in the depression, because the stock was split four for one after it had gone above 400 and stockholders had been permitted to buy extra shares at a price far under the market. Even as I write, the stock which he had bought for me at thirty-seven dollars a share would now be worth, including the accumulated dividends, nearly $2,000 a share, if I had held on to them and had not done anything about them except cash my dividend checks. Those who bought the stock on margin when it was selling around 400 in the hope of quick profit and who were sold out in the crash because they could not raise additional margins, lost money, but nobody who paid even as much as $400 a share for the stock and held on to it has lost anything. Instead, such investors have drawn more in dividends in eighteen years than they originally paid for the stock, and they still have the stock, which is readily liquidable at considerably more than they paid for it.

This explains how corporate ownership tends to contract and individual wealth tends to expand after a panic and recession of security prices: these individuals and corporations with large liquid assets dispose of their holdings in common stock when public participation pushes the prices of stocks to a point which discounts earnings for several years in advance. With the cash from their disposal of common stock they buy bonds which bring a higher yield in interest than in the dividend yield, per dollar price, of common stocks. Then when stocks drop to a point where the dividend income is greater than that from an equal investment in bonds, they switch from bonds to stocks in their portfolios. This is conservative investment policy as against speculation.

This point is not understood by many popular historians of the boom and crash of the twenties. They confuse in-and-out speculation on margin with investment in securities, without realizing that a drop from hysterical boom prices in a speculative market is from a price discounting many years of potential income from the stock, not from a logical view of the stock in relation to its annual dividend yield per dollar invested in it. There were an estimated 1,000,000 persons participating in the wild stock-gambling spree of the twenties, of whom nine tenths were greedy ignoramuses eager to get something for nothing. Some big speculators, such as Durant, Whelan, Cutten, Livermore, and Schwab, lost huge fortunes, and many small speculators, who answered the calls for additional margin and threw good money after bad during the early days of the debacle, lost their savings, their homes, even their insurance. But in spite of all the howls of welchers and bad sports, vast numbers of the small speculators lost nothing but "paper profits" and actually came out—if they withdrew cash from their accounts as the market moved on to higher ground—with more money than they put into it.

The people who really lose as a result in a panic that follows the collapse of a speculative orgy are the non-speculative, creative industrialists, whose production is curtailed by lessened demand for their products, the workers, and the general public. Their plight is not the consequence of the machinations of "economic royalists" nor of any unremedial fault of the capitalistic system: it is the consequence of abnormal mass psychology, wherein, say, ninety-nine out of one hundred play the stock market just as they drop quarters into slot machines hoping to hit the jackpot. Panics and depressions, too, are largely psychological (though that doesn't mean they are not real enough, just as a neurotic headache can be just as painful as one caused by indigestible food); and business paralysis, with resulting unemployment, follows the psychological effect of panic or mass hysteria.

The first issue of the *Bookman* (September 1927), which was bought for Seward Collins by his father, under my editorship had sold out on the newsstands, in response to considerable gratuitous publicity, and also because the first issue had pleased readers and commentators so much that the October issue then on the stands, issued on the twenty-fifth of September, had passed the *American Mercury's* peak circulation of 60,000. Subscriptions were pouring in at a very gratifying rate. When we took over the magazine, the subscription list had dropped to a little over 7,000 and newsstand sales had accounted for only about 2,000 more; and yet with our first issue the newsstand sales were over 40,000. (In order to get display and distribution by one of the great magazine-distributing agencies we had had to print twice as many copies as our anticipated sales and the agency had helped us to arrive at the number of copies in our printing order, fully expecting a considerable volume of returns on which we would have to pay cartage and storage charges for three months.)

Thus we were prospering from the first issue. Besides editing and writing for the *Bookman,* I had not yet dropped my syndicate work, which meant writing a daily column appearing in more than four hundred newspapers, or my weekly "Book-of-the-Week" review, syndicated in sixty-four newspapers; I was also writing an article each month for *Arts and Decoration* and the *Detroit Athletic Club News;* and I was editing *Morrow's Almanack for 1928.*

Although I was soon to drop my syndicate work because of the pressure of other interests I was not to become active in the stock market until a year's association with Seward Collins convinced me that we were hopelessly at odds about how the magazine was to be run.

Meanwhile, I had been studying the stock market academically and adding to my holdings but not doing any active trading. I seemed to be almost alone in this among my acquaintances. Everybody I knew, except stockbrokers, were in the stock market as daily traders—store clerks and traveling salesmen, bootblacks and truck drivers, but, above all, artists, cartoonists, novelists, playwrights, editors, musicians, critics, baseball players, actors, and press agents. At every literary "tea" (euphemism for cocktail party) the talk was of stocks, not of literary or intellectual matters; nearly everybody was boasting of killings he had made and exchanging tips on stocks.

Most of these people were carrying on their daily work but were in touch with their brokers several times a day. If they got a "hot tip" in a speakeasy or at an evening party they would call up their broker and ask about the stock. Almost invariably the reply would be, "It looks pretty good." Then the order would go in to buy. Or a novelist would call his broker around noon and ask how the market looked. Sometimes a customer's man would pass on a tip and the customer would put in a buying order. Very often the customer not only knew nothing about the company whose stock he had bought on a margin account but also did not know the real name of the company, many of the active stocks having nicknames, such as "Monkey Ward" for Montgomery Ward, "Big Steel" for United States Steel, "Little Steel" for Bethlehem Steel Corporation, and bawdy names for some of the others. Rube Goldberg, the cartoonist, once told me he bought 300 shares of "Pan Pete" on a broker's recommendation, under the impression that the company made some kind of pans; it was six months before he learned he was a stockholder in Pan-American Petroleum Corporation.

The postwar depression had begun to give way to some hope-

ful signs of recovery toward the end of 1922 and, after Calvin
Coolidge succeeded to the presidency on the death of Harding
on August 3, 1923, there began a slow but definite trend toward
a boom. There were setbacks in business activity during 1924,
1925, and the early half of 1926. But by July 1, 1926, General
Motors had replaced United States Steel as the "market leader"
and within a space of a month shot up from 146½ to 189½.
Then a statement by a Morgan partner started the bull market
on its tumultuous way.

On the evening of Saturday, July 31, Thomas Cochrane, a
partner in the firm of J. P. Morgan & Co., who had brought
about the reorganization of General Motors Corporation after
W. C. Durant had lost control of the company, sailed for Europe.
According to Cochrane (see *They Told Barron; The Notes of
Clarence W. Barron*, edited by Arthur Poud and Samuel Taylor
Moore, 1930) this is what happened:

"I went aboard the boat at eleven-thirty at night and Mr.
Nicholes (Morton Nicholes, ship news reporter for the *Wall
Street Journal*) came to me with one of our men and asked if I
would not please help him out with an interview. He mentioned
the name of my dear partner, Mr. Stettinius (Edward R. Stettinius, the brains of the House of Morgan after the death of
the elder J. P., and father of Edward R. Stettinius, a nine-day
wonder in the fast turnover of Franklin D. Roosevelt's favorites
under the New Deal), whom he had known. I think Nicholes is
also from the South and that rather touched my heart, and I
thought I would help him out. He asked me if I thought General
Motors had not gone up pretty fast. I said, 'Yes, but I think its
present price is justified by its management, its earnings, and its
prospects'—seventeen words which he wrote down. . . . I asked
him where this interview was to be published and he said, 'In
the *Wall Street Journal* Monday morning.'"

If Nicholes had quoted only those seventeen words of Cochrane, the bull market would have started from there, because

263

this was the first time in history that a partner in the powerful House of Morgan had expressed an opinion publicly about a particular stock or about the market in general. It was a go-ahead signal for the bulls.

The high point of the interview with Cochrane, as Nicholes reported it, appeared thus on Monday: "The rise in the stock of General Motors Corporation has been very rapid during the past week (it had gone from 169⅞ on July 26 to 189½ on July 31) but it is more than justified by earnings. I am convinced the corporation will earn more than $35 a share this year. . . . When the former proportionate prices of Associated Dry Goods, American Can, and General Electric are compared as to earnings, General Motors, with earnings running at such a rate, is cheap at the price and should and will sell at least one hundred points higher."

Following this interview General Motors rose to 201¼ on the date of publication. The House of Morgan, it appears, frantically radioed Cochrane asking him to deny the interview. He radioed back that he could not contradict the interview, part of which was true, but that he had been misquoted. Nicholes was fired. The *Wall Street Journal,* pressured by the House of Morgan, denied the interview, in substance, and printed an apology. But, according to Cochrane's own words (in confidence) to C. W. Barron, publisher of the *Wall Street Journal,* on October 14, 1926, after Cochrane had returned from Europe, Cochrane had been more sanguine in his prediction about General Motors than Nicholes had credited him with. Nicholes quoted him as having said that GM would go at least 100 points higher than 189½, that is, 289½. Cochrane had really told Barron that he had predicted GM would go to $300 a share within three to five years. . . . It went to a high of 396¼ on September 3, 1929, that is, within thirty-one months.

By the early spring of 1928 I had familiarized myself enough with the psychology of the stock market, by careful study and observation, to embark as a trader. I had a cash balance of about $60,000 on an original investment of $2,000, after having drawn about $30,000 from the account in cash. My parents had insisted that we buy a house, they paying one half of the purchase price of $18,500, and I had it entirely reconditioned, reroofed, repainted, and furnished at a cost of about $15,000; I had bought a Buick; my wife bought gowns costing $250 apiece, and I had an overcoat and five suits of clothes tailored in London and evening clothes tailored by Wetzel; we paid a cook twenty-five dollars a week; we entertained considerably; and friends and acquaintances soon found that there was always a plentiful supply of liquor on our premises at 42 Stuyvesant Avenue, Larchmont. But lavish as I thought our spending was, we were mere pikers in comparison with many of those we knew whose earned income was no more than mine but who were active in the market. They had big houses, swimming pools, numerous servants, Cadillacs, ermine and mink coats, and cellars of vintage wines and bonded whisky.

I did not envy them, nor did I care particularly for what seemed to me the wasteful extravagance of our living. But the world seemed to have gone mad in a hectic frenzy of speculation and wild extravagance and I was interested in the phenomenon, especially since nearly all the other values of life had been engulfed by it. To retreat from it was to retreat from life itself. I had missed participation in the mad extravaganza of the Florida land boom, which preceded the stock market boom, and, from all accounts of participants who had lost their shirts in it, I had been rather sorry I had been able to learn of its fantastic gyrations only at secondhand.

The Florida land boom, although it followed the general pattern of inflation and collapse that has characterized all money-mad mass manias, was unique in one respect: it was the only one in history that began with a vision of beauty.

The man chiefly responsible for the sudden widespread interest in Florida land values—an interest that soon attracted a horde of large and small speculators, adventurers, schemers, camp followers, and plain, ordinary suckers—had quite honestly believed that Florida could be made a paradise on earth and had set about converting the swamps, marshes, and sandy flatlands of Coral Gables into a perfect city, the capital and metropolis of a visible and tangible heaven. There was nothing slipshod, hasty, or mercenary in his plans. Swamps were drained, artificial lagoons created, rolling hills built up to vary the flat monotony of the scenery; houses were made to conform to a strict standard of architectural beauty; shrubs and flowers, palms and verdure were as definite a part of the whole scheme as perfect sanitation, a plentiful supply of wholesome water, and wide, paved streets and tree-lined avenues.

That man was George Merrick, the son of a Nonconformist minister who had left the winter winds of Cape Cod to save the life of his dying wife, and on horseback, and with a wagon and team had trudged the long, arduous journey to Florida, carrying with him his family and chattels. The Rev. Solomon Merrick had staked out a one-hundred-and-sixty-acre claim near the village of Miami and started a fruit farm called Coral Gables. The farm prospered, and by the time George Merrick reached manhood he was able to go to Columbia University. There he made the beginning of a literary career by winning a prize offered by the New York *Herald* in 1912 for the best short story of the year. American literature, however, was destined never to know what further promise there was in George Merrick, for he was soon called back to Florida to administer the estate of his father who had suddenly died.

George had not been home long before he became possessed, like all saints, madmen, and geniuses, with a fixed idea. That idea, which occupied his mind, energies, and resources for many years, was that of establishing an earthly paradise on the very spot where his father had dreamed of a heavenly one. The idea bore fruit abundantly. Others caught the glamor of the scheme. Arthur Brisbane, the Hearst mental mentor to millions, having bought up vast acreages of Florida land at a cheap price, began to trumpet the virtues of Florida as a garden spot of the world and as an investment which, he said, would grow fabulously in value; the Mizner Brothers, with Wall Street backing, began to elaborate on Herrick's dream and build a dream city of riotous color and Spanish architecture.

And the rush began. Thousands upon thousands of people, attracted by the stories of wealth overnight, began the hopeful trek to Florida. In cities and towns men sold out their small shops, disposed of their homes, quit their jobs; on western prairies and New England hillsides families gave up their holdings; waiters, clerks, salesmen, writers, lawyers, mechanics, medicine men—all fevered by dreams of easy wealth—formed an astounding cavalcade of teams, trains, and motorcars, dribbling from all parts of the Union into the glutted highways of Florida. Sanity fled the scene; Tom o' Bedlam was uncrowned king; caution and common sense were out of hand and out of mind. Folly was rife to wreck George Merrick's half-realized dream of an earthly paradise.

Here is the Florida boom in a nutshell, given in the Barron book:

1896. C. W. Bingham bought 3,000 feet of ocean-front property near Palm Beach at $4.65 per front foot.

1915. He sold part of this at $27.50 per front foot.

1917. Paris Singer bought part of Bingham's land at $90 per front foot.

1918. Dr. W. L. Kingsley bought Singer out at $160 per front foot.

1924. Mrs. Horace Dodge bought Singer's part at $888 per front foot.

1925. Mrs. Dodge sold to speculators at $3,300 per front foot.

1927. They failed and she resold at $1,400 per front foot.

But that doesn't tell the whole story; nor do the figures showing the terrific drop in stock market prices during the October-
November 1929 debacle tell the whole story. Even though there
were numerous failures of Florida banks which had loaned money
on inflated mortgages and even though an estimated 60 per cent.
of the late-comers to the scene of the boom lost their houses by
foreclosure, the net and far-reaching results were that a great deal
of Florida land was permanently redeemed from swamp and
marsh land, roads were built, prosperous towns and cities were
founded, the citrus-fruit industry was enormously expanded to
add to the productive wealth of the country.

The losers were, in the main, those who had put up only $150
or $200 in cash in the first place and given mortgages on their land
for an initial payment for construction of their houses and, in
turn, had issued first and second mortgages on them. They had
been stuck for taxes and special assessments for the construction
of water mains and electric power; but during the boom they had
also been given unusual opportunities for earning money, through
inflated wages and the sale of commodities at inflated prices. The
water mains, paved highways, power lines, the trees, the shrubs,
the houses remained. Real wealth had been created, even if
people no longer traded two $30,000 cats for one $60,000 dog (as
the wags had it at the time), and a sense of reality concerning
the medium of exchange had returned to normal.

Nor was the stock market boom altogether dire in its ultimate
effects: the normal growth of our productive wealth remained a
constant 6 per cent throughout the depression, just as it had
remained 6 per cent throughout the boom; industries, in many
cases, went into bankruptcy through overexpansion when the
demand for goods contracted, but the plants and facilities remained for productive use under reorganization and under the
resumption of buying power; Iowa farm lands (and fertile land
elsewhere) had risen in price during 1919 to such fantastic prices
that efforts to make them yield an annual profit in crops was like

purchasing a lot in downtown Manhattan in the expectation of growing potatoes on it for profit, but the introduction of scientific methods in agriculture in order to narrow this spread between acre-price and produce-yield enormously benefited the country at large; installment buying, so deeply deplored by many commentators during and after the boom of the twenties, raised American standards of living, lessened the difference between the comforts and luxuries of the haves and have-nots (foreclosures on installment-bought products during the depression were negligible), and the truth is that the depression of the 1930s was more the result of the economic paralysis of Europe, following World War I, than it was the result of an overoptimistic expansion of domestic productive effort and crazy mass speculation.

During my intensive study of economic theory and my observation of its practice I concluded that economics is, by and large, pure mythology and that any economic plan is workable just so long, and only so long, as it is sustained by faith. Let faith be shaken and general doubt prevail and the plan collapses. Bullion is deposited in the ground at Fort Knox and the illusion is created and sustained that the United States is on the gold standard, which it is not; with credit grants from Great Britain and the United States Hitler could create the illusion that the paper money he issued against the theoretical wealth of a prostrate and bankrupt country was actual wealth and out of this he was able to build his war machine, pay his Gestapo, his Storm Troopers, and his army, and sustain a sort of prosperity—it was faith in fiat money that made this possible and, without defeat in war, the economy of the German Reich would have collapsed at any point when that faith weakened. It was Hitler's (or his advisors') foreboding that this faith was weakening which, I believe, caused him to gamble on an aggressive war.

As an observer of the psychology of the stock market boom, it did not take me long to discover that, either in a bull market or a bear market, the word "value" as used by brokers and commentators has no meaning whatsoever, and yet it is a word constantly employed by them. "Value" is a subjective, intangible, inestimable thing which is erroneously associated with "price." The "value" of anything, from a can of beans to a Gainsborough portrait, from a share of General Electric to a Conrad manuscript, from a Picasso to a Gutenberg Bible, is exactly the exchange price of it at the moment of exchange of ownership.

"Values" fluctuate according to supply and demand, and supply and demand are governed by the psychological mood of the moment. For instance, there was a boom in Joseph Conrad manuscripts at the time of the Crosby Gaige auction sale and the boom reached its peak at the Quinn sale, in which the Quinn collection, including some former Gaige items, brought a fortune. The Conrad manuscript boom collapsed shortly after the Quinn sale and Conrad manuscripts are now "worth" only a fraction of what they once sold for. Of course another boom in Conrad manuscripts may develop in which prices may soar above the prices at the Quinn sale. I cite this only as an illustration that "value" is an abstraction in the economic mythology.

I have read a great many books on economics, from Adam Smith to Sully, from the Krafft-Ebing of economic pathology, Karl Marx, to Keynes, from Henry George and Bellamy to the latest mumbo-jumbo of high priests of the New Deal economic myths. Those who can write English with any degree of facility (a rare gift among economists) are entertaining and often even plausible; but even as cogent a thinker as Keynes proved himself to be in *The Economic Consequences of the Peace* (an analysis and a warning that went unheeded; hence the creation of the possibility for the rise of such a paranoiac scoundrel as Hitler) has more recently shown that his economic views are strictly conditioned by the desirabilities of the ruling class of England whose blind and disastrous (to the world) greed he once condemned.

The only economist during the twenties who commanded my

entire respect was Carl Snyder, chief statistician of the Federal Reserve Bank in New York and author of the bank's bulletins. As long as Snyder had Benjamin Strong to back him up as governor of the Federal Reserve Bank, he was able to keep the economy of this country on a pretty even keel. Strong had halted the war boom just when it threatened to get out of hand in 1919 by following Snyder's suggestion for the gradual contraction of credit. He thus prevented a really disastrous collapse and lessened the duration of the postwar depression.

Had Strong not been stricken in February 1929 with an illness that proved fatal, I believe he would have enforced the credit contraction suggested by Snyder in the famous Federal Reserve Bureau bulletin "warning" and the wild orgy of kiting stock prices, which followed the defiance of the Snyder warning, would not have occurred; the stock prices would have subsided to normal level, the speculators, no longer able to borrow money at 15 per cent in the call-money market for stocks overpriced by 30 per cent, would have slowly withdrawn and the October collapse would have been avoided.

This country lost a great, if very obscure and almost unknown, man when Carl Snyder died in 1940. His book *Capitalism: The Creator* is, in my opinion, the soundest and most enlightening analysis of the advantages of a free society over that of a totalitarian state I have ever read. It is a wise and brilliant explanation of how our country grew great. I had admired Snyder's erudition and type of mind ever since 1916 when I first encountered his *World Machine*. That book had been published nine years before but had fallen flat. A connoisseur of rare books had recommended it to me as a source of Theodore Dreiser's utterances on the mechanistic conception of life, and I had, after considerable search, bought a secondhand copy for $12.50—because only a few hundred copies had been sold and the book had long been out of print—to find out what Dreiser had derived from it. It had, in a superficial sort of way, conditioned Dreiser's thinking, as I discovered when I read it; but it is a much more profound book than Dreiser discerned.

Snyder had also written *New Conceptions of Science* (1903) and *Business Cycles and Business Measurements* (1927) and his FRB bulletins, written for the information of the member banks, were words of wisdom, but no one paid any attention to them. These bulletins were instructive and profitable reading to me, and would have been more profitable if I had had the nerve to hold my brokers responsible for declining to carry out my orders.

In January 1928, while I was visiting my parents in California, I read Snyder's Federal Reserve bulletin, which came to be known as the February "Federal Reserve warning," and I wired my broker to sell my entire list of holdings, which then would have yielded me close to $200,000 several days before the warning was released to the newspapers. I got no reply to my wire and therefore I assumed that my instructions had been carried out. But, it must be remembered, brokers do not buy or sell securities except as agents for their customers. It doesn't make any difference to them whether the market is going up or down; they make their commissions on each buying order or selling order; and the more active a trader a customer is the more money they make out of him. They hate to see a customer retire from the market and will use all their powers of persuasion to prevent him from doing so.

On my return to New York I discovered that my brokers had received my telegram and had discussed it in executive council, concluding that I had been ill-advised and that, in as much as I had first entered the market with my account guaranteed by the late H. S. Collins, mine could still be assumed to be a "discretionary account." A "discretionary account" is one in which brokers attempt to guard the inexperienced against the consequences of their own folly, refusing to execute buying or selling orders, for example, when a widow has obviously got a bad "tip" from some ignoramus at a bridge game or at a dinner party or has fallen into the hands of a swindler. They did not consider me on the same level as a nitwit female, because even the president of the firm had sought my advice time and again and I had enjoyed a reputation in the office for having phenomenal luck; but they rationalized their desire to keep me an active trader into assuming I had taken bad advice.

On the surface it seemed that they had been right. A sharp break had occurred when the FRB "warning" was widely publicized; but when Mitchell said he had $50,000,000 to lend at 15 per cent and he would lend it as long as there was a demand for it, FRB or no, the market rebounded sharply. Stocks were zooming again. The stocks I had ordered sold were up an average of about ten points since the day my order was given. The brokers, who had been bewildered and skeptical of the whole dizzy rise of stocks since August 2, 1926, had become convinced that there was no foreseeable end to it; that stocks would reach a still higher level and maintain that level without serious setback, permanently.

I didn't believe this and, moreover, was sick of the whole thing. I had proved to myself that I could trade successfully, as successfully, at least, as Marcel Proust, who for many years derived a very comfortable income (it was his only one) from speculation in the Paris Bourse, giving his trading orders by telephone from the sickbed in which he wrote his monumental *A la Recherche du Temps Perdu,* which made him world famous but did not bring him any appreciable income. In fact it had got around the brokers' rooms that I was uncommonly shrewd in judging the actions of certain stocks and, as a result, "Josh" Cosden, the oilman, and Theodore Marseles, the great merchandiser, whose accounts at the same brokerage house ran into the millions (making my account seem piddling in comparison), now and then sought my advice on the market in general and my opinion of certain specific stocks.

This was very bad for me, as I soon had sense enough to

realize. It inflated my ego in a way in which no one's ego should be inflated. With a few drinks I would start to brag about how much money I had made in a day's trading, and when others began to talk about tips they had got on this or that stock, I'd assume a superior, know-it-all attitude and begin to *tell* them instead of listening to them. Next morning I would realize what a boor I had been and resolve to keep my mouth shut. This behavior, though, gradually grew worse instead of better, and in my reflective moments I was thoroughly disgusted with myself in the role of a stock market gambler. Besides, my father had once told me, when I was in a terrible state of nervous anxiety at the time of the two-day collapse of the Bank of Italy stock (I did not hold any of that stock, but it affected the whole market), that he wouldn't go through, even for one day, what I went through, if he never had a dime in his life. He said such a life was *indecent*.

The excitement of trading in a hectic market kept most of the gamblers as well as those who executed their orders in a high state of nervous tension. From the balcony of the Stock Exchange I had occasionally watched the floor traders on an active day, and I was not surprised to learn that nervous breakdowns and stomach ulcers were the occupational ailments of the clan and that the average floor trader's endurance was six months, at which time he would be ordered by his doctor to take a vacation. A floor trader's work combines a maximum of physical strain and a maximum of mental strain five hours a day five days out of the week and two hours on Saturday. On a million-share day it is as if a marathon runner were doing it in sprint time, engaging in rapid calculations and undergoing a memory test all at the same time. A runner will present him with a sheaf of buy-and-sell orders involving a dozen different stocks; he has to go from post to post (for stocks are assigned to certain posts), signal to each specialist, note the stocks and the prices, and report results accurately to the runner who takes them to a clerk who phones them to the brokerage office.

Exchange workers and brokers' clerks, on busy days, ordinarily take only half an hour out for lunch. They usually eat standing up in one of the numerous short-order restaurants in the financial district, where almost the entire patronage of a day is jammed into the hours between 11 A.M. and 1 P.M., many of them serving only that one meal. The food, and especially the coffee, in these restaurants is the very best and consists, in the main, of roast-beef sandwiches or double-decker sandwiches of ham and cheese on rye. The choice is limited to the few standard demands, including soup, but the portions are generous. The downtown restaurants, indeed, differ entirely in character from the restaurants uptown or midtown, where the bulk of the patronage at noon consists of women shoppers and workers, whose demand is typified by the cucumber-and-lettuce salad and tea.

During the twenties, at the end of the day, after books had been cleared following the three o'clock stock exchange closing, speculators, floor traders, clerks, and executives crowded the numerous speakeasies of the district—most of which were luxuriously appointed, serving the very finest brands of drinks. After four and until six these places were always filled with men discussing the market and events of the day; and, although most of them consumed inordinate numbers of drinks in the course of an hour or so, I never saw anyone obviously under the influence of liquor. Talkative and excited, yes, but not drunk; most of them were so wound up by the strenuous work of the day that not even a dozen scotches could relax them. Brokers and their customers' men, by the way, were rarely to be seen in such speakeasies. To places that were noted for their food and then only at noon, a broker or customers' man might take a client and order one or at most two cocktails. Brokers and customers' men did not work at as high tension as clerks, runners, and floor traders, and apparently, whatever drinking they did, they did in the evenings after getting to their homes in the suburbs.

I was resentful of that dodge about the "discretionary account" and within a day or two disposed of $69,000 worth of stock, handing my order slip to the clerk myself instead of passing it on to my customers' man. I had had more than enough of that madhouse, and although I did not then dispose of all my holdings, I reduced my debit balance by that much and was thus prepared for any setback in the market that was not completely disastrous. I stopped talking about the stock market, even stopped thinking about it. I would rarely even turn to the quotations in the financial pages and began to be so self-righteous about it as to hold a bit of contempt for those who grabbed each new extra off the newsstands and immediately turned to the financial pages.

But I have always carried pleasant and interesting memories of the associations I had formed in Wall Street. Brokers, customers' men, floor traders, clerks constituted as fine and as intelligent a type as I have ever encountered. They are also openhearted, friendly, engaging, and most of them frankly like the excitement of their work, even if they sometimes have a humorously cynical view of amateur and professional speculators.

For years after the stock market was a part of the dead past of many who had been active in it when the excitement of the boom was on, any gathering or chance meeting of those who had haunted the same brokers' offices was sure to produce tales of the comical and fantastic. For a speculative boom and collapse are, I am constrained to think, the nearest approach to that invention which William James so earnestly desired—a moral equivalent of war. James had observed that, say what you will about the carnage, the suffering, the waste, of war, it provides excitement and co-operative endeavor; it is a radical departure from the routine of being born, begetting, and dying. And I have often heard veterans of World War I say (in long retrospect, of course) that they hated to admit it but they got more fun out of life during their time in uniform than at any time before or since. As I write this, Robert C. Ruark, a navy lieutenant in World War II who saw considerable action in the Pacific, has just

276

recalled in his newspaper column that he and his old navy chums, "without exception," look back on the war as "a wondrously stimulating experience. For my age group, anyhow, it was a tight little oasis of complete freedom from care, with nothing to lose but your life—and statistics were against that."

I have even known men to whom World War I was the climax and culmination of their life's experiences; everything that has happened to them since then has been anticlimax. But I don't think Ruark or anyone else would find a war a "wondrously stimulating experience" after three or four years of it. Nor do I think that the excitement of speculating in a bull market would prove stimulating and interesting to anybody after three or four years of it. But while it was in progress (about three years and less for most of the participants) it was a mass madness like war without savagery, wholesale butchery, and destructiveness. It had its aftermath of depression and of sobering up—just as every war has. But a distinguished psychologist, Dr. Smith Ely Jeliffe, was inclined to agree with me, during the height of the speculative boom, that the phenomenon was a revolt against the drab repressions and monotony of ordinary life, particularly the life of taboo-ridden and regimented America, against which so many other revolts were concurrently being demonstrated, from the satire of Lewis's *Main Street* and *Babbitt* to the conspicuous defiance of the Prohibition laws, from the woman's suffrage movement to the rolled stockings and abbreviated skirts of the flappers.

In effect, I retired from active trading in July 1928 and, although I still maintained a fair-sized inactive account, I didn't —believe it or not—much care what became of it. In August the market reached its dizzy peak and my Montgomery Ward touched 447; but I had already suffered such a revulsion against the game that I paid little attention to it. I was in the office of my broker on that fatal Wednesday, October 23, when five billion dollars were clipped off market valuations within five hours, and on the next day when by eleven o'clock in the morning every bank in New York was technically insolvent, having loaned millions of dollars on stocks for which no price was offered and hence much of the bank's collateral was, for that day, worthless. But I was there only as a spectator. My paper fortune had shrunk in half in two days, but my credit condition was not endangered. I could watch the frenzied activity with the cool eye of an almost disinterested witness. A junior partner in the firm remarked to me as he dashed by (like the rest, he was trying to take care of the accounts of frantic customers and also trying to protect his firm by sending out margin calls by phone and telegraph) : "It must feel good to be sitting pretty in a panic."

The bankers saved themselves that day, but in saving themselves they had not, as the newspapers proclaimed, saved the market; they had merely passed the buck on to the brokers who in turn passed the buck on to the holders of stock on thin margin, hundreds of thousands of whom were unceremoniously sold out on Monday, even after they had raised additional cash on Wednesday, Thursday, Friday, and Saturday.

The cleanup really began on Monday and continued until November 15. I checked out at eleven o'clock on Saturday before the final deluge and even then against my broker's assurance that the market had steadied and that "Arthur Cutten and a lot of other big operators are reported to have stepped in with large buying orders." Mr. Cutten, indeed, had thought, along with many others, that the market had hit bottom on Thursday and that it offered attractive bargains. He and others loaded up to the extent of their borrowing capacity. They were broke by noon Monday. But on Wednesday, October 23, 1929, the wild party of the twenties was over, although a great many eminent economists and financiers did not realize it. The stock market was dead but unburied: it was doomed to lie stretched out in the parlor, decomposing and odorous for a long time.

Among the amusing experiences I had during the boom were those which resulted from the similarity of sound between my last name and the last name of John J. Raskob, chairman of the finance committee of General Motors Corporation, vice-president of the Du Pont Company, and treasurer (and holder of the bag) of the Democratic National Committee during the campaign of "Al" Smith for the presidency.

In the early fall of 1927, after the bull market had been in full swing for over a year and before I had become active as a trader, I attended a newspaper publishers' convention at the old Waldorf-Astoria. My syndicate boss, "Little Bill" Johnson, introduced me one afternoon to a group of delegates from Detroit. Their deference and cordiality were so marked that I was astonished and puzzled. A group surrounded me and began to talk about the weather and other trivialities. Finally one of them assured me he had got in on General Motors very early and had kept buying on a scale up. The others bent their heads in close attention when he asked me if he should hold or take his profit now. I told him truthfully and guilelessly that I didn't know. I added that I didn't own any General Motors myself, but I had a few shares of Montgomery Ward.

The group thereupon vanished without ceremony. I could not guess why until one of them returned a little while later and said, rather breathlessly, "I sold my General Motors. I put in an order to buy Monkey Ward up to the hilt. Thanks for the tip."

"What tip?" I asked. "I didn't give you any tip."

He patted me on the shoulder. "Of course you didn't! Of course you didn't! And I would never in the world say you did. I know! I won't breathe a word to a soul. Thanks just the same, though."

He strolled off just as another returned from having phoned his broker. The latter purringly said, "I had the great honor of playing golf with your father in Florida last summer. Wonderful man, your father."

I said, "My father indeed is a wonderful man, but unfortunately he has never been to Florida and he doesn't play golf."

279

The chap thought I was rudely high-hatting him. He said, "But I can't be mistaken. The man I played golf with was no impostor; I would recognize him anywhere from his pictures."

Then I asked, "What did this man with whom you played golf in Florida call himself?"

"Why, John J. Raskob, of course."

"That explains it," I said. "My father's name is M. L. Rascoe. R-a-s-c-o-e. I am a writer. I never even met a Raskob."

Chagrin and consternation registered on his features and he dropped me like a hot potato. Whether he bought back his General Motors I don't know. Later I saw him in a huddle with the others who had rushed to sell GM on what they considered a hot tip. I have no doubt that many a "hot tip" has just that much foundation—mistaken identity coupled with a chance remark such as "Raskob unloaded his General Motors and switched to Montgomery Ward. I got it direct from his son."

On a trip to Chicago on the Century a porter with a telegram bawled out my name in the club car. Within a few minutes an alert fellow had stolen a march on other occupants and had introduced himself, handing me his business card: he was vice-president and general manager of a cement company. He made conversation for some minutes and then whispered that he had some excellent scotch in his compartment and invited me to come have a drink with him. I accepted; we had several highballs. He wanted my opinion of various stocks, the general market trend, and the duration of the bull market. I gave him my opinion and then deliberately added, "Of course you are mistaken as to my identity. You think I am related to John J. Raskob. I am not. My name is Rascoe, not Raskob."

He pretended this was not the case and that he had introduced himself because he could see at a glance that I was an intelligent and substantial citizen; but his disappointment was so obvious as to be pathetic.

Epilogue

With the collapse of the national dream of perpetual prosperity in the bleak days of October–November 1929, a revolution had occurred, a creeping revolution rather than a violent one in this country. Our revolution was only the backwash of a tidal convulsion in Europe, but it ended an era just the same.

For nearly ten years a serious and somber mood was to settle upon the land, a mood that was not to be altogether dispelled by singing "Happy Days Are Here Again!" A reaction against the whole ebullient spirit of the twenties set in. Young men came of age in a period of vast unemployment and in an atmosphere of fear and pessimism. Many of them had enjoyed childhoods in which they had been pampered by indulgent and free-spending parents, now grown apprehensive, cautious and penurious.

There was ushered in another kind of revolt, differing from the revolt of the twenties, which had been a revolt against the Victorian taboos and restrictions exercised by parents, by the home, and by the conventions of society. The new revolt was of a youth which did not think their parents and society had taken their obligations seriously enough. The new generation wanted restrictions, they wanted guidance, and they wanted, I think, the sort of regimentation against which so many of their parents had rebelled.

Therein we had, I think, the beginning of the tendency to

281

substitute the state for the parent, the bureaucracy for the home, the government for the father, whose function it was to provide a liberal allowance and unlimited security in a hazardous world where all security is relative and is governed by chance and individual initiative. It was an acceleration of the movement toward collectivism or totalitarianism which may, or may not, be checked and dispersed by counter-revolt against the fatherhood of the state.

Already, of course, there is the beginning of the concept of the collective fatherhood of all states, which is presumed to guide, direct, and liberally provide for all of the earth's children. This concept may grow and prevail, undisturbed by any heretical notions that such a fatherhood is made up of integers which are quite palpably very fallible, and even contentious and intransigent, human beings. The capacity of people to believe in the godhead of their rulers was not limited to the Egyptians, the Romans of the Caesars, or the worshipers of the Mikado before he disclaimed his divinity: the ikons of Stalin are more numerous in Russia than formerly were the ikons of the Church.

Wherever we are drifting, or rushing headlong, however, I believe it is the part of sense for the adult-minded to look to the future without despair and as at a promise of excitement, just as he should look back upon the past without chagrin and as an experience that had its many moments of enchantment. We of my generation, like those of every generation, found the world that we were born into, and had to make our way in, was lacking, in quite a number of details, in the factors of ideal perfection. For one thing, it did not seem to be altogether a free and honest world but full of hypocrisies, bugaboos, and artificial restraints; it seemed to be too full of busybodies trying to regulate the conduct of others and trying to make others conform to their particular majority-group notions of what to eat, drink, wear, read, think, believe, and do. At least certain articulate numbers of us of the younger generation of the twenties, irked by these restrictions, set about very volubly to break them down; and we were aided by the great inarticulate majority of the members of our generation who had felt the restrictions and were happy to join in the work of demolishing taboos, by example as well as by precept.

It has been said of the generation which reached maturity in the twenties that we destroyed old ideals without creating new ideals to replace them; that we produced a chaos of mental confusion, cynicism, and ethical anarchy. Even some members of that generation who had grown older a little more rapidly than the rest, such as Joseph Wood Krutch in *The Modern Temper* and Walter Lippmann in *A Preface to Morals*, took an exaggerated view of what, after all, had been only a slight shift of emphasis on values, a change of styles of thinking more like a change of styles of clothing than like a revolution of the spirit. These commentators, and others like them, seemed to judge the life of the times in terms of the scandals and corruption revealed in the newspaper headlines. They forgot the French axiom that a happy marriage has no history and the newspaper axiom that it is not news when a dog bites a man, it is only news when a man bites a dog. They mistook the common phenomena of displays of anti-social behavior to be peculiar to their times.

Fundamentally, the younger generation of the twenties was like the younger generation of this and of all other times. It was under the disapproving scrutiny of certain members of the older generation who had forgotten what they were like when they were younger; and it was, as is usual in every age, scolded, admonished, and even deplored. But, on the whole, it was a generation that moved steadily into the category of an older generation with hearts as steady, illusions as fixed, principles as sound (and as flexible), faith as high, and a sense of obligation as tenacious as those of any generation that preceded it.

It was unfortunate in that it was followed by a younger generation of what seemed to be made up of prematurely old men, nagging, disgruntled, ascetic, and, in a way, zealously puritanical, holding that beauty, grace, innocent enjoyment, the arts, comfort, and relaxation were instruments of the devil. They didn't put it quite that way: they said that the arts should be the instruments of the proletarian revolution and that what we had been accustomed to enjoy as the cultural usufructs of a civilization were opiates designed by a capitalist society to benumb us while the masses were being exploited.

We are always thankful for some slight novelty in our mental fare, and fads come and go in literature and the other arts almost with the regularity with which the length of women's skirts are shifted. Communism, diluted or straight, became an ingredient of much of our literature during the thirties and we had to take it, whether we liked it or not, because it was about the only kind we could get.

To a certain extent it still is; but new generations have a way of growing up and elbowing the oldsters out of the way as obsolete and dodoish; and there are signs that this new generation will soon declare that many of the ideas which were touted and exploited and capitalized upon by a class-conscious younger generation of the thirties and early forties are as out of date as the whalebone corset.

The thirties and the early forties did not prove to be favorable ones to the creative or re-creative arts. The best writers of the period belonged to the twenties, during which time their gifts had come to fruition, and what they produced during the thirties was, as Somerset Maugham once described a new volume of his own, "more of the same." But the arts do not flourish during an era of revolution, an era of quick and violent change.

But whatever we may have lost in the way of the decorative arts and the amenities of life, during the years of depression which led directly into the years of war, the social gains were considerable. Labor gained new dignity, a greater solidity, a power to equalize the power of management. There has been no perceptible decrease that I can see in the gap which separates the haves and the

284

have-nots, except that some of the old haves are now among the have-nots but the ranks of the haves have been swelled by a great number of those who have had the ability and the enterprise to seize the opportunities that always seem to be at hand, in any age, for the aggressive and the acquisitive. And those who supply our comforts and conveniences have steadily made things more comfortable and convenient for us, from traveling to washing dishes.

Life, indeed, still remains an exciting adventure except for the ossified; and even the terror of the atom bomb is quite noticeably lessened for us who remember that for each new means of destroying his kind that man invents, he seems also to invent or discover some new means for preserving life, and that the life span not only continues to grow rather than to decrease but the productive years of the average life span continue to grow longer also.

On the Sunday following the panic in Wall Street my brother, my wife, and I drove up to West Point to see the drill. General Pershing was the guest of honor before whom the budding officers were to exhibit their clockwork efficiency.

We witnessed a minor tragedy. One young company commander in the flourish of raising his sword let go of it and it flew upward and fell to the ground. He was put to the awful humiliation of picking it up and resuming where he had left off. Not more than four ticks of a metronome had been lost in that beautiful perfection of rhythm.

But, said my brother, who had been to West Point, "That poor lad will carry the scar of that accident the rest of his life. On his soul, which is worse than an open wound. He is none the worse for it, nor is the honor of West Point or of the Army, but he will think so, and that will be the tragedy of it."

Let us hope that my brother was wrong in his forecast. Let us hope that the young man was sensible enough not to brood upon what, after all, might have happened to anybody; that he regarded it as of no consequence; and that he went on to show his mettle and do what was required of him, with distinction, when his nation called upon him to make practical use of his abilities and of his specific training.

For most of us, chests out, stomachs in, self-confident and alert, have, at one time or another, seen our swords speed out of our hands and fall with a humiliating thud to the ground. If we were overmindful of what others might think of us we have let such happenings cripple us, forgetting that the real business of life begins where parades leave off. If we are sensible enough to realize that people have their own affairs to think about and cannot concentrate too much on ours, we have recovered our swords, awkwardly or with grace, and gone on to acquit ourselves in the chore at hand with what distinction we can display. To whatever untoward event befalls us, not entirely of our own volition, we should say, in perhaps the wisest philosophical reflection in our present-day common usage, "That's that!" and think of happier things and pleasant events to come, even if we can pretty well foresee that such events will probably not be unmixed with events that are grim, sorrowful, and difficult to bear.

The general mood of the country, as I conclude this book, is so very much like the mood which ushered in the twenties, so like it in widespread strikes, rising prices, housing shortages, lowering of consumer demand, and other phenomena of unrest that maybe we are on the eve of another twenties, a bigger and better twenties in which there was a resurgence of national energies after a let-down which followed World War I effort; maybe we are in for another era of rapid expansion of industry and of a boom of mighty proportions. And, God forbid! another economic collapse. Even so, it should all be exciting while it lasts.

Appendices

Representive selections from "A Bookman's Daybook," the "Day-book of a New Yorker" and from contributions to magazines written by Burton Rascoe during the twenties.

Luncheon with
W. Somerset Maugham

December 1, 1923

I had lunch with W. Somerset Maugham at the Plaza the other day. He is shy, extremely reserved, and at first he gives one a sense of his being a very lonely person, self-isolated, a hermit of the spirit.

His early struggles to gain a livelihood by literature were bitter. He wrote plays for eleven years before one was produced, and it was through his plays only that he was able to make enough to live on until he passed forty. Fortunately he had a small income, so he was never financially distressed. *Of Human Bondage,* he told me, is a faithful record of the first thirty years of his life. He says he has little or no inventive faculty; that when he has tried to invent a story he has failed, as in the case of *The Making of a Saint* (a medieval romance written at twenty at the suggestion of the critic, Andrew Lang); and that in his other books he has put down only what he has seen or felt. *Mrs. Craddock,* a novel of great power and fine workmanship, which is an English *Madame Bovary* written with sympathy for the woman's side of the story, was, according to Mr. Maugham, a story he saw enacted before his eyes as a young man. *Lisa of Lambeth* is straight out of his experiences as a hospital interne in London.

Those who have read *Of Human Bondage* will recall that the germ of the theme for *The Moon and Sixpence* is embedded in one of the Paris scenes of that great drama. Mr. Maugham wrote *The Moon and Sixpence* in hospital after he had developed tuberculosis in Russia during World War I.

"I wanted to write a book entirely to please myself," he said. "And no one was more surprised than I when it turned out to be the greatest financial success I have ever had, the one book which advanced my royalties and created a demand for my stories. The book has a disagreeable person, a real blackguard, as the chief character, and the sentiments expressed by Strickland are calculated to arouse the hatred or disgust of women. The novel has no sweetness or light and is certainly not the sort of pap the great reading public demands. Yet it was a success, and I can't keep from wondering at it."

Mr. Maugham found the story for *The Moon and Sixpence,* of course, in the life of Gauguin and in the legends connected with the painter's extraordinary career in Paris and the South Sea Islands. The novel does not follow Gauguin's career accurately, but there is no reason why it should. The novel was merely suggested by Gauguin's career. It was not intended to be a biography. For all that, despite the carping of critics, I suspect that the artist's spirit as Mr. Maugham depicted it in Strickland is closer to the artist's spirit as it existed in Gauguin than is the cardboard figure evoked by the more factual biographers of the painter. It takes an artist to fathom an artist and Maugham is an artist.

"I try in my work," said Mr. Maugham, "to write as simply and as clearly as possible. I haven't much talent for word ornament and I don't like it. When I find that I have made a phrase which is more interesting as a phrase than as an expression of what I have in mind, I change it. In my youth there were held up as two great stylists whom all young men who wanted to write should copy those very precious and involved writers, Walter Pater and George Meredith. These writers are next to unreadable now. The life of a book is short enough in all conscience without a writer's deliberately shortening it by stylistic idiosyncrasies of one generation with which the next generation will have no sympathy. My favorites among the English prose writers are Swift, Jeremy Taylor, Addison, Dryden, and Hazlitt—all of them men who are as readable today as they were in their own time because they wrote directly, forcibly, clearly, simply.

"From the great body of work which every writer turns out, only a very small portion of it, sometimes only one book, or only part of one book, survives. We must judge that writer by his best work. In England a novelist who tries to make a living by his pen must turn out a novel every year or he will starve. This means that during his creative period he must write a great deal of stuff which posterity will forget. In England it is very difficult to earn a living as a writer."

Mr. Maugham, who is forty-nine, says that he has reached the period of life when he wishes to write essays. "That means," he said, "that I am beginning to think about life rather than to feel it. It is a sign of age to wish to write essays. It means that the emotions are no longer as capable of stimulation as they once were. It means that I am withdrawing to the side lines of life and taking up the point of view of a spectator."

Joseph Conrad Comes to Town

September 1924

When Joseph Conrad died at his home in Kent on August 3, 1924, English literature lost one of its few modern novelists who are indubitably of the first rank. Not even Hardy's fame rests more secure than that of the seafaring Pole who knew no English until he had grown to manhood and who was thirty-eight years old when he began writing.

It was probably with some premonition that his writing career was at an end that he authorized his American publishers to bring out the Concord edition of his collected works which they are just completing and that caused him last May to carry out an old wish to see New York's skyline from the harbor.

He came to America neither to lecture nor to gather material for a book. He wanted to see the New York skyline; he wanted to view the city and its environs from the tower of the Woolworth Building; and he wanted to pay a visit to his friend Frank N. Doubleday, the publisher, whose company had sent him the first considerable check he ever received in royalties.

He was ill most of the time he was here. He had been attacked by lumbago and gout on the voyage over and when he arrived here, and throughout his brief visit, he was a sick man. Except for a few automobile trips he spent most of his time at Mr. Doubleday's estate on Long Island.

I have never seen a group of newspapermen more reverent toward any person, no matter how exalted in rank, than was the little crowd of them, of which I was one, which set out that May morning at dawn on the revenue cutter to board the *Tuscania* while she lay at Quarantine.

Conrad had come over on the liner commanded by his friend, Captain David W. Bone, who is himself an author of two books of sea stories, *Broken Stowage* and *The Brassbounder*. Each reporter had brought, it seemed, his favorite Conrad book, hoping to summon enough courage to ask for an autograph. I had a limp-leather copy of *Lord Jim*. It is inscribed now with Conrad's signature and also with this legend: "Captain Joseph Conrad duly delivered in New York Harbor in good order and condition by David W. Bone, Master., R.M.S. *Tuscania,* May Day, 1923."

When we finally clambered aboard the *Tuscania* we learned that Conrad was in the captain's quarters. Awed more perceptibly than newspapermen are wont to be, we formed a hasty council to consider ways and means of effecting an interview without frightening the great man into silence, because we had heard he was shy and timid.

We delegated one of our number to break the ice gently and in a roundabout way, agreeing that in that way only could we coax him into a confiding mood. We filed through the door of the narrow cabin, hats in hand, respectful and awkward, as if we were latecomers at obsequies, and ranged ourselves in a solemn circle around the frightened little genius.

He was still suffering from some of the effects of his voyage. He was swathed in a white silk muffler and a black overcoat. He wore a white stiff-bosomed shirt with a high collar without wings, a dark four-in-hand tie, a suit of brown cheviot, brown woolen hose, low black shoes with square toes, and a black derby hat.

He was about five feet eight inches in height, slightly stooped. His head sat lown on his shoulders and slightly forward. He had a gray mustache and a close-cropped white beard, trimmed to a point. His hair and eyebrows were coal-black; his eyes deep brown. He wore a monocle which distended the lids of his right eye, while the lids of the other eye were narrowed to a slit.

His face was weatherbeaten and ruddy, with the red tracings of fine veins making a network on his cheeks. His forehead was very low and receding. His head was broad above the temples and shaped like an interrogation point in the back. He enunciated his words largely through movements of his lips, and had more than a trace of a foreign accent, with a tendency to stress all words on the last syllable.

I learned afterward that he was conscious of this accent and was pained to have it noticed; but it gave a piquancy to his vocal language which I have since found interesting to apply to his written work while reading it aloud.

He was visibly frightened by the presence of the interviewers. His hands and lips trembled and his mouth expanded in a nervous smile. His glance darted from one to another apprehensively. He had the appearance of a man of the most delicate sensibilities, shy, modest, sensitive, even humble before strangers. The interviewing got on badly, for we were all at a loss as to what to ask him. There raced through my head some of the beautifully worded aphorisms which are embedded in the fine texture of his prose and, remembering them, it seemed a desecration to demand that he reword them in the bald colloquialisms of an interview when he had been at such pains to express himself perfectly in his work.

I knew how he felt about life, about women, and about men. No one, except himself, had ever adumbrated Conrad's feeling about life clearly and concisely. Both his skepticism and his convictions are devastatingly pessimistic; and his pessimism consists precisely in this, that he believes man to be the victim of his own codes of conduct and of his own unattainable ideals. All man's tragedies are based upon those things—not, as many critics have said, upon man's blind battle against fate—and because Conrad sees in those tragedies the beauty of aspiration and defeat he conveys that beauty to us magically.

While these thoughts echoed in my mind, I heard the informal patter of a great writer courteously obliging importunate newsmen with such answers as these:

"I had a touch of lumbago and an attack of gout in my left hand; I didn't get up in the bridge as much as I should have liked . . . This is the largest ship I was ever on . . . I left the sea in '94: ships have changed since then. All life has changed. Captain Bone was kind enough to show me all the new contraptions which ships did not have when I was at sea. . . . Yes, I still hold my master's ticket: it is in the family archives. Captain Bone insisted that men address me by my title. At first I didn't know who they meant when the officers said, 'Do this and that for the captain.' A pretty compliment. It pleased me very much. . . . Americans have an enviable enthusiasm. Enthusiasm which makes life interesting. . . . No, I am not much up on American literature. You see, I don't read much fiction, and my mind is not critical. I couldn't say much about writers because I haven't got any general culture. Twenty years at sea when one is a youth do not fit one with a critical type of mind. I am not a literary man. . . . You see I have had three lives: until seventeen a boy in Poland, twenty years at sea, and the remainder as a writer. I thought of drifting back to sea, even after I was married; but after *The Nigger of the "Narcissus,"* I made up my mind it was the end of my life at sea."

We were on the captain's bridge and Conrad had forgotten his interviewers and was rapt and ecstatic in contemplation of the spires of Lower Manhattan which were becoming visible through the thin, bluish mist. Captain Bone's brother, Muirhead Bone, the etcher, was at one end, working away for dear life with crayons, trying to catch the harbor scene as viewed from an incoming liner. Conrad kept exclaiming, "Wonderful! Magnificent! Beautiful!"

My final impression of him was that he was a very complex and determined man under an exterior of simplicity in manners and, beneath, an attitude of courteous deference.

He knew human nature; he had created character in the grand

manner; and he was very sure about himself and his work in the world, whatever appearance he gave of humility.

He was a man, I thought, whom it would be very difficult to know, for he lived in the ivory tower of his own thoughts and dreams—thoughts and dreams which he committed to paper.

As a ship's master, as also I imagine in all of his duties and concerns with daily life, he was doubtless a rigid disciplinarian and a severe taskmaster. He had, I suspected, a capacity for hard work and was impatient with laziness and procrastination in others. But that he was gentle and kind, tender and compassionate, there could be no doubt.

First Meeting with Dreiser

December 18, 1922

This afternoon I went to see Theodore Dreiser, who had just come on from Hollywood and is living in St. Luke's Place, next door to Sherwood Anderson. Although we had exchanged brief notes from time to time for several years I had never met him.

The ground-floor flat in which he lives has a large living room, about forty feet by twenty, with a fireplace, over which there is a mirror in a scroll frame; the room is almost bare of furniture, except for an office desk at the rear of the room and some chairs; no rugs. There is a huge portrait of Dreiser in mandarin coat and posture and a very fleshy reclining nude on the walls. I saw none of the rest of the apartment.

Dreiser is more youthful than I expected him to be, remembering that he published *Sister Carrie* more than twenty years ago. He is tall, without superfluous flesh, and only slightly stooped. His hair is gray, his eyes deep-set, his cheeks so full as to seem puffy, his lips thick. He has no gestures and is the most immobile writer I ever saw, apparently capable of sitting at ease for an hour without moving a muscle. His voice is well-modulated, soft and without any nasal quality. He speaks slowly, with an average stammer, and there is a certain air of humility and gentleness in his bearing. I got from him the same sort of impression of dogged, persistent honesty, sincerity, frankness, and hungry curiosity about life that I get from his writings. He greeted me with the friendly casualness one has toward friends of long standing. He had a sheaf of manuscript in his hand, and after he had got a match for my cigarette (he doesn't smoke) he sat down and explained in a timid and bashful manner that he had been writing poems and that he was anxious to know what I thought of them. He said he would like to send me the batch of poems he had written over a long period of years and have me make frank notes of comment on each one.

"They are free-verse sort of things," he said. "Just moods and impressions and attempts to get into a few words something I feel about the color and beauty and strangeness of life. I have been writing them off and on for years. I don't know whether they are any good or not, but they are things I had to write just the way they are written."

I asked him to read some of them to me, knowing that I had been much more sympathetic toward Sherwood Anderson's *Mid-American Chants* after hearing Sherwood recite them than I had upon reading them in *The Little Review;* but Dreiser picked out five and handed them to me. I had almost wanted to laugh when he told me he was writing poetry, so redundant, cacophonous, and deficient in word values is he in his prose; but these strange pieces had life and heart in them, like his plodding, cumbrous novels, and, moreover, they had the impress of authentic poetic emotion. Here was an ineluctable sadness, a poignancy in no way rhetorical, glimpses of beauty caught in images from life in a city street— astonishing things, really, yet somehow in character, somehow the sort of fumbling grasps of poetic essentials one would expect of him did one ever think of him expressing himself in verse, free or otherwise.

He works daily, he told me, from ten until three or four, uninterruptedly and without lunching. He is still writing *The Stoic* and the third volume of the trilogy which includes *The Financier* and *The Titan*, and he has also written eight of a series of fifteen portraits of women, which is to be a companion volume to *Twelve Men*. That book, *Twelve Men*, he said, is apparently the best liked of all his books; more copies of it have been sent to him for his signature than of all the others combined.

He recited to me without bitterness, indeed with an amused

297

resignation, the rebuffs he had had, the difficulties he still encoun-
ters in finding a market for his writings; the hostility of the reviewers, the trenchant personal abuse that has been heaped upon him
gratuitously by critics, the hard time he has had in making a living. Of the series of fine and original portraits in *Twelve Men* he
was able to dispose of only one to a magazine, although, he said,
"I hawked them all in every editorial office. Everybody said they
were no good until after they came out in book form and critics
here and there began to praise them. Then editors wanted me to
write more like them."

Dreiser's tenacity of purpose in the face of all possible odds
against him has been not the least noble aspect of his writing
career. Against a storm of critical derision, moral indignation, the
hounding of the vice society, rejection slips, insufficient financial
returns, discouragement and abuse, he has made no compromise
whatever; he has expressed himself unequivocally, sincerely, as he
felt. He is at once a proud and humble man, without arrogance or
a sense of martyrdom, driven by a desire to write of life as he sees
and knows it as well and as truthfully as he can.

He moved, a pathmaker, with heavy, crunching, powerful
steps, through the brambles and thickets of American literary
prejudice, making way for a host of more graceful but less powerful writers who follow him, and who in the blithe heedlessness of
youth will never be properly grateful for the work he has done
until it turns out, as it reasonably may, that he has done not the
most artistic but the most significant work of his period in America's age of democratic industrialism, that it was his genius which
most accurately reflected the peculiar aspects of his age.

Dreiser Party a Flop

June 23, 1926

With a blandly naïf indiscretion, Llewelyn Powys describes in his new book, *The Verdict of Bridlegoose*, a party that has become famous in the sub-rosa annals of New York literary history because of its ghastly and abject failure. Powys's impression of the evening is interesting as being that of a visiting Englishman who plainly did not know what it was all about and who not only did not grasp the fact that the party was a dud, but knew nothing about the factors which contributed to the peculiar events of the evening.

Since Powys has spilled the beans, it is well to give his testimony:

"One evening I was asked by Dreiser to meet some friends of his. He stood in the very center of the room, entirely ignorant of the fact that the guests he had brought together were not mixing well, and ready at a moment's notice to forget all of us as he followed the flounderings of his own wayward imagination, which, like a mammoth whale, with snortings and spoutings, plunged over the limitless ocean of life to the Isles of the Blest. Suddenly there entered upon us a youth, a little the worse for drink, whom everybody called Scotty, and who, I learned afterward, was the novelist, Scott Fitzgerald.

"There was something about this young man, who came in from Tough Man's Bend with a bottle in his hand, that I liked extremely. He had evidently never met Dreiser before; and, far gone in his cups as he was, he addressed the elder novelist with maudlin deference. It was as though some young Dick Lovelace had come bursting into Ben Jonson's room; only, when one looked more closely at this boy's face, one noticed that it had a weak,

299

blue-eyed, modern look that would have been curiously inappropriate in more heroic days.

"Mencken, Carl Van Vechten and Ernest Boyd were among Dreiser's guests. I always had liked what I had heard about Mencken, but I never expected to meet anyone so squat, a veritable Tweedledum, with curtailed schoolboy jacket making schoolboy jokes and talking schoolboy talk with a kind of boisterous bonhomie. Though I saw at a glance that his nature entirely lacked that finer edge which some of us perhaps rate too highly, I felt that there was no nonsense about him. I felt, in fact, that he was in possession of a far sounder intellect than, for example, that other zany of God's Nordic circus, Mr. G. K. Chesterton.

"Carl Van Vechten sat silent on a hard chair, his clever head drooping slightly to the left. Indeed, I have never been in the company of this famous wit when he did not appear to me like an aging madonna lily that had lost its pollen and had been left standing in a vase which the parlormaid had forgotten to refill with fresh water."

So absorbed was Powys in assimilating the above impressions of these famous literary personages he had heard about that he did not notice that the party was dying on its feet and that presently it keeled over with a most pathetic flop.

What had happened was this: Dreiser, who was not given to gregariousness, was not a social being in the sense that he enjoyed company just because it was company. He, who rarely attended any sort of literary gathering, decided, on the eve of the publication of one of his books, to give a party inviting some of the distinguished critics, essayists, and novelists of the city.

As it happened, few of those invited had ever met before. This may astound those who live outside of New York and who imagine that all of the writing folk of New York know one another, but it is a fact. Dreiser received in a long, wide room in his apartment in St. Luke's Place, where the chairs were arranged around the walls as though there were going to be a dance. Dreiser was blissfully ignorant of the fact that his guests were unacquainted with one another (for he, too, having been buried away with his writings, imagined that the lit'ry folk all lunched and dined together ever so often), and in consequence he neglected to introduce new arrivals to those who were already there.

To make matters worse, Dreiser provided nothing to drink to enliven the spirits of his embarrassed and self-conscious guests. They sat around like so many well-behaved school children at a party waiting for something to happen, and especially waiting with their tongues hanging out for the host to offer some kind of a drink. In anticipation of the shindig, most of them had had a cocktail at dinner, but the effects of it had worn off, leaving them dull, lumpy, and listless. Dreiser, who does not smoke and only very rarely drinks (and then only to be sociable), had not an ounce of liquor, vinous or spiritous, in the house.

Suddenly there broke in upon this curious wake F. Scott Fitzgerald, his eyes not focusing well enough to pick out his host (even from photographs) among the faces that swam before him and brandishing a bottle of very excellent champagne. He had idolized Dreiser as the dean of American novelists and, overwhelmed by the invitation which Dreiser (whom he had never seen) had extended to him to attend the party, he had gone in search of a suitable present to the master. It had taken him much time, going from speakeasy to speakeasy, and in his colloquies with the bartenders in each as to where he might pick up a good bottle of vintage wine, he acquired quite an edge. With the treasure finally tucked firmly under his arm, Fitzgerald made his way to St. Luke's Place and burst in upon what looked like a row of wax dummies.

Teetering from one guest to another, inquiring which was Dreiser, he finally found his host and presented his gift with an eloquent speech of homage.

Dreiser listened through the tribute, took the bottle, and put it in the icebox. After an hour or so of waiting, each separate member of the dismal party finally made up his mind, regretfully, that Dreiser was never going to take the champagne out of the icebox, and with an air of vast disappointment bade the host good night.

On the sidewalk outside one or two writers who had hitherto been hostile to each other held a parley to decide the question as to whether it would be proper to ask Dreiser to open up the bottle, and finally polled in the negative. Thereat they dragged their feet down the avenue as if they were pallbearers in a cortege.

Ellen Glasgow at Home

September 1928

Miss Glasgow's home is at No. 1 West Main Street, Richmond, a tall, square, gray-walled mansion in a most incongruous setting. The house is old and spacious and is situated on a plot of ground shaded by magnolias and enlivened in the summertime with a profusion of flowers. There is a high wall in the rear and an iron fence encloses the yard on the side and front. But this charming old residence is surrounded by garages, chain stores, lunchrooms, bakeries, laundries, fruit stores, and small shops. For "commercial progress" has overtaken the old residential section of Richmond, and the house at No. 1 West Main Street is one of the few ancient houses of the section that have not been demolished.

Miss Ellen Glasgow was born in this house. All of her novels, with the exception of *Life and Gabriella*, were written in a room on the second floor which is set aside as her workroom. The sides of this room are occupied by bookcases, except for a niche in which fits a cabinet of glass and mahogany, where she keeps her collection of porcelain dogs. There is a fireplace, a Hepplewhite couch, a straight chair before which sits a small table, on which stands a typewriter directly under a shaded light supported by a wrought-iron standing lamp.

In one corner, where the sunlight falls through two windows, is Miss Glasgow's work desk, a heavy, beautiful piece of old colonial design. On this desk there is a china vase containing a great number of cork-bodied pens with stub points. Over the mantelpiece there is a Botticelli print and about the room there are many paintings and pictures of dogs. Miss Glasgow loves dogs, and, besides her collection of china dogs, paintings, bronze medallions, and photographs of dogs, she has two large and fluffy and very animated Sealyhams.

The walls of the hallway and living rooms are ivory and gray and the furnishings of Sheraton and Hepplewhite, with Chinese hangings and oriental rugs adding touches of color.

Miss Glasgow uses a typewriter and usually makes her first draft by typing it out herself. This draft she submits to a thorough revision with her stub pen and gives the result to Miss Bennett, her secretary, to retype. She invariably attends to her correspondence in longhand, writing large, full-bodied letters, slanting slightly to the right.

She as a person is witty and charming, with an unquenchable spirit of gay irony. Her eyes twinkle with an amused vivacity, and her conversation is studded with general and specific ideas expressed with subtlety and verbal resourcefulness. One of the subjects about which she grows grave and indignant is that of Prohibition. She told me that it embittered her to hear old Virginia gentlemen who once prided themselves on their knowledge of the various grades of bourbon talking about their new shipments of "corn," their palates ruined, their urbanity coarsened, and their mint juleps a vile parody of the mint julep of former times. And over the murders committed by Federal Prohibition enforcement officers she flames with the anger of outraged justice. A most gracious and hospitable hostess who entertains her guests in the grand manner of old Southern traditions, she took precaution to stock a fine collection of wines and spirits before the Eighteenth Amendment went into effect, and it is a source of anxiety to her that this cellar is steadily diminishing with no hope of its being replenished with anything like its quality.

The authoress is unorthodox in her opinions and as free from sentimentality as was Jane Austen. She made her somewhat sensational debut as a novelist at eighteen, when she published *The*

Descendant, a novel in which she broke away from the sentimental tradition in American fiction. She has lived through the
final stages of Victorian hypocrisy and has seen the expansion of
the privileges and rights of women; and she has seen the South
emerge from its old lethargy and take part in the brisk go-getterism
of the North. And she has reservations about both eras. She finds
many of the professed ideals of the Victorian age preposterous;
but Fundamentalism, Prohibition, and real-estate subdivisions she
finds have destroyed one of the old rules of life in the South, which
was to live and let live.

Miss Glasgow has dedicated her most recent novel, *They
Stooped to Folly*, to James Branch Cabell. Mr. Cabell had dedicated *Something About Eve* to her. They are old friends, and the
Cabells are often guests at Miss Glasgow's home and Miss Glasgow is often a guest at the Cabell home in Monument Avenue.

She tells me that every time she publishes a novel, some of her
readers in Richmond accuse her of having used real persons in her
book; but all the events she has ever recorded in fiction have been
imaginary and although, like other novelists, she draws upon the
character of this actual person and that one for traits, none of her
characters has existed as a whole except in her imagination.

They Stooped to Folly Miss Glasgow describes as a comedy of
morals. It is more than that. It is the lively history of three generations in the South from the days when, as she says: "Being ruined
was not a biological fact but a state of mind," to the present, when
the whole is a personal affair, one's own business. *They Stooped
to Folly* is being sponsored by the Literary Guild for August. It is
characteristic of Ellen Glasgow that she sympathizes not with
Poor Aunt Agatha who stooped to folly in an earnest age, nor
Amy Dalrymple, mid-Victorian flirt, but with Milly Burden, a
young stenographer, who sinned as if it were her own private
affair; and that she blames Southern men for the "harlot or
Madonna" concept that has brought tragedy to so many Southern
women.

Miss Glasgow is plump and bronze-haired; she has brown eyes and a short but ample nose, slightly retroussé. Her lips are neither thick nor thin, although they appear thin when stretched into her frequent and engaging smile. She likes to dress in lively colors and to carry of an evening a large purple fan of ostrich feathers and to wear brightly colored shoes.

Her favorite poet is Alice Meynell and her favorite novelists are Tolstoi, Dostoevski, and Jane Austen, all of whom have influenced her work. She is generous and benevolent, intensely feminine, and endowed with that complete ignorance of money matters, which, somehow, miraculously enables her to get the fattest sort of contracts and the most desirable terms from editors and publishers. She is ruled over by a kindly despot, her secretary, Miss Bennett, who sometimes seems to regard her as an improvident child.

One night when Mr. Cabell and I were admiring Miss Glasgow's collection of porcelain dogs, Miss Glasgow, in a burst of generosity, offered Mr. Cabell one of the dogs he expressly admired. Mr. Cabell collects representations of all sorts of creatures: cows, lions, horses, dogs, elephants, rhinoceroses, cats, lizards, in glass, amber, bronze, porcelain, terra cotta, and plaster of paris. When he got downstairs with the treasure Miss Glasgow had given him, he took care not to let the porcelain dog out of his hands for more than a few seconds and not to let Miss Bennett have it at all, for he rightly feared that Miss Bennett would at once restore it to its former owner and tell him that he could not have it. For Miss Bennett upbraided Miss Glasgow for giving it to him.

Bertrand Russell, the Philosopher, At a Party

May 30, 1924

I met Bertrand Russell, the philosopher and mathematician, at the Algonquin today. Horace Liveright had him and Horace M. Kallen in tow and asked Hazel and me to sit with them. Russell is a thin, wiry man, a little below medium height, with a hatchet face, furrowed cheeks, a Scot's ruddy complexion, and a heavy shock of white hair. He looks a little like Henry Ford. He has a quizzical smile and an alert look of intense curiosity. He has a fund of anecdotes and tells them well. One was about Lytton Strachey. He had gone to a lodginghouse in the country where Strachey had put up several weeks previously. The landlady, in telling Mr. Russell of Strachey, said that when Strachey first came she thought he was a tramp, he looked so disreputable. "I discovered later," said the landlady, "that he was a gentleman—though an odd one."

After lunch we went to Liveright's office, where Horace called up a number of people and in a short time the party was on. T. R. Smith called a caterer and gave him instructions for canapés and sandwiches; and Liveright's office is always well stocked with liquor for any emergency. A four-piece Negro orchestra appeared out of nowhere within half an hour and people began trouping in —Mayor Jimmie Walker, Theodore Dreiser, Edna Ferber, Paul Morand, Joseph Schildkraut, Maxwell Bodenheim, Otto Kahn, Art Young, Sinclair Lewis, Louis Kronenberger, Manuel Komroff, Isador Schneider, Harry Kemp, Lillian Hellman, and dozens of others whom I did not know, including a flock of very pretty women.

As the party got going good late in the afternoon, Russell was obviously having the time of his life. This renowned logician and authority on the atom flirted and danced like a young collegian. He didn't miss a dance throughout the afternoon and evening, except when Dreiser drew him aside and asked him, "Why didn't you say something in that article of the *Nation* on 'New Morals for Old'? You beat about the bush—nothing concrete." Russell said he would like to talk to Dreiser about it sometime but got back on the dance floor as fast as he could.

Tonight, while reading Russell's little book about the future, *Icarus,* I again was confirmed in my belief that what a writer thinks is to be sought in what he writes, not in conversation with him. Conversation with a writer and observation of his response to his surroundings give one a set of impressions more or less reliable about his personality and about the factors determining his character. What Bertrand Russell thinks about science and the future, however, is not to be got from him over a luncheon table or at a party. It is to be got when he expressed himself thus in *Icarus:*

Science has not given more self-control, more kindliness, or more power of discounting their passions in deciding upon a course of action. It has given communities more power to indulge their collective passions, but, by making society more organic, it has diminished the part played by private passions. Men's collective passions are mainly evil; far the strongest of them are hatred and rivalry directed toward other groups. Therefore at present all that gives men power to indulge their collective passions is bad. That is why science threatens to cause the destruction of our civilization. The only solid hope seems to lie in the possibility of world-wide domination by one group, say the United States, leading to the gradual formation of an orderly economic and political world government. But perhaps, in view of the sterility of the Roman Empire, the collapse of our civilization would in the end be preferable to this alternative.

The increase of organization in the modern world has made the ideals of liberalism wholly inapplicable. Liberalism, from Montesquieu to President Wilson, was based upon the assumption of a number of more or less equal individuals or groups, with no differences so vital that they were willing to die sooner than compromise. It was supposed that there was to be free competition between individuals and between ideas. Experience has shown, however, that the existing economic system is incompatible with all forms of free competition except between states by means of armaments. I should wish, for my part, to preserve free competition between ideas, though not between individuals and groups, but this is only possible by means of what an old-fashioned liberal would regard as interference with personal liberty. So long as the sources of economic power remain in private hands there will be no liberty except for the few who control these sources. Such liberal ideals as free trade, free press, unbiased education, either already belong to the past or soon will do so.

AE (George Russell)

March 1928

In that trilogy of superb malice and almost flawless art, *Ave, Salve, Vale,* at least one man escaped ridicule and, more than being let off, was sainted by a chap who was worthy to officiate only because he writes so well. After many years in Paris and London, George Moore had returned to a Dublin that quite patently did not want him. When he proposed to honor the *Claidheam Soulis* with some writings, the assistant editors told him that the next few numbers of the magazine were full up but if he had any notions, to work them into an article and take his chances with the caprice of the editor. And he had got no encouragement from renting agents in his search for a place to live.

"I followed the pavement along Trinity College Gardens," wrote Moore, "my feet instinctively taking me to Æ, who settles everybody's difficulties and consoles the afflicted." And in three days Æ had found him a house, a capacious eighteenth-century house in the center of Dublin within a few minutes' walk of Stephen's Green, and with a convent garden adjoining it, in which Moore noted, with characteristic indelicacy, that the nuns' underthings were hung out to dry. . . . And again: "It is a great good fortune to have a friend whose eyes light up always when they see one, and whose mind stoops or lifts itself instinctively to one's trouble, divining it, whether it be spiritual or material."

"I wish you would tell me why I am coming to Dublin. . . . Nobody wants me here, Æ. . . . All I hoped for was a welcome and some enthusiasm; no bonfires, torchlight processions, banners, bands, *Cead mille failte's,* nothing of that kind, only a welcome.

310

It may be that I did expect some appreciation of the sacrifice I was making, for you see I am throwing everything into the flames. . . . Isn't it strange? You understand, but the others don't."

Æ, who was always taking out his watch and saying he had to get back to his office, took out his watch at this point and said he had to get back to his office. But he had divined, meanwhile, that God (or whatever is the equivalent of God in Æ's metaphysics) had sent Moore to Dublin as an affliction for certain sins of the Celtic Renaissance—though Moore never knew he was an instrument of correction—and so Æ accepted the ordainment and aided Moore in the accomplishment of his mission. "There is other work to do here," said Æ, "besides the Gaelic league." Moore's job, although Moore did not know it, was to provide comedy relief in a drama that was in danger of becoming altogether too tense and serious. Æ knew that; but then he knew everything.

I had asked James Stephens when he was over here what Æ looked like. "He is an enormous man," answered Stephens, "inconCEIVably covered with whiskers." And as I looked at Stephens, who is like a leprechaun out of *The Crock of Gold*, five feet three about, I had a picture of that anomalous boon companionship—that of the giant Russell walking along the streets of Dublin deep in conversation with the gnome-like Stephens, who comes no higher than Æ's elbow.

Everybody speaks of George Russell with a sort of reverence. Even Boyd, Ernest Boyd, a mocking cynic who views his fellow men with an eye to their absurdities, becomes grave and mellow and deferential on the subject of Æ. "There is nobody in the world like him," says Boyd. "He wins the heart of everybody. He knows how to inspire people to do things. Talk with him for a few minutes and he knows exactly what you are capable of doing and supplies the ideas for you to work with. When I went down to the boat to meet him he had not got on the dock before he shouted, 'Boyd, I have got an idea of a book for you.' And with customs inspectors shoving him around and Irish compatriots bawling in his ear, he told me the whole scheme of the book then and there. He has a thousand ideas a day."

We were riding up Fifth Avenue in a taxicab to Judge Richard Campbell's house, after the P.E.N. Club dinner. Æ was to join us there later. "Ernest," I said, "as I listened to him tonight I found myself wishing that it could be possible for my son when he gets to be seventeen or eighteen to come under his influence. I wish he could see him and talk to him now and then. I am sure that he would bring out every potentiality he has. I have never seen anyone with such serenity, naturalness, and simplicity." And I thought of Moore's phrase about Æ's "hope-inspiring eyes," but did not voice it.

"That charm of his," said Boyd, "affects everybody. At a dinner of great financiers and high moguls of politics and diplomacy the other night they were all dwarfed by his personality and rendered speechless by his superior knowledge of the very things they are supposed to know."

At the P.E.N. Club dinner Russell had told us that the Irish literary Renaissance had developed out of the fact that the Irish were poor, they were ignorant, they were unorganized, and they were behind the times. Since they were poor, he said, the writing profession was so great a hazard that only a few could go in for it as a means of livelihood and only those few about whom there could be no mistake concerning their literary talent. It was a case of the survival of the fittest. Since they were ignorant, he said, they were not handicapped in the flowering of their talent by that sense of the futility of writing which overcomes people who have read a great many books and have contemplated the enormous stream of literature of all ages. Since they were unorganized, he said, each man developed his individuality to the fullest.

"There is no such thing as a 100 per cent Irishman," said Æ. "An Irishman is never standardized; he never conforms to any rule. On account of this, Dublin is full of characters. And Irish literature is full of individualities. You would never mistake the

312

writing of one Irishman for that of another. If you saw an un-signed page by James Stephens you would immediately know that it was Stephens's, and so also with a page by Synge or Yeats or any other Irish writer."

And since they were behind the times, he said, they were not affected by the accelerated tempo of modern industrial life, but were leisured, lazy, primitive, and at peace.

Later, at Judge Campbell's, I noticed that same trait in Æ that James Stephens has—an alertness of interest which permits his mind to travel from the sublime to the ridiculous and from the profound to the absurd with little indication of any transition. Civilization has left no mark on either of them : they are untamed, uninhibited, and without fear. Stephens would recite some lofty lines from Yeats and in the next breath recite a ribald limerick by Oliver Gogarty with the same relish and gusto in each perform-ance. And Æ's mind would move lightly from problems of grave concern to humorous anecdote and back again without any effect of incongruity. There is this difference : he is a spiritual leader and his role has been to instruct, inspire, console, and reassure, whereas Stephens's mission has been to enliven and to entertain.

Moore tells that when Sir Horace Plunkett was trying to awaken Ireland to the advantages of co-operation, Yeats had told him that Ireland was deaf to his economics because he did not know her folk tales and could not croon them by the fireside. What Plunkett needed was a poet and Yeats had in mind the right man, a poet at the time earning his living as an accountant at Pim's. "His personal influence," said Yeats, "pervades the whole shop, from the smallest clerk up to the manager, and all eyes go to him when he passes." And Yeats went on to tell a story, how a young man, a ne'er-do-well, had once seen Æ crossing from one desk to another with some papers in his hand and had gone to him, saying, "Something tells me you are the man who may re-deem me." And Æ had saved this young man, not by preaching to him, but by inspiring him with hope. And so Plunkett called upon him at Pim's and drafted him into the work of bicycling about the countryside, establishing creameries, and preaching the message of co-operative marketing of farm products to the husbandman. That was how George Russell came by his pseudonym "Æ": Plunkett had turned a mystic poet into an Agricultural Economist. And Æ, a poet, painter, and philosopher, accepted his destiny and, as always, did his job well.

George Russell was not satisfied with Moore's portrait of him in *Ave* and *Salve* and complained that Moore had represented him as the blameless hero of a young girl's novel. "Why have you found no fault with me?" he asked. "If you wish to create human beings you must discover their faults." And so Moore meditated upon the possible flaws in Æ's character. He recalled that he was indifferent to money and had often said, "I came into the world without money or possessions, and I have done very well without either. Why shouldn't my children do the same?" And Moore thought for a moment that Mrs. Russell might not feel the same way about it and might be nagging her husband into "making more of himself," for it is "the common belief that a man's life is not his exclusive possession to dispose of as pleases his good will, but a sort of family banking account on which his wife and children may draw checks." But Moore remembered Æ's wife and remembered that he chose her for her intelligence and that in Mrs. Russell's eyes there is no blemish in Æ's character. And so the portrait in the trilogy remained a "silhouette," for Moore could find no fault to make it human, except a tiny one: John Eglington had recalled to Moore, when they were trying to rake up something against Æ, that Russell had not known that Athenian society was founded on slavery. Moore began to speculate upon Æ's private life along lines that would occur to Moore and to no one else, but before he got very far he gave up his imaginings as too inappropriate even for his indelicate mind.

Part of George Russell's beautiful serenity may come from his belief in reincarnation, with its corollary that our bodies are lent to us for a brief space of time to accomplish some definite mission in a long education and shriving of the soul. But Æ has a chuckling mind even in gravity, and he would never be positive about any belief that rests upon undemonstrable theory.

Willa Cather

July 1924

I met Miss Willa Cather in March 1924; she had returned from a year's residence in France, during which time she had written that beautiful little masterpiece, *A Lost Lady*. At an evening with Ernest Boyd, Thomas Beer had told me that he was having Miss Cather to lunch on a Tuesday and invited me to join them. I suffered some delay in getting away from the house, and Beer and Miss Cather were waiting for me on the much too prominently placed settle at the Crillon, which faces the dining-room doorway—a restaurant appointment having the advantage of throwing you into immediate contact with the person you are seeking, but having the disadvantage of forcing the person who has to wait to remain on display like an object in a shop-window.

My tardiness ruffled the composure I had been at some pains in attaining at the prospect of meeting the woman whom I consider to be the finest artist of her sex now writing in English. I was not put any the more readily at my ease by my discovery that she was amazingly unlike my conception of her as a person. I had somehow expected her to be wistful—though if I had troubled to recall her biography I should have known that no woman could have once been a telegraph editor of a daily newspaper and later managing editor of a magazine and still be wistful precisely. Miss Cather is quite the reverse of that; she is alert, alive, quick-witted, vigorous-minded, and assertive, not at all dreamy, preoccupied, self-isolated, or diffident.

I believe the first thing I noticed about her was the forceful masculinity of her hands; they are strong hands without the

316

so-called artist taper—which, by the way, I have observed very few artists possess.

Her features are bluntly decisive in line; her eyes are pale blue and set wide apart, with eyebrows high enough to give her ordinarily a look of challenge and appraisal; her mouth is ample, with full, flexible lips whose movements are as expressive an accompaniment of her speech as are the gestures of a Latin; and her nose is a nose, not a tracery.

All the pictures I have seen of her amount almost to libels, for they portray a faintly sullen expression about her mouth, and such an expression she is not guilty of, I believe, ever. Hers is a mouth capable of sternness, severity, stubbornness, perhaps, but not sullenness.

I like the way she sits, relaxed without slumping, free, easy, assured, without tension. She wears her hair parted slightly to the right of the middle and drawn up in a loose knot in the back. She has the extraordinary courage to wear at the same time salmon and green, and she does it with complete success. I can now very easily imagine that she has sat for Leon Bakst's most successful portrait; whereas I had wondered why the women of Omaha had chosen that artistic Tartar barbarian, of all painters, for the honor of doing her likeness as a memorial to her as Nebraska's eminent novelist, there is probably no portraitist who would be more understanding and appreciative of the strength and subtleties of her character and handsomeness.

I was not surprised to hear her expatiate with the keenest admiration upon the character and personality of a woman who is pretty much her own direct opposite—Ellen Terry, a talented, capricious, intensely feminine woman who has pirouetted gracefully and radiantly over the surfaces of life, learning nothing of its sordidness apparently (if we are to judge from her memoirs) which she might not have learned as a charming, imitative, ingenuous child in the nursery.

Histrionism and mimicry, playing at life and finding it enchantingly colorful, an escape into an imaginative world where drabness and time-serving are forgotten in the illusion of adventure—these are the things which attract Miss Cather to the singers and actresses who figure so prominently in her stories. And because she has emotional understanding as well as intelligence, sympathy as well as insight, her stories have warmth and poetry in them. They touch both the heart and the intellect. Mrs. Forrester, the heroine of *A Lost Lady,* is one of the few women in fiction whose author has endeavored to convey the idea of a heroine who is irresistible, and whom you *know,* you *feel* to be charming, radiant, attractive, and beautiful—not through any description but because of the effect, carefully observed, that she is depicted as having upon men. Miss Cather knows her decorative women of electric energy and she knows the other sorts too.

Her conversation is staccato; she chops her spoken sentences out incisively, in short, neat links. In this respect she reminds me somewhat of that other dynamo of creative zeal, Miss Amy Lowell. It is impossible to register and recall as a continued or amplified discourse any topic she touches on, because she disposes of any topic that interests her with expedition and economy of words.

One remembers only the high points—"One of those women with round chins. Women with round chins have terrible tempers. . . . Sarah Orne Jewett was too much cuddled by her family. They'd have kept her in cotton wool and smothered her if they'd had entirely their own way about it. She was a very uneven writer. A good portion of her work is not worth preserving. The rest, a small balance—enough to make two volumes—is important. She was a voice. She spoke for a slight but influential section of the American people. She was clearly a voice, an authentic voice. . . . Suzanne Lenglen plays perfect tennis, entirely on her nerves, not on beef and muscle. She has no American conception of sportsmanship: she goes in simply to win and if she loses her confidence in herself for a moment before a match,

318

she goes into hysterics and refuses to play. She is a superb player, though, when she has control of herself. . . ."

Miss Cather is interested in good food; she is proud of her cook; she walks a great deal for the exercise; she is fascinated by the spectacle of life; she is a capable businesswoman, or at least gives the impression of so being; and she is without sentimentality, prudery, or false values of any sort. She uses such good, sanguine words as "muttonhead," "cub," "scamp," and "ninny" with delightful colloquial effectiveness.

She provokes in me the belief that she early formed a just and reasonable estimate of her gifts and decided to cultivate them pretty much to the exclusion of everything else. She was, I believe, intelligently aware of her genius and had the will to bring it to fruition. On the strength of her work she has already accomplished I think that she is more secure to posterity than Mrs. Edith Wharton, whose great lack as a writer is that of human warmth.

A Glimpse of Galsworthy

August 1926

My first interview with John Galsworthy was in Chicago during 1912 when I was a newspaper reporter attending college. He had not been reached by other reporters and had gone directly to the home of a professor in the University of Chicago for dinner. I learned where Galsworthy was dining, and with the temerity of a young man anxious to make good with the city editor on a self-imposed assignment, I called the professor's house on the telephone and asked for Mr. Galsworth. To my happy surprise I was not asked who I was. Galsworthy came to the phone. I explained matters and asked for an interview then and there. Galsworthy was prepared to give it to me, but we had difficulty in understanding each other. Afraid, probably, of affronting his host by remaining too long at the phone, he told me that he would be at the Congress Hotel at ten-thirty in the evening and that we might talk more satisfactorily there.

Shortly after ten-thirty I was in the hotel lobby telephoning to his room. No answer. I strolled down Peacock Alley prepared to await his return. Near the fountain in the Pompeian Room I spied a man and a woman seated at a table. The man wore a monocle. In those days, and even now, a monocle is something in the nature of an unexpected event in Chicago. Only Englishmen wear monocles, so I reasoned: Galsworthy is an Englishman; ergo, the man in the monocle is Galsworthy. I could not make up my mind. While I was meditating upon the advisability of having Mr. Galsworthy paged, the man with the monocle, with the lady on his arm, left their table, came out into Peacock

320

Alley, and entered the elevator. Sure enough, the man with the monocle asked for the floor on which was the Galsworthy suite. I rushed up, introduced myself, and said that I had come for the interview he had promised.

It was not much of an interview. Galsworthy was slow in answering my questions; his mind was not made up on a number of things; and ever and again he would appeal helplessly to Mrs. Galsworthy to answer the questions I asked. His courtesy, it seemed to me, was the most innate and charming I had ever witnessed. So many of my questions, it was obvious, were wholly unexpected and out of the realm of his meditations. Yet he seemed anxious to oblige me. He sat there, a calm, medium-sized man, with a large head, partly bald, white hair, and a pale skin, while his wife, a colorful woman, removed her hat before a mirror and straightened her hair, following the conversation between us, and answering the questions, when her husband was at a loss, without ever looking around.

All that emerged concretely in print from that interview was that Galsworthy had read and had liked Jack London, Edith Wharton, and Theodore Dreiser; that certain reforms in which he had been interested had been brought about in the English courts and prisons; and that it was wise for Americans to pay no more attention to the editorials in the British reviews that sneered at or condescended toward America than is paid to the editorials in England. I had been annoyed by a number of these editorials and with an impetuous sort of resentment I asked Galsworthy, "Why do your leader writers and reviewers even on the best-informed and most readable reviews persist in referring to America as though we were a nation of coarse and vulgar illiterates?"

"Those things," Galsworthy informed me, "are written by crabbed old men who have never been thirty miles from Fleet Street in their lives. They meet no one; they have no experience of life. They are living on the same meager stock of ideas which they took secondhand when they first entered journalism. If they are ill-informed about America and impervious to knowledge, they are equally ill-informed about what is going on at the present time in England and equally unamenable to instruction."

I have since talked to Galsworthy on two other occasions (he is a fairly frequent visitor to these shores) and nothing much came of these talks that showed up well in print. I doubt whether it is possible to get an exciting interview out of Galsworthy. He is too impersonal. He is the sort of man in whose presence you become aware that you simply cannot ask him a question touching himself, and so you are forced to talk of general matters. It used to be G. K. Chesterton's habit (it still may be) to come out to the gate to greet his visitor and inquire, "Do you believe in God? The question is very important." Not even Chesterton, I daresay, would ask that question of Galsworthy.

Joe Gould and Other Eccentrics

May 25, 1927

One of the most interesting of New York's many eccentrics is Joseph Gould, one-time press agent of the Republic of Albania, an authority on the American Indian, and a scholar of extraordinary parts. He was graduated at Harvard in the same class with John Reed, now buried in the Kremlin in Moscow, and of Walter Lippmann, now buried in a syndicated column.

Joe has written a history of the world. Or, rather, he is writing one, for the history is not yet finished. He has not yet found a publisher, although he has already written enough to fill ten volumes. His history promises to be unique because he conceives history as a series of events radiating from himself. We can know nothing definitely about the remote past, he says, except what our imagination tells us; and our experience is an aid to our imagination.

Joe is especially fortunate as a historian in that he can give us the evidence of an eyewitness to ancient episodes, since he is a believer in reincarnation. It might almost be said that he is a believer in galloping reincarnation, because he may be Cromwell one minute, Louis XIV the next, Cagliostro the next, Archimedes the next, and King Tutankhamen the next.

Joe was Cassius on the occasion of the assassination of Julius Caesar. He was "yon Cassius," remote from the scene, but not too remote for him to exercise the function of a reporter for posterity. He was Alexander the Great at various stages in that great warrior's career. He was present at the Diet of Worms; he sat in the tribunal with Robespierre; he was Button Gwinnett, who signed the Declaration of Independence and signed so few other things that his signature is worth $60,000.

Almost any day Joe may be seen in Greenwich Village—moving. He has an armload of books so large that he has to peer around the side of them to see where he is going, and on top of these books is placed, as a tantalus to the caprice of the wind, his hat. These are his worldly possessions; but in that amazing egg-shaped head of his, from which long, dry silver hairs wave sparsely, there teem great, glorious worlds of information and ideas.

He knows more about Albania than do all the Albanians. He knows the history and ethnology of Abyssinia backward and forward. I once gave him a small book about the American Indians to review and he brought me back enough manuscript to fill two quarto volumes of ordinary thickness. I had asked him to write three hundred words. But there is nothing meretricious about Joe. When I told him that I could not use all or even part of what he had written as a review, he was not distressed or angry. He had had his say about the book and that, so far as he was concerned, ended it.

Joe is a sublime and benevolent soul, patient, wise, benign, courteous, and just. Were he to tell me that the spirit of Buddha dwells within his breast, I would have no difficulty in believing him.

Eccentrics interest me more than normal people. Perhaps that is because the world is made up mainly of normal people and true eccentrics are rare. There is novelty about them. Your true eccentric, I have found, is almost never interested in money. His fixed idea is all-important to him and, although he sometimes tries to make money out of his fixed idea, the motive is secondary. He wants converts to his idea and nothing you could pay him can compensate him so much as patient and interested attention to what he has to say.

324

In my capacity as editor there came to me once a man who had written an 800,000-word treatise on forest conservation. He had a theory, which it had taken him 800,000 words to sustain, that the decadence and downfall of every nation in the past had been due to the decimation of the forests.

His theory was quite simple, fundamentally, and quite plausible. Trees breathe in and are sustained by carbonic-acid gas, which human beings exhale, and trees, in turn, give out oxygen, which is necessary for human life. When trees are destroyed, the supply of oxygen is diminished, and human beings become effete, sickly, neurotic, and without courage and ambition. A nation made up of such people is soon destroyed by more virile hordes from lands where there are trees. He brought to witness Syria and the lost glories of Nineveh and Tyre.

When I told him that his thesis was too long and too recondite for popular consumption, he was not disturbed by that. It did not matter whether he sold the treatise to me or not. That was not the point. Money was no object. But it was obvious from his fervor that he wished to convert me to his idea. When I pleaded lack of time, he did not heed me. It was not until I told him that I was utterly and completely convinced that he was right that he desisted in unloading upon me the enormous number of detail from his 800,000-word manuscript.

New York is full of eccentrics and quasi-eccentrics. Some of them are geniuses or near geniuses and some are charlatans and some are plain goofy. There is a rich and famous theatrical producer who is a little cracked on mechanical toys. He has two rooms full of them in his suite of offices. Some of them have been designed especially for him at great expense. Some are simply toys, like miniature grain elevators with electric trains and contraptions for loading grain into the trains; and some elaborate sets of rooms with mechanically propelled dolls going through strange motions. The producer will sit on the floor—and he is a big, hulking man with a broken nose and cauliflower ear from his days as a prize-fight trainer—playing with those toys for hours at a time, while movie magnates, famous theatrical stars, and hopeful playwrights cool their heels in the anteroom, having been told that the producer is "in conference."

Amy Lowell and Her Critics

August 1925

Clement K. Shorter, the critic and *causeur* of the London *Sphere*, has accused Sir Edmund Gosse of killing Amy Lowell. The critics did not kill Keats, he writes, but they did, in effect, kill his biographer. In support of his assertion he refers to a letter Miss Lowell wrote him just before her death. It was, he says, the letter of a heartbroken woman who had been stricken by the venom of Sir Edmund Gosse's review of her biography of Keats.

Mr. Shorter's gallantry has, I believe, led him into an indefensible presumption. Sir Edmund's review of Miss Lowell's book was not a favorable one; it challenged a number of Miss Lowell's conjectures; but it was not a scathing attack. Few of us who ever listened to Miss Lowell, ever watched her in action, can credit the notion that she could be mortally wounded by any attack, however severe. Her self-confidence was such that even though she may have been exasperated by Sir Edmund's criticism, she would never for a moment allow that it was justified. It would be more like her to say, "Gosse is a silly old man; he doesn't know what he is talking about," and then defend her position with great skill and energy.

She had weathered ridicule, calumny, and abuse in the early days of the introduction of *vers libre* into America, and had thrived upon them. She loved debate, although with her singleness of mind and absence of doubt her part in a debate was usually but an emphatic statement of her point of view, concerning which she was impervious to attack. It is true that during a

327

debate in Philadelphia she once broke down and cried; but it was in anger at what she considered the inflexible stupidity of an audience that remained unconvinced and slightly ribald in the face of her most earnest efforts to enlighten them.

Lest Mr. Shorter's accusation gain too much currency, it should be said that Miss Lowell died after an operation for a rupture which became dangerous a few days before she was scheduled to sail for England where she was going to enjoy the triumph her book on Keats had earned for her. Galsworthy, Bennett, Wells, and others had cabled their congratulations and had urged her to come to England for a celebration they meant to hold in her honor. With one or two exceptions, the English reviews of Miss Lowell's book had been laudatory, even enthusiastic. In all the literary supplements and magazines a great deal of space was devoted to serious examinations of her contribution to Keatsian theory and interpretation. The courtesy accorded her over there is all the more remarkable when it is remembered that Miss Lowell was a woman, an American, and had not only entered the field Sir Sidney Colvin had staked out for himself, but had effectively challenged the traditional view of Fanny Brawne.

That Miss Lowell was annoyed by Sir Edmund's review is natural enough, and even in a weak moment she may have written a letter to Mr. Shorter reflecting the psychophysical state induced by her anxiety over the impending operation. But Miss Lowell was too indomitable a warrior to allow any critical thrusts to kill her. If she were alive she would, I believe, resent the way in which Mr. Shorter has championed her. It was never in her to question the validity of her inspiration.

Miss Lowell quarreled at one time or another with most of her fellow poets, but poets are often quarreling among themselves, and eventually those who crossed swords with her in print or by mail came around to a deep admiration for her personality, a sincere respect for her talents, and even to an affection for her as an eager, generous, witty and amusing woman.

It was a treat to be invited out to her house in Brookline and an experience to test the wit and nerve of the timid. Miss Lowell always took the trouble to inform herself as to the views her guest had in regard to literature and especially in regard to poetry and, if they did not coincide with her own, she was ready for her attack as soon as she set eyes upon her guest.

Miss Lowell habitually slept during the day and worked during the night. One was never invited to luncheon or to tea at her house. One came to dinner at eight. One was met by her secretary and often enough one sat down to dinner before the hostess put in an appearance. One would be through the soup and fish courses and entering upon the roast when Miss Lowell would come in like an imperious and excited mandarin, seat herself, catch up with the progress of the dinner by an amazing gustatory dexterity, and launch in, between mouthfuls, on her guest's ideas.

"I hear, Mr. Rascoe, that you think very highly of T. S. Eliot's *The Waste Land*. Mr. Eliot is not a poet, Mr. Rascoe; he's an intellectual. An intellectual can never be a poet. The two concepts are contradictory. *The Waste Land* is an interesting fabrication, but it is not a poem."

Emphatically it was, for Miss Lowell, not a poem. I had been warned by friends in Boston that I would find the evening more pleasant if I permitted Miss Lowell to have her say and not take issue with her. I disregarded the tip. She and I had it hot and heavy, all through dinner. We did not come to terms until we were before the fireplace of her magnificent library, the library that contains the marvelous collection of Keats manscripts.

She offered me cigars from two boxes. One box contained Corona coronas; the other contained a special brand of Manila cigars she imported for her own use. They were not "long, black cigars" as the story usually has it; they were medium-sized cigars, rather light brown in color, and exceedingly mild. I had never smoked a cigar that satisfied me so completely and I told her so. That set me very much aright in her eyes; I had good taste in cigars at least, whatever deficiencies I might display in poetic understanding and appreciation. We talked until long past midnight. My conclusion was that had Miss Lowell gone in for politics she could very easily have been governor of Massachusetts; had she gone into jurisprudence she might have sat on the Supreme Court bench; had she gone in for finance she might have been a rival of Mr. Morgan's. She was magnificent, tremendous, a dynamo of energy. Deeply hurt by Sir Edmund Gosse? Nonsense. She was capable of sailing into the French Academy and knocking together the heads of the forty immortals. For was not Miss Lowell, after all, a Boston Brahmin, of the Lowells who spoke only to God?

The Grim Anniversary

From the New Republic, October 29, 1930

The Great Panic was unprecedented in duration, in volume of trading, and in extent of liquidation. It quasi-officially began on October 24, 1929, and ended on the morning of November 15. Meanwhile the New York Stock Exchange, the Curb Exchange, and out-of-town exchanges had closed for two days, November 1 and 2, and from then on until November 14 trading was restricted to the hours between 10 A.M. and 1 P.M. The panic was precipitated by an extreme urgency. Its long continuation was enhanced by a ruse. And its end was brought about by a gesture which did not cost the maker a penny and seems to have been the idea of Mr. Ivy Lee, a press agent.

The panic really began about eleven o'clock on the morning of Thursday, October 24, 1929. At that hour a sinister omen occurred. An alarming number of stocks listed on the New York Stock Exchange were offered at the market and there were no bids for them. Heavy liquidation had preceded the panic for nearly a month and a half, and on Wednesday there had been an avalanche of selling which had clipped off five billion dollars in the market valuation of the stocks listed on the New York Stock Exchange alone. But until that Thursday morning there had been no stocks offered at the market for which there were no buyers at any price.

On these stocks which were valueless that morning, and on other stocks listed on the stock exchange which had suffered severe depreciation—one stock had dropped ninety-six points and some bank shares, which are dealt in over the counter for cash, had dropped $500 a share in valuation—the member banks of the Federal Reserve in New York City had loaned at the close of business on Wednesday afternoon $6,634,000,000 to brokers and dealers—or, in other words, two billion dollars more money than was in circulation in the United States during the whole of last year and only two billion dollars less than the entire stock of money in the country, including the amount held in the Treasury against gold and silver certificates and against Treasury notes of 1890.

On that Thursday morning, then, because of the number of stocks that had become worthless on which the banks had loaned money to brokers and dealers, and because of the number of stocks which had depreciated in value below their lending value established by the banks, there was probably not a large bank in New York City that was not technically insolvent. (Bankers, brokers, investors, speculators speak of "real" or "intrinsic" value of stocks and bonds. These are mystical terms. All market values are relative and governed by opinion. The value of any commodity or anything at any time is precisely what you can get for it. Its value is established at the given moment of exchange, even if, at the next exchange, its value shifts markedly up or down.) In lending money to brokers and dealers with securities listed on the New York Stock Exchange (and on some curb stocks) as collateral, the men who govern the lending values of stocks do not speak of "real" or "intrinsic" value; after the close of each market day they make a guess at the lowest possible point to which any given stock might drop in twenty-four hours, and lend money to the brokers, who in turn lend it to customers, to the amount of that lowest possible point. That is to say, on a stock which has been selling around $165 a share on Tuesday, the banks had guessed at the lowest liquidation point as $100 and had loaned that much money on it. But on Thursday morning this stock might have been selling at $75 a share or offered for sale at any price with no takers.

This situation called for quick thinking and desperate strategy. After the panic had been raging for nearly an hour, officials of four New York banks, summoned by Thomas W. Lamont, somewhat ostentatiously entered the impressive squat building occupied by J. P. Morgan and Company at Broad and Wall streets and went into extraordinary session with Mr. Lamont. News of the conference had been duly announced to the press and flashed all over the country to brokerage houses on the Dow-Jones news tickers.

What really happened at that conference was not divulged to the public until January 16, 1930, when some astute reporter wrote for the New York *Times* what he had been able to learn from Mr. Lamont. Although that scoop was of great historical significance, I later saw no evidence that any editorial writer or writer of financial news had read it, or, having read it, understood the momentousness of the disclosure. There were not even follow-up news stories on it. Of this conference more anon.

At one-fifteen on that Thursday afternoon in October, Richard Whitney, then known as the floor trader on the New York Stock Exchange for the Morgan firm, walked to the post where United States Steel (the market leader) was traded and bid 205 for 25,000 shares of Steel. A moment before Steel had sold as low as 193½. Word of this spectacular action was shouted by order clerks through direct-wire telephones to every brokerage house in the city and news of it went out all over the country on the tickers. That was the first indication to the public that the bankers had taken steps to "bolster up the market." Simultaneously other floor traders, acting under instructions from the bankers, began to create a market for the stocks which had been valueless in the morning. Immediately the rest of the market responded to the action of the bankers' consortium. American Can, which had dropped to 137, rallied and closed at 157½. Steel closed at 206. American Telephone and Telegraph, which had dropped to 245, closed at 269. General Electric, which had dropped to 283, closed

333

at 308, off only six points from the previous close. Montgomery Ward, which had opened at 84 and had sunk to 50, closed at 74. United States Industrial Alcohol, which had opened at 203⅞ and had sunk to 169, closed at 176. Columbian Carbon, which had opened at 260 and had dropped to 210, closed at 231. International Harvester, after being down twelve dollars a share from the opening, actually closed with a gain of 8⅜ points.

In Washington that afternoon a Federal Reserve meeting was called, attended by Secretary Mellon. The meeting lasted two hours but no action was taken that the public knew about. The Treasury Department reiterated its contention that "business is fundamentally sound," ascribed the panic to bear raiding, and pointed out, as a fact, the irresponsible rumor that Jesse Livermore, the biggest of the bears, had been buying all morning— which goes to show to what trivialities the Treasury Department was capable of stooping. Colonel Leonard P. Ayres, the loquacious financial wiseacre of the Cleveland Trust Company, gave his opinion that the break was "a security panic, with no economic basis. The stock market probably hit bottom today and a rally tomorrow is in order." Senator Carter Glass of Virginia gave out a statement that the panic was "entirely due to Mitchellism." (Senator Glass had demanded that the Federal Reserve Board oust Charles Mitchell after Mitchell had defied the board's edict against advancing reserve credit to support the market and had relieved the tight money situation in the call-loan market by offering National City Bank money in $25,000,000 lots on a ten-point graduating scale from 15 per cent.) Mr. Mitchell gave out an optimistic statement and said, "I still see nothing to worry about." The harried writers of market letters for customers of brokerage houses took strength from all this cheeriness and that night composed opinions voicing the belief that the "worst is over," that "the reaction was technical," that "the market is oversold," and that "the panic was largely psychological and had nothing to do with business conditions, which are basically

334

sound," and that "now the better grade of stocks are on a sound investment basis."

The next morning the newspapers carried a statement from President Hoover in which he said, in part, "The fundamental business of the country, that is production and distribution of commodities, is on a sound and prosperous basis." He continued in that strain a statement as to conditions which were not borne out by later events. Overnight statements had been gathered by the newspapers from financial and industrial leaders, all of them reassuring. Arthur W. Loasby, president of the Equitable Trust Company, said emphatically, "There will be no repetition of the break of yesterday. I have no fear of another comparable decline." M. C. Brush, president of the American International Corporation, said, "I think we are all indebted to the four gentlemen who met on the corner yesterday and through their action steadied the whole situation. I believe that the very best stocks can be bought at approximate present prices." Walter C. Teagle, president of the Standard Oil Company of New Jersey, said, "There has been no fundamental change in the petroleum industry"; and others were equally misleadingly optimistic. Charles Schwab made a speech, occupying two columns in the newspapers, saying that the country was vastly prosperous and that the steel business was never better.

Samuel Vauclain, chairman of the board of directors of the Baldwin Locomotive Works; George M. Reynolds, chairman of the executive committee of the Continental Illinois Bank and Trust Company; Dr. A. H. Giannini, president of the Bank of America, and other presidents and chairmen of the boards of banks and corporations each put in their mite of optimism. Arthur Reynolds, chairman of the Continental Illinois Bank of Chicago, said, "This crash is not going to have much effect on business." The newspapers on Friday morning all carried stories to the effect that a big bankers' consortium, composed of six members, had been formed to give support to the market—"not to buy stocks to put up prices," according to the *Times,* "but to furnish a cushion of purchasing power against the recurrence of any such condition as Thursday." (This comparatively guarded statement was, nevertheless, typical of the misapprehension of the power and scope of the consortium. These bankers could not legally use depositors' money to gamble in stocks, nor did they: the banks have subsidiary investment trusts with large cash funds which they can use at their discretion and large investments which, as trustees of the investment-trust shareholders' funds, they must protect.)

Next morning, Friday, United States Steel opened up at 207 and the whole market steadied. Optimism had been restored, mainly by what was supposed to be the action of the bankers' consortium. Impaired margins were bolstered up by affected customers who raised money to protect their accounts, thinking everything was going to be rosy again. Speculators who had been out of the market rushed in to clean up on stocks which supposedly had hit bottom. The rally continued throughout the day with only a few declines. At the close there were some spectacular gains on the day: United States Industrial Alcohol closing with a gain of 21 points, International Business Machines with a gain of 13¾, Warren Brothers with a gain of 14½, American Bank Note with a gain of 11, Cuymel Fruit with a gain of 18½, and other gains of five and ten points. On the Curb Exchange the Aluminum Company of America (Secretary Mellon's company) gained 50 points on the day; Duke Power Company, 33 points, and American Light and Traction, 20½ points.

The action of the bankers' consortium was kept pretty much a secret. When asked by the reporters what action had been taken by the bankers, Mr. Lamont said he did not know, although the Thursday conference and the Friday afternoon one, which George F. Baker, Jr., joined, had been held in his office.

What actually happened Mr. Lamont recalled on the fifteenth of the following January. Although he did not say so in so many words, he said in effect that the banks had saved themselves from closing their books that Thursday night "in the red," and after that let the market take care of itself. Six banks, on behalf of their subsidiary investment trusts, pledged $40,000,000 each, $240,000,000 in all, to "fill the air pockets"—that is, to create a market for the stocks which had been offered and nothing bid for them and to bid up stocks which had dropped below their lending value at the banks. About $100,000,000 of the pledged amount was used on Thursday afternoon. With a hundred million at one's disposal, one can mightily affect the trend of the market, as the event proved. But with the buoyant market created in the late afternoon and the next morning, when confidence had been restored by these purchases and by the reassurance of the President and others, the consortium quietly fed back into the market nearly all of the stock—at a fair profit to themselves.

For his feat in bidding 205 for 25,000 shares of United States Steel on that momentous Thursday afternoon, Richard Whitney was voted a tribute of honor by his fellow members of the stock exchange. (As I write, Steel is selling at 145½. It is interesting to note, by the way, that Mr. Whitney's predecessor, E. H. H. Simmons, then president of the exchange, refused point-blank to add to the bogus optimism of the time and would make no comment on the market or on business conditions.) The newspapers began to refer to the "Big Six" bankers as "Saviors of the Market," and actually still refer to them as such.

What happened to the market after they had "saved it" is almost too painfully in the memory of everybody except financial writers. The bankers had got out. Of course, if they had not, the severity of the panic would have been more violent, if not so protracted. We would have got everything at once instead of having the pain stretch out for a year. Indeed, we might have had it over with. If the consortium had really wished to save the market as such, they would have used some of that $240,000,000 on the following Monday. But having saved themselves on that

337

historic Thursday, that night the banks drastically revised downward their estimates of the lending value of stocks. Thus they passed the buck over to the brokers, who, in turn, had until Monday morning to pass the buck on to the public.

On Monday, October 28, the real debacle began and it continued unremittingly until November 14. On that afternoon, after the close of the market, during which Standard Oil of New Jersey had got down to 50¾, John D. Rockefeller announced through the press that he had placed a standing order for 1,000,000 shares of the stock at $50 on a share. This was a gesture probably inspired by Mr. Ivy Lee. Of course the next morning Standard Oil of New Jersey opened up two points above its close and it never after that dipped to 50. Mr. Rockefeller did not have to spend a penny.

In the face of world-wide depression, increasing unemployment, sharp declines in commodity prices, suspension of dividends, and a steady down curve of business activity, the stock market gained some heart from the Rockefeller gesture and started advancing, with an occasional "technical reaction," reaching its peak last March. It had been aided periodically by statements from President Hoover or members of his Cabinet saying that business was on the upgrade and unemployment was on the decrease.

Finally the absurdity of these statements in the face of known and published facts began to be seen even by the holders of securities and speculators. Anyone with the reasoning power of a low-grade moron knew that a sinister situation existed and, in fact, had existed ever since early in November while the panic was still on—due to the fact that a great number of smaller interior banks were loaded with "frozen securities," and that a great many brokerage houses had been forced to carry their biggest customers, with accounts running into the millions, at their own risk because they could not afford to sell these customers out. (Here be it remarked that the "sucker," the small trader with limited capital and resources, was not affected by the panic, except in so far as all of us were by the depression in its wake: he had been sold out at least a week before, and in some cases weeks before the panic began.)

Fortunately the older established houses had officers who had been in the Street long enough to plow earnings in boom times back into company surplus to tide them over in the event of a panic and so no important brokerage house failed at the time. But it was this strain upon company surplus, in carrying large accounts against the time when the market would stage a comeback, which finally did for the important but comparatively young house of Prince and Whitely. The situation was indeed precarious. President Hoover was optimistic in his May Day speech, and the next morning the market fell flat on its face with an expiring gasp. The decline has continued ever since until, as I write, the average prices of all utilities and industrials are considerably below the panic lows and the rails are lower than they have been since 1926.

Meanwhile one guesser, Roger Babson, who had gained a vast reputation for prophecy by hollering "Panic" in the summer of 1929, a full month before the utilities reached their dizzy peak and three months before the panic, made another bid for fame as a prophet by predicting in September of this year a rapid business recovery. In Cleveland, Ohio, on September 30, Rome C. Stephenson, vice-president of the American Bankers' Association, told his buddies (and the newspapers) some things he had cribbed right out of the guess of the once-right Babson. He said that a speedy return to prosperity was at hand; in fact, it was only a matter of a few weeks:

There is as much money in the country as a year ago. The trouble has been that those who had it would not spend it. As soon as they are satisfied that the business revival is on the way they will begin spending again. The depression of the stock market impressed the general public with the idea that it would

339

depress general business. Because of a psychological consequence, it did, but it should not have. There are 120,000,000 persons in the country and at the maximum not more than 10,000,000 were involved in stock market transactions. The remain 110,000,000 citizens suffered no loss.

Mr. Stephenson, who had cribbed from Mr. Babson, was himself parroted a few days later by President Hoover; but it is amusing to analyze the paragraph I have quoted from Mr. Stephenson's speech. It is a masterpiece of tosh and ignorance or duplicity. He says that there is just as much money in the country as a year ago. As if that had anything to do with it. There was also more money in the country in 1923 and 1924 than there was at any time during the stock market boom, including last year. His corollaries are too absurd to analyze. Then he says that because only ten million persons were involved in stock market transactions, the other hundred and ten millions suffered no loss. He had just admitted that the entire country *had* suffered a general depression in business. His statement about the psychological consequence of the panic being what it shouldn't be is like the statement of the lawyer who was summoned by a client who was in jail. When he heard what the fellow was in for, he said, "They can't put you in jail for that." Whereupon the fellow insisted, "But I am in jail." Even panhandlers and pickpockets have suffered losses from the crash, not to speak of six million unemployed.

As I write, there is a lot of hokum in the newspapers about short selling. There are so many superstitions involved in finance, so many myths, that it is necessary, now and then, for unofficial spokesmen of the stock exchange to say something or do something about short selling as a gesture. They made this gesture on November 11, 1929, when the stock exchange sent out a questionnaire to brokers regarding the commitments on the short side of their accounts. When the returns were in, it was revealed that the short commitments were less than one eighth of one per cent of the total commitments. It would have been a miracle if there had been any more that late in the day. And lately there was a report that something was to be done about short selling or bear raiding. That is as sensible as if the Casino at Monte Carlo made a ruling that people couldn't play the red any more, they would have to pay the black. Short selling is a necessary corollary to trading on the long side. Stop short selling, as President Whitney pointed out, and you prevent a free and open market for securities and Wall Street would have to close up shop. That might not be a bad idea, but if it did, a lot of other things would have to close up too, including the government at Washington.

The "experts" on finance, the amateur economists, and the financiers were for a long time engagingly varied in their opinions as to why the crash occurred. There is one school of great thinkers who said that the cheap money of the Federal Reserve Board was responsible for the stock market boom and subsequentially for the crash—a bit of cerebration that is positively dazzling, especially since the Federal Reserve rediscount rate for months has been lower than it has ever been in Federal Reserve history and this has created no conspicuous boom. Other great thinkers laid the panic to the multiplication of investment trusts and still others to the tendency of industries to finance their expansion by common-stock issues and so on. In explanation of finance you can hear anything, including the faint tinkling of bells.

The payoff is this: When the Federal Reserve Board issued its warning against stock market speculation in February 1929, a warning which precipitated a minor panic, the important thing in the warning was apparently overlooked by everybody including, of course, the administration officials, who kept giving out optimistic statements to offset the reaction it had caused. The financial and political world and the public knew only that the Federal Reserve Board had probably stepped out of its proper function and given the stock market a spanking. But the real gist of the report was that the prosperity talk was a myth, that there had been no more than a normal increase in business activity following the depression of 1921, and that "prosperity," so far as world production and consumption are concerned, is relatively normal always, even though there are periodic waves of speculation inspired by imagination and based upon universal human greed and love of adventure.